WICKED SPEED

By the same author

Chase the Fade (Blandford Press, 1982)

ANNIE NIGHTINGALE

WICKED SPEED

SIDGWICK & JACKSON

First published 1999 by Sidgwick & Jackson
an imprint of Macmillan Publishers Ltd
25 Eccleston Place, London SW1W 9NF
Basingstoke and Oxford

Associated companies throughout the world

ISBN 0 283 06197 9

1 3 5 7 9 8 6 4 2

A CIP catalogue record for this book is available from
the British Library.

Phototypeset by Intype London Ltd
Printed and bound in Great Britain by
Mackays of Chatham plc, Chatham, Kent

for

Lucy
Alex
Bill

CONTENTS

ACKNOWLEDGEMENTS

For help in preparation of this book, thanks are due to Jo, Simone, Nikki, Maggie Noach, and editors Ian Paten and Susan Hill, especial thanks to her for her saint-like patience and understanding. I also thank all my friends and colleagues whom I have driven up the wall talking about rather than getting on with writing the book. And to Irvine. With an 'e'.

A FOREWORD IN
TWO PARTS
DISCO

1
1976

In a small council flat on the outskirts of Edinburgh, a gangly teenage boy is watching *Scotsport* on the television. His father is sitting in the armchair opposite, shifting his attention between the screen and the side of the boy's face which is exposed to him. In this profile the face of the Teenager is disfigured by one massive scab which stretches from underneath his right eye, across his cheek and almost to the corner of his mouth.

The Teenager is aware that his father is watching him. He finds it hard to concentrate on the game. He intermittently feels the coarse roughage on the side of his face. Then his mother enters the room carrying a tray with cups and a pot of tea on it, setting them down on a teak-veneered coffee table. The mother catches the Teenager self-consciously touching the scab. 'Ah telt ye no tae pick it. It'll never get better if ye pick it,' she informs him for the umpteenth time that day.

'How regular are yir bowel movements? How often do you do a shite?' his father asks.

'Eh!?' the Teenager replies incredulously.

'Well, if ye dinnae keep yir bowels moving, that's what happens, the shit comes out in your face. That's why you've got such a bad pluke.'

'That's nothing tae dae wi it,' his mother snorts. 'It's cause he's been picking that scab.'

'Aye, ah ken that, but wi the plukes in the first place, they come aboot through no moving your bowels regularly. That's the key.'

The Teenager is saved by the ring of the telephone in the lobby. It is his Best Mate on the line. 'Missed yirsel at the Americana last night. Brilliant. The fanny was fuckin amazin. Comin oot the waw's!'

This depresses the Teenager further. He touches the scab again. That fucking curse! He's forgone a three-two home Hibs win and now he's missed a top night out and a romantic opportunity. He has to ask. 'Anybody bag off?'

'Eh . . . well . . . naw. We aw goat too pished doon Rose Street. Ah wis in wi this wee blonde piece, but then A Certain Cunt Who Shall Be Nameless dropped his fuckin keks oan the dancefloor. The bouncers wir straight over n it wis oot the door. Hud tae back um up, so wi goat tanned outside. On the wey hame wi ran intae these Clerie cunts n it aw went radge. Ah hud tae go up tae the hoaspital eftir, five stiches above the eye. Brilliant! Some fuckin night man, ye really missed yirsel.'

The Teenager touched his scab again. 'Aye. Ah wis skint, eh.'

'Ye gaun doon the pub later?'

'Eh . . . naw. Still skint.'

'Suit yirsel. Ah'll catch ye later. Ah'm gaunny listen tae Annie Nightingale. See ye.'

'Right.'

The Teenager felt a bit better as he put the phone down. It was indeed time for Annie N's request show. Annie was more than a DJ; she was a surrogate cool big sister to the Teenager and most of his friends. He went into the small bathroom with its tiles and vinyl wallpaper and ran the bath, taking the tranny in with him. As he relaxed in the warm water, Annie's voice coming through the steam was familiar and reassuring amidst his anxieties, and her tunes were always uplifting. Sometimes the Teenager would sit with a pencil and piece of paper to take note of her reference to a song he'd particularly liked, and nip over from his work to ARDS record shop in Leith's Great Junction Street to purchase that tune. Annie was always there to provide that respite, through those unspeakable Sunday horrors of anticipating school and then work on a Monday morning.

In spite of his despondency, his fear that life was passing him by and that he would never, ever look normal again, the Teenager was starting to feel more positive. Yes, he'd have to go in tomorrow and face his workmates' ridicule because he couldn't take any more time off sick. But it would all be a laugh. He'd tough it out. But then his heart sank when he considered the lassies in the office. He couldn't face them. Oh God.

Another tune though. Maybe it's not so bad.

The steam from the bath filled the small room. The tiles, still cool against his cheek. Then the Teenager was aware of something out of the corner of his eye. Something dark. He turned and looked at it, almost jumping out of his skin. It was like a rat, a squashed, flat rat. It wasn't moving. He stared at it.

There was a massive feeling of joy and elation as the Teenager touched his cheek. Instead of the coarse scab, he felt smooth, taut, fresh skin. He stood up out of the bath and brushed the heavy condensation from the mirror. There it was staring back at him: a face with two matching sides! Both pink and crystal clear!

He picked up the scab and flushed it down the toilet. He kissed the radio in appreciation of Annie's healing powers. Then he dressed up in Saturday night gear for a Sunday night out with his mates down the pub. Well, you never knew who might be out, and it was no bad thing to make an effort. Maybe one or two of the crew might be persuaded to make a night of it in town. There was supposed to be a new Sunday nightclub at Pipers in Lothian Road. It was good to be alive.

2
1997

In Broadcasting House, Great Portland Street, the Teenager is now older but no wiser. This Old Teenager is still into disco music. In fact, he's in Broadcasting House being interviewed with his friend, the Even Older Teenager, about the disco single their band has just released. The DJ who is hosting the show is asking them about their influences and it's all going well, Nile Rodgers and Chic are being well-referenced. The Old Teenagers have been drinking all day in the West End, and are a bit pissed. When the DJ mentions some of the criticisms of the single, the Even Older Teenager gets testy. 'They haven't got a clue,' he says dismissively, 'they don't know what disco is. They just don't understand where we're coming from. All they're concerned about is their careers in journalism, while we're in the studio down in Brick Lane having it large!'

They leave the studio and move through the open-plan office where they are delighted to run into their friend Annie, who is a DJ with Radio 1. They sit down together and talk about tunes and more tunes. The Old Teenager and the Even Older Teenager think that Annie is looking really well, and is continuing to come on in leaps and bounds since that terrible incident in Cuba. The Old Teenager is thinking about her incredible spirit and how, since that incident he's never seen her down or in a negative frame of mind. Maybe in the back of his mind, he's thinking about a scab and music and healing powers. Most likely though, he's thinking back more generally to that time when the flatulent sounds of loud, boring, thick and egotistical men strafed the airwaves and Annie's cool funky tones always stood out and how it's funny, or maybe not, that those men are now all long gone and she's still here in this BBC office.

After a bit, the Even Older Teenager suggests they head for the pub. Annie says, in her thoughtful way, 'I suppose we really should . . .' as if not to do so would be highly irresponsible.

During her convalescence period at her son Alex's house, Annie tells the Old Teenager that in addition to forcing his friend to take an interest in gardening (Alex *has* already mentioned this to him) she has written her autobiography. The Old Teenager says, 'Aw Annie, that's brilliant. I'd really like to write something for it. Some kind of appreciation . . .'

He thinks it's his way of saying thank you. The stupid wanker doesn't, in the moment, even consider that there are thousands of people better qualified to write something for this book than him. He doesn't, in his enthusiasm, not arrogance, even think about that. He just wants to say thank you. At first for the music, but it's even more than that. Then he starts thinking about the scab, and reading through the manuscript, with Annie recounting all her broadcasting adventures and travelling experiences without any bitterness or rancour towards anybody. Most of all he thinks about the conversations he's had talking to the people who know her as a friend and those who don't, but who've listened to her over the years and how that huge but so often misused word 'respect' always seems to loom so large. Then he realizes that it's really about saying: 'Thanks for being there.'

Irvine Welsh

PS: Note on the text.
Irvine is with an 'e' (always an e) and not a 'g', although I've been known to have a 'g' of charlie.
A trainspotter.

INTRODUCTION

This book is about adventure. It is not a kiss-and-tell book and it is not a book of name-dropping, although you will meet, I hope, some interesting people along the way. All I would like to do is inspire you, the reader, to give anything a whirl, because if you don't you may always regret it. I have had, I think, some extraordinary experiences, taken some risks, and met some amazing characters, not all of whom I've been able to weave into this particular tale. I have been inspired, and I would like to inspire you. If I can do it, so can you.

In 1983 Prince made a track called '1999'. Immediately I began, on my radio show, to discuss plans for the New Year's Eve 1999 Millennium party. Some people wailed, 'It's sixteen years away – I'll probably be *dead*.' I replied to them, 'Well, you probably *won't* be dead. It's a lot more likely that I shall be.' Certainly there was a greater likelihood of me being dead than most of my young listeners, but it didn't stop me beginning to plan. For years, beside my bed in my house at Montpelier Road in Brighton, I had tacked up a torn-out newspaper headline. It read, 'DON'T WASTE YOUR ENERGY.' I took this to mean, 'don't waste your resources on being angry or negative. You might get walked over, trodden on, ripped off, cheated, lied to, deceived, taken advantage of, fucked over . . . but then, who hasn't been? Just don't let anyone stop you – go change the world.'

Right, that's enough of the homespun philosophy. Now let's get on with the story.

London, June 1998

PROLOGUE

Grip. Will-power. Mend. Join. Stop grinding. Hold. Will-power. I used both hands to hold the flesh of my right thigh as tightly as I could. A bone or some bones were broken, grinding together in a manner that felt sickeningly serious. If I could just hold, clamp, bind together what was smashed inside, surely the broken bits would fuse, somehow – stick, mend, join, come back together again. Somehow. If I could just lock the bones together by gripping tightly with the span of my hands. Just hang on like this for long enough.

The pain was pounding relentlessly, and I could feel it draining my strength, my will and my resolve. But there didn't seem any way out of this nightmare. I had lost track of time, but I guessed it must be now about seven or eight o'clock in the morning of 23 December 1996.

The swift, savage attack had happened around six hours beforehand. Dark, ill-lit Old Havana is known to be a mugger's paradise at night. The streets are lined with magnificent, towering, colonnaded but crumbling buildings, each with crusty remains of once bright blue or yellow, pink or green paint peeling away in great curlicues from the derelict dark façades. Behind the black portals, though, there was furtive movement, signs of human life going on in the tall-chambered ruins of these once-splendid Spanish mansions. Way back in the depths of some uncurtained hall, the narrow beam from a loose-hanging fluorescent tube threw a sharp perpendicular slash of cold white light across huddled, fugitive shapes, caught in silhouette like plaster figurines. In the silent streets, sounds of footsteps and of the wheels of predatory, circling cycling gangs were muffled by the dust of the soft dirt on the unsurfaced road, the colour of dried blood. There was an unmistakable presence of menace, but at the same time an atmosphere redolent of some swashbuckling *Boy's Own* adventure book. The musty but elegant buildings, with their huge pillars and trellised balconies, the theatrical but ineffective spots of light thrown at irregular intervals by old coaching lamps perched high on street corners, gave Old Havana the look of a C-circuit touring-pantomime set, or a garish fifties B-movie lot. It was no coincidence that Errol Flynn's photograph took pride of place at the Ernest Hemingway watering hole La Floridita, a few streets away. All the guys hanging around on the street corners looked ominous all right – ominously likely to break into some camp chorus from an Ivor Novello musical, rhyming 'come over here' with 'jolly buccaneer'.

But this was no 'Desperadoes of the Caribbean' Disney-world ride. And I'd been to enough financially starved Third World countries to know the danger signs. Yet the cheap, almost glamorous sleaze had fooled me. Graham Greene had struck again. *Brighton Rock* had shaped three decades of my life; now I'd been lured to his setting of *Our Man in Havana*! And this was not virtual reality, this was confrontation with the capital of Cuba, a country block-aded and strangled to within a piss-taking peso of its very economic existence. Any credit-card-carrying tourist or wedged-up dollar Westerner was potential prey. The dodgy geezer posing in each doorway on every street corner was the children's adventure-book bogeyman come to life, waiting to reach out, grab your cash, and, if necessary, beat the holy shit out of you.

It was the fact that I was strolling along with a native Cuban, a cosmopolitan entrepreneur, a middle-aged, responsible, worldly man, whose name was Angel, for Christ's sake, which that night made me a little less on my guard against bag-snatchers. There was absolutely no warning of what came next. I was carrying, swinging from my right shoulder, a small plastic silver-coloured rucksack. Suddenly there was a sharp, shocking and desperate wrench of the strap from behind me, and I spun half round to my right in an involuntary twist to grab at the bag. But it was already too late. In that split second my unseen assailant smashed into my right thigh with what weapon I'll never know – a cosh, a baseball bat, a knee, a boot – tore the bag away from me, and was gone. Now I was on the ground. The thief was off around a corner, and Angel gave chase. Some minutes later he returned ashen-faced and empty-handed. The mugger had broken his collarbone rather than let go of my bag, and had escaped into the myriad dark alleyways that criss-cross Old Havana.

I

My great-grandfather was killed being thrown from a
horse-drawn cart on a farm in Darwen, near Blackburn,
Lancashire, with the result that his son, John James Nightingale, my paternal grandfather, seven years old at the
time, had to kiss goodbye to full-time education, and work
to help keep the rest of the family. Not an unusual situation, I assume, in 1880s rural England. In any event, J.
J. Nightingale rose above any shortcomings of formal
learning and, married with two daughters and two sons,
became a textile bigwig, moved to France around the turn
of the century, and ran the French division of the giant
Sanderson wallpaper company in Paris. Before the family
set sail for France, and before my father was born, J. J.
took in a young lodger – sort of an early version of a boy
au pair – to the family house in Chiswick. He was an
eighteen-year-old French boy employed by Sandersons as
a translator and befriended by my grandfather who
reduced the boy's 'keep' in exchange for French lessons.
The young man kept a detailed account of life with the
Nightingales, which included never being given enough
food to eat and finding young Englishwomen unsexy as
they didn't wear corsets. The young man's letters and cards
to friends and family have since been published. But it

was his book *Le Grand Meaulnes* (*The Lost Domain*) that immortalized him. The young man's name was Alain-Fournier. He died in action in the First World War at the age of twenty-eight. My grandfather was a flamboyant, extravagant, wine-drinking spender of a character, who loved entertaining, big-time, even if he hadn't the money to do so. It was apparently left to my grandmother, Annie, to juggle the books to keep the family in food and clothes.

Incredibly, living as they did in some style in a house near the later site of Orly Airport, in southern Paris, J. J. Nightingale insisted that the household lead as English a life as possible, and my grandmother was obliged to bake English bread and cook Lancashire hotpot throughout all the years the family lived in France. I remember him only in his last few years, smoking a pungent pipe and sitting beside an ornate marble fireplace at the last Nightingale family home back in England – The Retreat, in Brentford, west London. My grandfather had split with Sanderson, set up his own wallpaper company and it was the onerous task of my father, more a natural artisan than a businessman, to carry it on.

I was the only offspring from any of John James Nightingale's children. Which meant that I was spoilt rotten as a child by them. They all had eccentric nicknames. The eldest daughter, Alice Clara, was known as 'Mazzie', as she resembled the photograph of a girl with curls on a Mazawattee tea packet. The second daughter was named Florence Nightingale, after the famous nurse, and was trounced by a team of experts she tried to outwit on a TV quiz game called *The Name's the Same*; in any case, she was always known as 'June' or 'Friday'. My father was Basil, corrupted by the family to 'Basle', after the Swiss city, or

'Tiny', on account of his above-average height of six foot two. The youngest child was named Harold, always called 'Bill'.

My mother, Celia Winter, was one of six children, one or two of whom did produce offspring, but it was her elder, childless and, eccentric sister Dora to whom I warmed most. She was into health foods and astrology, and later in life became extremely paranoid about the considerable wealth she and her husband, Ted, had apparently built up growing black-market farm produce during World War II and the austere post-war years of the late 1940s – to the extent of burying share certificates and jewellery in their garden. Sometime during my childhood she upped and left the smallholding she and my uncle had worked, however illegally, in Hanworth, near Heathrow Airport, and moved to Peacehaven, a shambles of a shanty town tottering precariously on the cliffs between Roedean School and the port of Newhaven, and conveniently close to Brighton. My mother and her sister would argue fiercely when we stayed in Peacehaven, usually about my aunt's unusual mealtime arrangements, which were to me pleasingly erratic. I would wander off into her huge garden with its beds of prize-winning dahlias and inadvertently free her brood of a hundred or so penned-up ginger-coloured chickens, which then had to be rounded up and corralled before any of us could have lunch or supper.

I loved the trips to Brighton on the green-and-cream double-decker Southdown buses, which trundled dangerously close to the blustery cliff edge, past Saltdean and Ovingdean and the few solitary cafés dotted along the coastline, their orange-tiled roofs painted with the word 'CAFE' in huge white letters – to attract interested airmen, I assumed. Everything else here seemed to be turquoise –

the painted railings along the seafront; the pointy-roofed beach huts; the stripes of the deckchair canvas; the blue-green-shadowed sea swirling sinisterly beneath the Ghost Train at the far end of the Palace Pier.

I was a product of the North–South divide. My mother's family lived around Richmond upon Thames, and my mother, petite and dark-haired, had apparently been known as the Lass of Richmond Hill, which is also the name of a famous pub. Although my father's family had moved south from their Lancastrian base, they remained Northerners in attitude. As a Surrey person, my mother thought Northerners were 'over-familiar'; she loathed being called 'loov', and she despised what she called their 'lavatorial humour'. But what irked her even more was the habit of her in-laws, especially Mazzie and June, of speaking in French in her company. This wound her up appallingly, as she was well aware that they knew she could not understand them.

My mother, when she was single and before I was born, trained as a chiropodist with the famed Dr Scholl. He had, she told me, wanted to take her to work with him in the United States. *Her* mother forbade her. Even as a child, I could not understand this. 'Why didn't you just *go*?' I was forever asking. Not that I'd wished to be of any other nationality, and certainly I wouldn't swap dads with anyone.

Counteracting the effect of being 'spoilt' and indulged by my aunts Mazzie and June (both married, but both seemed to have returned to the family home rather than live with their spouses), the first ten years of my life were spent in the enlarged faux family of a cul-de-sac over-shadowed by a towering sound stage which was part of Twickenham film studios, later to be made truly famous by the Beatles, who made their first movie there. There were children galore, growing up, playing and fighting together, probably doing me the world of good as surrogate brothers and sisters, preventing me from becoming a really obnoxious spoilt only child. Even so, I was known as 'Bossy Anne' on occasions.

My mother was deeply suspicious of our neighbours. The family that lived in the flat closest in our block, Kelvin Court, were vegetarians and spoke Esperanto. This, as far as my mother was concerned, made them card-carrying members of the Communist Party. On the floor below lived a German-born woman with her blond son, John. My mother was convinced that they were still active Nazis.

School provided me with my first experience of class distinction. I was decked out in a head-to-toe navy-blue-and-white uniform to begin my education at St Catherine's Convent.

The rest of my playmates were being sent to St Stephen's, a local state school, which did not expect its pupils to wear any uniform except a black blazer. For the first time I felt the cold breeze of resentment from my peer group. I was not being sent to St Catherine's for any religious reasons. My parents were not Roman Catholics, nor were they bringing me up to be one. I think their motive was that St Catherine's had a reputation for turning out nicely spoken young ladies.

The school premises were fairly spectacular. The convent – red brick, with a cream-and-brown tower pro-truding from its midst like a missile from a launching pad – had once been the home of Alexander Pope. It was set right by the riverside at Twickenham, with an arched, cloistered but open-sided play area often flooded by a high Thames tide. The main attraction was the school's underground grotto, linking it to an annexe and playing fields across a main road. As schoolgirls, we were convinced that the roughly hewn walls of the grotto were encrusted with large chunks of precious stone – diamonds, rubies, amethysts – and we would surreptitiously give the walls a good kicking on each journey through it, in the hope of dislodging some of these gems. At its far end the grotto was covered with thick, curling ivy branches, which hid an infestation of stag beetles. In some lunatic display of bravado I had, on one of my first schooldays, declared myself unafraid of these shiny, black, pincered beasts, which could also *fly*, and fly straight at you in the darkness of the tunnel, so thereafter I would habitually be sent into the front line by my gym-slipped peer group to lead them through.

Often in winter a great, thick, white-green fog – a 'pea-souper' – would come rolling in off the river, dense enough to silence your footfall and for your outstretched hand to disappear in front of your face. Then we would all be sent home early before darkness and fog stopped the buses running.

I loved the fog and the fear of getting lost in it. Nuns I wasn't so sure about. They wore floor-length dusty black dresses and starched, white, tight-fitting headpieces, like balaclavas, which left only the area of flesh between eyebrows and chin exposed, giving no clue as to their age. They had a soap-scrubbed, leathery, chalky, cotton- or linen-yarn smell about them, and all their names began with the prefix 'Sister Mary', which seemed unnecessarily unimaginative and repetitious.

The first Mother Superior at St Catherine's that I remember was Sister Mary Ignatious, a tall nun who boomed at me on our first meeting, 'You don't like me, do you?' 'No,' I replied. But what I did like, what I embraced whole-heartedly, was the Roman Catholic religion. Five years old, and I bought the whole package. Jesus and Mary, the first pop stars. I was totally seduced by their glamour. There were pictures, statues, effigies of them all over the convent. Hung on the wall in my first classroom was a black-and-white painting of Jesus adorned with his crown of thorns. Sister Mary Denis, the form teacher, told us that if we looked hard enough at Jesus's eyes in the picture we would see them open and close. Well – Hail Mary and Mother of God – it worked! Their eyes did open! A miracle! After that I was hooked.

In the school chapel, I would spend free time 'doing' the stations of the cross. I thought that Lent, when all the statues were draped in purple cloth, was fab. I was obsessed with being almost within reach of the mysterious gold box, the tabernacle, with its set of miniature doors on the front, which stood on the altar and, right here in Twickenham, Middlesex, had a bit of God inside it. Great concept, great design. I bought Holy Pictures with my pocket money, and had them blessed with Holy Water by the local priest, Father Gordon. Great marketing. I was really proud of the fact that I had more than one rosary, the most prized consisting of crimson polished wooden beads linked to a silver crucifix. Then the images, the icons! I thought the Virgin Mary was really cool, always wearing a long blue gown and carrying a single white lily. Most of all I was impressed by her halo, which seemed to stay on the back of her head without any visible means of support.

The main attraction of Jesus, later in my life to be seen as his very rock, very André Agassi tennis player look (long hair, good cheekbones, dazzling eyes), was his Sacred Heart – bright red, and pulsating with rays of neon-bright pink light shooting outwards from his bared breast, like a psychedelic firework display or a laser show at a Who concert. Pwhooaaar! All this could make you forgive the beard and the sandals.

My parents were appalled. They could now foresee the unthinkable happening. I was taking God far too seriously, and had all the makings of a future nun. One day a gang of 'rough' boys hurled some half-bricks at me from across the street on my way home from school, having spotted my distinctive navy-and-white uniform, which marked me out as going to a posh school. I thought that I would use this incident as a test. I prayed, and pretty rapidly, that Jesus would protect me from being hit, and sure enough – wowee! – the bricks sailed past and missed me. Proof! God existed, and was a really reliable bodyguard.

The nuns taught us a jingle that went, 'It's better to die than tell a lie.' I took this to be a literal statement. On a solitary occasion when my mother briefly left me alone at home, and instructed me not to tell any callers that I *was* alone, she returned to find me terrified, in tears, and convinced that I was about to hit the highway to hell. In her absence a caller *had* knocked on the door and I had told a lie. I was inconsolable, and my parents took the opportunity to whisk me away from the convent (attended also by Dirk Bogarde and Patsy Kensit at different times). In later years I was to display all the wild behaviour associated with ex-convent girls, yet I had never been a sworn-in Roman Catholic. I've always felt that I copped all of the guilt but none of the glory.

I was immediately admitted to and spent a totally undistinguished six years as a pupil at Lady Eleanor Holles School for Girls. Fenced off from an identical-looking boys' school next door, it looked more like a factory than a school, and was indeed a factory of academia. Now it has a reputation as holding Britain's second-to-top girls' school academic record, after St Paul's, and its ambitions were heading that way while I was there. I did not strike the staff as Oxbridge material, even though I had won some sort of scholarship to the school. I didn't shine at all in any subject, and indeed was so bad at mathematics that I became the first pupil in living history allowed *not* to take maths at O-level. I thought I'd scored a great triumph there! In the end I managed a respectable number of passes, but my image at school was so flighty, so much that of the 'raver', that no one expected me to do well, or even to be considered for higher education or university.

Many of the other girls came from quite wealthy – if sheltered – backgrounds. This became apparent to me during a French lesson when the class was asked to draw a plan of their homes. One girl put up her hand and asked, 'What's French for billiard room?'

After school there seemed to be the following options available: go to university and become a scientist; for the intellectually challenged, go straight from school to the St Giles without Cripplegate Secretarial College in the City of London (on the site of the original Lady Eleanor Holles School); or else, if you were a real halfwit, grab yourself a steady boyfriend, get married as early as possible after leaving school, and have kids. I knew I wanted something else, something more – a helluva lot more – from life, although I have never been able to understand why such a typical middle-class suburban girl from such a typical middle-class environment should have yearned so passionately for adventure and felt so different in my expectations from my contemporaries. Rock 'n' roll 'n' politics, I suppose, were influencing me deeply. It wasn't just the music; it was – still is – the attitude.

I was a proper teenager, I guess, rebelling against a society that by my mid-teens I really abhorred. To see my mother being made unhappy because she didn't have the trappings of English suburban middle-class society just sickened me. She would not invite her acquaintances to our home – and we had by now moved up the social ladder to a four-bedroomed house in Strawberry Hill, another area of Twickenham – because she was ashamed of the state of the furniture in the 'lounge', or because the gas cooker was an extremely out-of-date model. The idea of competing in materialist terms with neighbours, or even worse with friends, I found pointless and repugnant.

I had a number of jobs during the school holidays. I tried the outdoor life, working at a nursery, picking tomatoes and disbudding chrysanthemums. I'd go to bed at night unable to sleep for seeing chrysanthemums. I also worked for a time in an ice-lolly factory, on the assembly line, and I will never be able to touch such frozen delicacies again, as the girls I worked with took delight in licking the lollies before they were bagged and boxed. I tried waitressing in Richmond, and working as a clerk for the Milk Marketing Board at Thames Ditton when they needed to do a census of all the cows in the UK. Counting cows was about as inspiring as counting sheep. Or counting crows. I was eliminating the sort of job I didn't want for the future. I tried being a shop girl at C & A, in Kingston upon Thames, working in the cocktailwear department during the January sales. I couldn't quite grasp the concept of being paid on commission. In fact I didn't grasp the concept of selling at all. When a middle-aged woman customer with bloated skin the colour and consistency of white blotting paper asked my opinion of a lemon chiffon frock with diamanté straps I would tell her honestly that it didn't suit her. Well, I didn't know you were supposed to *lie* and flatter the customers. The other shop assistants were utterly appalled by the amount of money, or rather the lack of it, that was in my small brown pay packet at the end of my first and only week. No one working at C & A had ever earned so little. So a career based on salesmanship was not for me.

For a while I worked in a record shop, but didn't fare much better. I thought it was a heavenly job, playing records and getting paid for it (and I have continued to believe this for many years afterwards), but my shift was a lone one, and, having been shown the ropes once, I had no one to ask about such technicalities as reordering. Thus, when we were down to our last copy of my current favourite, I would say it had sold out. When the shop's profits began to plummet, the owners soon found the flaw – me. But at least I'd found out early on what I couldn't do, or wasn't going to be very successful at.

After his own schooldays, my father had become a student at the Regent Street Polytechnic (as later would I), where he took an unusual combination course of art and chemistry. He told me that most of his time was spent making stink bombs with his friends the Shand-Kydds, one of whom later married the Princess of Wales's mother, Frances, and also combing the electrical shops of nearby Soho for parts to make radio sets. Throughout my childhood he was meticulous about tuning a radio precisely. I was fascinated by the bubbling, underwater gurglings of the short-wave band, and would often stare enraptured at the place names on the dial, wondering where Hilversum was, or Prague.

The radiogram in the corner of the living room was the source of all entertainment, apart from books and the flicks. I adored putting on and handling records. I loved the smell of the heavy, breakable, scratched, twelve-inch-wide shellac, and the tunes from Rogers and Hammerstein musicals, or 'The Dream of Olwen', 'The Hall of the Mountain King' or Bing Crosby. I was captivated by the design and colours of the labels: His Master's Voice, red, gold and white; Decca – such a voluptuous-sounding word – a dark-blue background with silver lettering; and Brunswick, black-labelled, overprinted with gold.

My father's insistence on teaching me how to tune a radio and in due course his buying me one of my own was symptomatic of his attitude towards me. As I was his only child, he treated me both as a girl and as a boy. He taught me how to swim and how to row a boat, both on the Thames and at sea. He was surprised that I declined his offer to teach me to drive as soon as I was sixteen years old. By treating me as a person, not in terms of being a girl or a boy, he gave me the expectation that I could achieve anything I set my heart on. I had no elder brother whose needs would have to be put first, no elder sister whose hand-me-downs I must wait to wear, no siblings with whom I must share the attention and resources of my parents. Vassar College once carried out a survey among its female students which showed conclusively that 'only child' girls made up the largest group of high- and over-achievers when they reached adulthood. I believe that my father, treating me as he did, perhaps gave me the incentive to achieve what goals I have achieved, led me to not accept no for an answer and to breach areas previously considered exclusive male enclaves, even with my inexplicably extreme low level of self-esteem.

I had been a fat, untidy-looking child (see what I mean?), and was now an ugly teenager. My nickname during my years at secondary school was 'Treetrunks', on account of my straight, shapeless legs. My best friend, Sheila, had everything that, at fourteen years old, I did not. She had short, dark curly hair, whereas mine was lank and straight; she had good looks, to the extent of possessing a professionally photographed model's portfolio; and she had a stunning older brother. Her parents were in the fashion business. Their house had double glass doors to the sitting room, and they served delicacies such as gherkins, which I had not heard of before, and which I did not know how to eat. Because of her parents' profession, she always wore sumptuously glamorous clothes, such as a white winter wool coat, and of course she had a perfect figure. I'd do my best to compete, wearing Teenager at C & A, and Sheila's mother would look me up and down, pricing what I was wearing. It was most humiliating. (It was no less so some years later when Joan Collins did the same thing to me at a party for the Scandinavian actress Julie Ege, a friend of mine. Not that by then I was wearing Teenager at C & A, of course.)

Sheila, blissfully aware of the torture I was going through, and me believing that I was the most hideous adolescent since the study of anthropology had been established, would throw the odd crumb of comfort my way. One of her many male admirers had commented that I had a nice personality. Personality? PERSONALITY! I leapt upon this apparent compliment with alacrity. If I was not to be blessed with good looks with which to attract the opposite sex, then I would develop this other means. I interpreted 'personality' to mean being pleasant to people – being ultra-pleasant in fact, agreeing with everything anyone said to me. I did this at every possible social occasion for the next seven years, till I realized what a prat I was being and made up for lost time by picking an argument at every available opportunity.

Gradually I lost my hideous pudding-bowl hairstyle, grew my fair hair long, and washed it with 'Sta-blonde' – the choice being between that and 'Brunitex' shampoo, as advertised on Radio Luxembourg. Little did my father know when he bought me the tiny white Bakelite bedside radio what a profound effect it was going to have on me. Through the erratic signal of the maddeningly difficult-to-locate 208 metres on the medium waveband I discovered a new and secret teenage culture. New, wild music: American pop stars, rhythm and blues – Chuck Berry, Howlin' Wolf. My extracurricular activities involved hanging out in coffee bars, record shops, clubs and cinemas, and going to gigs and parties (which all seemed innocent enough to me), and I was already well into film culture – Brando, Bardot, Juliette Greco, James Dean. Now here was a soundtrack to go with it. I loved the idea of being part of a teenage 'cult' that dressed differently, thought differently, and read different books and listened to different music from the squares at school or in the 'hood, even if, as a suburban English schoolgirl, it was quite difficult to emulate moody Hollywood movie stars such as Natalie Wood, or wear anything that remotely resembled James Dean's red windcheater in *Rebel Without a Cause*.

Before long I found my 'cult' identity. I was a 'Bo' – a Bohemian. Which meant wearing a home-made butcher's-stripe blue-and-white tube-shaped dress, with my dad's shirt worn over the top, its tails tied together round my waist. I'd carry a woven straw 'fish basket' instead of a handbag, wear black eyeliner and white lipstick, and either walk barefoot or wear only flat Indian gold-printed leather sandals. I eschewed pop music, listening only to jazz, and got very precious about Jean-Paul Sartre, Paul Klee and existentialism. And Twickenham, despite being the stulti-fying kernel of suburbia as far as I was concerned, did at least have in its environs the ill-reputed Eel Pie Island club.

Eel Pie is a small islet in the Thames, and was home to many early raves. Hidden from the river by trees and bushes, in the centre of the island was a ramshackle building that had been a fashionable hotel for the Thames boating fraternity in the thirties. Now the ballroom, with its original sprung floor, jumped to a different tune. Jazz and later some of the first music created by the Rolling Stones blared out across the island, which had gained a huge notoriety even before the Stones arrived on the scene. 'Nice' girls did not frequent Eel Pie Island. It was said to be a place where a young girl would be sure to lose her virginity, so dense were the myriad dark pathways overhung with willow-laden branches and leafy unlit glades – natural girl traps.

Understandably, Eel Pie's notorious reputation drew me like a magnet. The original chain ferry that linked the island to the 'mainland' had been replaced by a narrow arched bridge after the ferry sank one Christmas, drowning the ferrymaster and a number of others. As a toll was charged to cross the bridge, I made every effort to make it to the island without paying the toll. Conveniently I had a voluptuous friend, Marion, who lived on the island and would row me across in her boat. I can't remember ever being inside the club – I was probably too young to be allowed in – but the fun was dodging the weird geezers stalking through the bushes.

Although my virginity remained intact, my social terrain was expanding. A coffee bar called L'Auberge in Richmond, overlooking the town's spectacular river bridge, was a major west-London Bohemian stronghold. This in turn had close links with Cy Laurie's jazz club in Windmill Street, Soho – exposed by a Sunday tabloid as being a drug-taking den of iniquity the week after my first visit to it. I also spread my fledgling wings out to Kingston, where close on a hundred ravers would gather on a church green opposite the Kenya Coffee House every Saturday summer evening, to descend in our gate-crashing hordes on any party within a thirty-mile radius.

Such was the academic snobbery at my school that no one among the staff showed any interest in or offered any encouragement regarding my future, given that I clearly wasn't university material. But I wasn't giving in to parental pressure to go to secretarial college either. 'It will be something to fall back on,' they would say. I had no intention of 'falling back' anywhere. I had made my mind up that I wanted to be a journalist, and I found a course at the Regent Street Polytechnic in central London. With that I launched myself into Soho life.

II

Once I got to the Polytechnic it became obvious that it was
the art students who were the coolest. The girls wore
purple dresses and black stockings, and had their hair mid-
shoulder length and woefully unkempt. The boys, in beige
suede and drainpipes, danced like demented daddy-long-
legs. After one term I had successfully infiltrated their
clique, and now my personal party network included
the delights of all the leading London art colleges: the
now Central St Martin's, the Royal College, Chelsea and
Hampstead. These were populated, for the most part, by
teenagers like myself, all innocence.

Then I discovered Sam Widges, the strangest daytime
hangout in Soho. This was frequented by such characters
as Ironfoot Jack, who indeed stumped in on an iron arti-
ficial leg, a billowing black cloak flying out behind him. In
one corner of the premises the Astrologer set up shop, a
painted wooden sign on the table in front of him. The
jukebox blared out Ella Fitzgerald's 'Ev'ry Time We Say
Goodbye' and Dave Brubeck's 'Take Five', and I sat waiting
hour after hour, day after day, for a bloke called Dave, on
whom I had an unrequited crush. Gradually, suburban
just-out-of-school girl that I was, I was accepted by Sam
Widges's clientele.

My still-home-to-Strawberry-Hill-at-night naivety knew no bounds. Little Joey, son of a famous folk musician, befriended me, and often asked me to take care of mysterious packages secreted in a Little Red Riding Hood-type basket while he disappeared for several hours at a time. On one occasion he told me he'd been chased out of a house and had had to scale a ten-foot wall to escape. It just never occurred to me what the perpetual paranoid glances over his shoulder could possibly mean. Similarly I never thought twice about the occupation of a young woman with whom I'd share the window seat and stroke the in-house cat. She wore the heaviest black eye make-up I'd ever seen, which gave her eyes a hooded, sinister look. Around four o'clock each afternoon she would depart with a cheery but matter-of-fact farewell and say she was going to work. It took me years to realize she was a full-time hooker. As for those male customers at Sam Widges who wore bewilderingly flamboyant women's clothes, I didn't know what to make of them at all.

Though I was the youngest in the class on my journalism course, it soon dawned on me that I was going to learn more about life, and maybe journalism, hanging out in Soho than attending lectures at the School of Journalism in Great Titchfield Street. Especially as the witch-like, claw-fingered shorthand teacher decided to concentrate her skills on those students who already had a rudimentary grasp of Pitman's shorthand, rather than a total novice such as myself. When the awkward occasion of annual exams came around, she just encouraged the incompetents among us to cheat blatantly. Which wasn't a lot of use when it became necessary to carry out verbatim court reporting.

It became clearer and clearer that the rest of the course

I was studying wasn't an awful lot of use either. In fact it became evident, towards the end of my one and only year as a full-time student, that the course was, if anything, *worse* than useless. It appeared that if I should tell any prospective newspaper owner/employer that I had taken part in this meaningless diploma course I would never get a job in journalism at all. Ever. The reason being that most, if not all, news editors and other hirers-and-firers in the reporting and sub-editing game had 'come up the hard way'; they were usually dour Scots or spoke like *The Archers'* Walter Gabriel, had struggled their way up from being a lowly copy boy or teamaker, and didn't hold with any of this new-fangled college-taught journalism. The sentiments of such gnarled, hard-bitten, cynical, living, breathing, walking B-movie clichés were later perfectly captured by the Monty Python 'Four Yorkshiremen' sketch. As it goes, they were probably right. But I had yet to find this out.

One of the set books on my course, together with a large dollop of Hemingway, was Graham Greene's *Brighton Rock*. Within a year of college I was packing my bags and leaving home to live in the infamous seaside town. The taxi driver who helped me pile my belongings out of the family home in Strawberry Hill said casually, 'You going back to school, love?' I was furious. I wanted to say, 'Actually I'm going to live in sin with a married man in Brighton.' Which I was.

This had come about through my first job after leaving college, which was as a trainee reporter at a news agency. This agency sold news items, as distinct from a newsagent's, which sells newspapers. Gruff-voiced tipsters would leave cryptic phone messages telling of bullion raids at Heathrow, botched bank robberies in Hounslow, multiple pile-ups on major dual carriageways near Kingston upon Thames, fatalities in fires in Feltham – any item of potential national news interest which had happened in south-west London was our business. Being the junior, I was not the one to roar off in a sports car or bark 'Hold the front page' down a sizzlingly hot phone line when a story broke. In those pre-fax days it was my job to dictate the same news story or tip-off item to every national newspaper and agency. I couldn't drive a car, so the only way I could become a newshound myself and follow up a running news story was to do all interviews and detective work by phone. I learned pretty quickly that, in terms of doorstepping, it's a lot easier for a potential interviewee to hang the phone up on you than to shut the door in your face.

My early shift would start at 6 a.m. with routine calls to local police and fire stations. All I had to work with was the telephone and my voice – talking people into being interviewed at 6.45 in the morning about a neighbour's chimney fire, or asking them to run down the street and get the fire victim to come to the phone. On the extremely rare occasions when I would be allowed out of the office to follow up a story in person, the interviewees would be, without exception, surprised at my youthful appearance. 'Ooh,' they would say, 'we were expecting someone much older.'

Without realizing it, I must have been developing a quality in my voice which communicated well on the phone. And that, it dawned on me a long time later, was how I had unwittingly taught myself the rudiments of broadcasting. I still say to all would-be radio presenters that broadcasting is precisely like making a phone call. A radio show might have millions of listeners, but they are not all massed together in a giant stadium. They are either alone or in a very small group, and you address them individually, because radio is an intimate phone-call performance, not in any way similar to Adolf Hitler addressing adoring Nazis at a rally in Nuremberg.

One evening while I was working late, a reporter called me from the *Daily Express* to ask me to file a story on the local situation in what was at the time becoming a national flu epidemic. This was an entirely routine situation. What was not routine at all was that the *Express* guy called me back later to ask how I was getting on with the story. Tough-talking Fleet Street journalists just did not do this. I was still a very naive teenager and I didn't realize he was chatting me up. He called back again, and then again, each time dropping some amazing piece of information about himself, such as that he had written proper, published books by the time he was in his mid-twenties, and that he had been thrown out of Egypt for spying. I was not just wildly impressed, I was swept off my feet. And totally unprepared for the circumstances that were to follow.

Until this time I'd been happy to hunt with the pack, or hang around with a gang of kids my own age or younger. At the end of my college year I'd had an idyllic holiday in the south of France with three art students, a girl and two boys, one of whom, Janice Ashby, now a revered New York designer, has remained one of my most cherished friends. I'd developed a romance with Leslie Spitz, one of the boys. It had been pure and beautiful innocent teenage stuff. The collision with this Fleet Street man was quite outside my experience. I felt almost as though fate had wrapped itself round me and that I had no choice but to do its bidding. Absolutely the last thing I had planned was to get involved with an older man – married, as it turned out, and the father of a three-year-old daughter. What then ensued was a messy affair, his marriage breaking up and the two of us almost literally running away together to get plotted up in Brighton. Not too much later I was to marry this man myself, and he became the father of my two children, Alex and Lucy. He had a powerfully persuasive personality, was a clever and talented writer, but had a tendency to volatility which after seven years of emotional see-sawing became too much to deal with. I had been far too young and immature for my years to enter into an adult relationship, and too young and immature to realize it, but I was also headstrong and felt that, despite my wish for independence and a career, destiny was taking hold. I do not regret what happened, because by having my children so young in life I now enjoy a brilliant relationship with them – more as if we are siblings rather than mother and children. And those first few years in Brighton were full of action. It was George IV who, when Prince of Wales, 'created' the town as a seaside health centre and an operational HQ for his nefarious activities with women, and the place has never lost its air of raffishness.

The wonderfully named Victor Gorringe was editor-in-chief of both the *Brighton Evening Argus* and its smaller sister weekly paper, the *Brighton and Hove Gazette*. Victor had a bristly ginger moustache, wore ginger-tinged spectacles, and commanded his newspaper domain, hands clasped behind his head, leaning backwards, from a creaking, lichen-green, leather button-backed chair. He struck me as a pompous iconoclast, and on the first and each subsequent occasion I was summoned to his office I willed the chair to collapse under him. I had applied for a job as a general reporter on the *Evening Argus*, at that time so prestigious a provincial paper that its journalists were almost automatically headhunted by Fleet Street. Such was my brief, inadequate and sleazy experience in journalism that he roared at me, 'With your background I shall *never* give you a job on the *Argus*.' I must have looked so crest-fallen, having moved to Brighton with little prospect of work as a journalist in the town outside of the Argus group, that he then conceded begrudgingly, 'Well . . . you can have one month's trial on the *Gazette*.'

The editorial department of the *Brighton and Hove Gazette* was entirely comprised of male sports fanatics. As I wasn't male, couldn't play cricket, and wasn't initially a fervent fan of ice hockey or football, I soon realized that my ability as a journalist would be judged solely on the only other passionate pursuit of the *Gazette* staff – drinking. My arrival coincided with the annual staff Christmas pub crawl through the picturesque village of Rottingdean. Reporting skills were irrelevant. If I could drink the *Gazette* staff under every pub table between Rottingdean seafront and the South Downs, I'd got the job.

A year later almost to the day, and gloriously contented being the girl *Gazette* reporter, I was summoned to Victor Gorringe's office. 'How would you like a job on the *Argus*?' he said, beaming broadly. 'But I thought you said . . .' I began, and then surprised myself by continuing, 'No, thank you. I'm very happy where I am.' Victor rocked violently back in his creaky chair and exploded: 'People would give their right arm for an opportunity like this.' (A little tactless as a metaphor, since the chairman of the Southern Publishing Company, which owned the *Evening Argus*, had indeed given his right arm to the job when he'd lost it in a printing machine accident.) 'There'll be no argument,' continued Victor. 'You'll start as a feature writer on the *Evening Argus* next Monday.'

So a job turned into a career. Gorringe had upped the ante, and I had now to prove myself among a sparklingly talented peer group. They included Jack Tinker, who was to become a legendary theatre critic, and John Pitman, later a fly-on-the-wall investigative TV reporter. I knew instinctively that this was a specially talented group of people, destined for brilliant careers. Wit flew like paper darts across the open-plan reporters' office. I drank 'gin and sin', a lethal concoction of spirit and white Cinzano, every lunchtime, afternoon and evening, and threw up all over the bed at night. My job included writing a 'women's page', film reviews and court reports, and covering the meetings of Peacehaven Parish Council. This last assignment was punishment meted out for bad behaviour by Jock Miller, the (dour Scot) news editor. The biggest piece of news that could possibly emanate from a meeting of Peacehaven Parish Council would be its chairman or treasurer dropping dead from a heart attack mid-meeting, so to spend an entire evening making notes about its petty pontifications was pure purgatory. 'I'm eighteen and my life is ebbing away,' I would write in my scroll-top notebook.

Of course, I realized later that making a story out of a Peacehaven PC meeting was the best form of journalistic training I could possibly have. Learning to make something from such small occasions meant that the big news stories wrote themselves. I would directly attribute the twelve-year success of my Radio 1 request show to my ability to scan a listener's letter and find a story or an angle to it, based on my days as a Brighton reporter scrabbling for a one-paragraph news item.

But what had attracted me to journalism, namely a lack of daily routine, still held good. One day I might be covering Peacehaven Parish Council; the next conducting a film-location interview with my childhood Goon idol Peter Sellers, or with Sean Connery, the new James Bond screen sensation. Sometimes I was too drunk to complete my film reviews and John Pitman would write them for me. When John and I took over writing the *Argus* gossip column I was all for going to the beach all day and writing our column at night. It was John who would say, 'Annie, we write the column first, *then* we go to the beach.' If I did manage to stagger to my desk opposite his during the day, he would often look me straight in the eye and say, 'Did you have sex last night?' I'm sure this was where his peculiarly intimate but forthright style of TV journalism began.

I had by now met quite a few of the 'Darling, you were wonderful' brigade of actors, artists and aristos who lived in the Kemp Town end of Brighton. And, at this stage still married, I moved there as soon as possible from the staid Strawberry Hill-like shores of Hove Actually (so called because the snobs of Hove, when asked if they live in Brighton, reply snootily, 'No, Hove, actually!'; you can even get Hove Actually rock) to an apartment at the top of a house in a gorgeous Georgian terrace at Black Rock. There my new landlord was Count William de Belleroche. This was a Belgian title which had mysteriously jumped a generation or two, as Willie's father, a contemporary of Picasso in Paris and a fellow painter, had been known simply as Albert de Belleroche. Willie was highly eccentric, agoraphobic and also a painter. His speciality was painting freshly caught dead fish. Then he would eat them.

Willie would think nothing of telephoning me upstairs from his ground-floor flat to ask what the weather was like. As this phone call was as likely to be at 3.30 a.m. as at any other time of day, I would wearily suggest that he should look out of the window. He would then ask me downstairs for a glass of wine. When I arrived at his apartment there would be no wine. There might be a pretty-looking young man Willie had met during his nocturnal-only ventures into the outside world, the odd detective inspector or two (to be kept sweet, I guessed), Willie's playboy friend the Honourable George Kinnaird, or a fishmonger who had delivered Willie's latest subject and had stayed on to party through the night. I felt as if I were starring in *Annie's Adventures in the Twilight World*. The actress Hermione Baddeley lived in the basement ('She's terribly jealous of the *other* Hermione [Gingold],' Willie would remark wickedly), another apartment was reserved exclusively for Willie's six cats, and in yet another flat in this huge house lived Viscount Peter Churchill. He was a godson of Queen Victoria, by his own admission the 'black sheep' of the Churchill family, drove a green 'n' white 'n' chrome fifties Oldsmobile, wore black polo-neck sweaters, and cut his white hair in a Beatle fringe before the Beatles did. I was later told that he ended his days penniless in Tangier. Peter I regarded as the height of cool, and it was he who was to provide me with the subject matter for my first radio documentary.

Once Laurence Olivier had set up house with his wife, the actress Joan Plowright, in a black-tiled mansion in Royal Crescent, a gently bowed terraced row of exquisite houses set back from Kemp Town's seafront, the social pecking order in Brighton worked its way from the Oliviers downwards. The scramble among Brighton's actors and aristos to make friends with the Oliviers was undignified and embarrassing. 'Larry', later to take the title Lord Olivier of Brighton, must have been the biggest fish to land on the beach at Brighton since the eighteenth-century Prince of Wales. The world's most famous actor was nest-building after his disastrous relationship with Vivien Leigh. He became the country's best-known commuter, travelling supposedly incognito in farmer's plus-fours, after a successful publicity campaign he ran restored kippers to the breakfast menu of the Brighton Belle after this item had been cancelled.

The Brighton Belle (its carriages with their cream-and-chocolate livery now belong to the trans European Orient Express) was so spectacular a train, on a journey that was such endless daily and nightly fun, that its owner, British Rail, of course killed it off. But even after the Belle was replaced by ordinary rolling stock with a lowly buffet car, the party spirit of the former train, with its wood-panelled carriages and art-nouveau lamps, carried on. The train took on a personality of its own, and I was later to forge some of my most enduring friendships with people I met travelling from London to Brighton: Barry Langford, an antique-silver dealer who was later to become an innovative pop-TV producer – the man who put all the Rolling Stones as guest reviewers on *Juke Box Jury* at the same time – who would stagger on to the Belle when it pulled out of Brighton at 9 a.m. with his pyjamas under his trousers and £3,000 worth of Georgian silver teapots clanking in plastic bags; the Mad Hatter, the mad male milliner who would scream at innocent passengers, 'Don't think you can sit in this carriage wearing *that* combination of cotton and tweed' (they say it was inhaling all the hat glue that made him so crazy); Michael Heath, the cartoonist, sometimes in a benign silent rage because he'd got to think of three different gags for three separate publications in the one hour before the train reached London.

* * *

From film and book reviewing on the *Gazette* and *Argus*, it was a small step to reviewing pop records, and I developed a music review column which carried the excruciating strap line of 'Spin with Me'. I had no qualifications for reviewing pop records, but I did have a fascination with and a never-ending passion for music. Working briefly in the record shop during the school holidays had been one of my least disastrous forays into the future world of work when I was a young teenager. Now I was poised beautifully and quite accidentally to surf in on the huge tidal wave of the beat boom and the Beatles.

Maybe I wasn't in Liverpool, but I was an hour away from London and I had a pop column on an influential provincial evening newspaper. I was already building contacts with the record business, arranging interviews with pop stars, as well as writing reviews of their records. When 'Love Me Do' hit the charts in 1962 I don't think that anyone had any idea of what was to come. (The sixties didn't begin in 1960, nor did they end at the actual turn of the decade.) Historically, it's quite easy to see why it happened as it did – a matter of geography, Liverpool being a home port to sailors who worked the transatlantic ships and brought back rhythm-and-blues records from the United States and made the music accessible to young groups like the Beatles.

All the cool music until the Beatles arrived on the scene was American: Elvis, Little Richard, Fats Domino, Muddy Waters, Miles Davis. All we teenagers had in Britain were cover versions, or tenors left over from the fifties. But we had force of numbers, we had opinions, we had a voice, through our disposable income and teenage demands, and if you were cheeky enough you could get something going even if you weren't a deb and didn't speak like the Queen.

As it had been before, it was radio that was my link with the music.

I'm extremely pleased now that in the midst of all this I got pregnant. If I hadn't started having children at a young age, I would have found myself in the predicament that so many women have encountered since, particularly in the eighties and nineties, where they are well into a career, reach thirty-five, and find the biological clock ticking away and become desperate to have children.

I was the first person among my peer group to get pregnant. I had no idea what I was doing. Basically I felt that pregnancy shouldn't make any difference – it was just part of life going forward. I had a boat on the beach at time, and I even carried on dragging this up and down the shingle. I didn't go to any classes and stayed away from pregnant women – I didn't want to hear any off-putting stories. I did, however, go freelance, which enabled me to keep on working. The only real difficulties were in my head – I was self-conscious with friends, thinking they'd find it all very boring.

I treated myself to a private nursing home in Hove for the birth. Count Willie was terribly excited when I went off in the middle of the night. He wanted to come with me, and volunteered to be the child's godfather. I declined, believing him to be potentially a 'bad influence'. If I'd known then of Alex's later wild experiences, I would have realized that even Willie would have been a restraining influence and would have given in gracefully.

Childbirth gave me my first experience of hard drugs. Pethidine, it was called, and, apart from making me throw up, it made me high as a kite and I loved it. Back at home, I soon sobered up as the weight of my responsibility for another human being bore down on me. Here we were in this freezing cold flat, during a very cold winter, no central heating and I was sure Alex was going to die and that it would all be my fault.

By the time Alex was six months old I was literally jumping up and down all over the furniture to the Beatles' music, waiting and listening out for *Saturday Club*, a show on BBC radio which seemed to feature the Beatles more often than other programmes. At that time the BBC would just slot them into conventional showbiz programmes, which I found weird. (As I did the fact that during the first tour I ever saw them on they were supporting Helen Shapiro, a tiny Jewish girl in her very early teens, Britain's very own Brenda Lee, with a deep, resonant singing voice and an image belonging to the fifties.) The Beatles, though, were definitely of a new era. They looked like the London art students I'd hung out with on Hampstead Heath and at the all-night parties in the cherry-blossomed avenues off the Finchley Road. I recognized the look, the attitude and the vibe.

I first met the Beatles at the Brighton Hippodrome, a magnificent theatre, now a bingo hall – naturally. It was set at front and back between two of the oldest thorough-fares in Brighton – Ship Street and Middle Street – which dated back to the fishing village of Brighthelmstone and still sported their original grey-Sussex-pebble frontages. The day the Beatles came to town the police put up crash barriers across Ship Street. I'd never seen this before. People had begun to gather in broad daylight, hours before the group was due to play. I had in my hand a letter on headed notepaper from NEMS Enterprises, Brian Epstein's management company, authorizing me to be admitted backstage to interview the band. The police pulled back the metal barriers to let me through. As I climbed the stairs I got my first view of a Beatle in the flesh – it was Paul McCartney, standing next to Brian Epstein. They both looked so unexpectedly *tall*.

It had occurred to me that during the course of their interviews the Beatles were being asked the most trivial questions, day in, day out: 'What's your favourite vegetable, George?'; 'What do you say to a girl on the first date, Ringo?' How unutterably tedious it must have been for these clearly intelligent, witty and irreverent young men. My plan was to somehow entertain *them*, make it a two-way intercourse. It's a maxim I've stuck to ever since. When my turn came to be interviewed by callow young journalists I'd never give anything to the blank-faced cold fishes who would stick rigidly to their written questions, never look you in the eye, and never give anything of themselves. I wanted the Beatles' interview with the *Brighton Evening Argus* to be not just pleasant but memorable. Or at least provocative. 'So, John, you're the difficult one, then?' I said to John Lennon. It worked. 'Eh?' he responded, looking at me sharply. I had succeeded in getting his attention, even though it was Paul McCartney of the velvet brown eyes and perfectly shaped semicircular brows that I was melting inside for.

The Hippodrome was the first of many meetings with the Beatles, and I always got on well with them. I believe the Hippodrome is where I also had my first meeting with the Rolling Stones, when they were down-bill on a Charlie and Inez Foxx tour. David Bailey had admired my new tan corduroy trouser suit, before I was inexplicably thrown out of the backstage area by the Stones' security team. I was bewildered. I couldn't *possibly* have been mistaken by manager Andrew Loog Oldham's gang as a hooker or an undesirable. Perhaps I hadn't looked enough like a hooker or even undesirable enough.

Once I had had my first child I felt the hideous tentacles of conformity trying to smother me, stifle me, drag me down into mothers' meetings, women's circles and coffee mornings, like mournful sirens saying, 'No more fun for you – you're a mother now. You're one of us.' I wasn't having any of it. But it was harder now to rebel. None of my friends had had children. They were still out there being make-up artistes, actresses, public-relations people. I thought my baby was cool (he was!) – we had a rapport, and he never cried.

At least I'd retained enough independence to be a regular freelance for the *Evening Argus*, and I continued to write the record review column. Once the avalanche of the Beatles' initial success happened, more and more bands came along in their wake. I had a feeling much, much later that going to live in Brighton had diverted me from a path which would undoubtedly have brought me into contact with the Rolling Stones at Eel Pie Island, or the Station Hotel, Richmond, had I still been living in that area. But the diversion didn't take me too far from the musical revolution, as it was going on everywhere. Brighton itself had several established venues for live acts, and they all came to play there. My pop column gave me immediate access to the upcoming stars in terms of interviews, and national record companies seemed surprisingly cooperative in putting a lowly provincial reporter (as I saw myself) in touch with their new stars. I was up for it and wildly enthusiastic. The arrival of pirate pop radio was the toffee on the pudding.

Then events began to happen very fast. A local councillor, Ray Blackwood, called me at home as a tip-off, to ask whether I would be interested in auditioning for a BBC television reporter's job in Southampton. Working in television had never crossed my mind before. I was crazy about contemporary music, but I could see no way then of becoming involved. If I could have sung, I'd have been a singer; if I could have played guitar, I'd have started a band. What I lacked most of all was self-confidence – so much so that it never even occurred to me that any options in pop music were open to me.

When I got in front of the camera at the BBC's studio near Southampton Docks, I thought, 'This is all right, I feel comfortable with this.' What I liked most of all was that as a reporter for TV you worked direct to camera, without having to write anything down. I was offered a job, with the proviso that I move to Southampton. This was impractical. I had a husband and a small child to consider – facts I had omitted to mention before the audition. But the experience had planted in my head the realization that there were other avenues I might explore in broadcasting. Like radio.

As a student at the Regent Street Polytechnic, I had passed Broadcasting House every day for a year, but, never ever thought that this strange piece of thirties architecture, with its white prow like that of a stately liner jutting into Langham Place, would be where I would spend most of my working life. The BBC was a huge, powerful, unapproachable monolith to me. To work for the BBC would be similar to having a Cabinet post – a distant, unattainable Establishment role. But now I'd had this one experience of being in a TV studio, and feeling so at home with it, I had a little more courage. Only a little. The fortress of BH was manned and womanned by forbidding names like

Grace Wyndham Goldie and Joanna Scott Hyphen Moncrieff. Hopelessly intimidating.

Then I discovered BBC Regions, who not only made programmes transmitted to their own local area, but also fed programmes into the national network. Music was my passion, but initially the only way into broadcasting seemed to be by creating small news features. I found an ally in Bristol, HQ of BBC West. Whoever had mapped out the original BBC areas had made Brighton the border of the West region. So it was that Bill Salisbury, a producer in Bristol, helped me make my first forays into radio journalism.

I worked from an unmanned studio inside the extraordinary Royal Pavilion in Brighton. The velvet ropes that cordoned off visitors to the palace would be drawn aside, and I made my way up winding stairs, like Princess Irene, my favourite character from my favourite childhood book, George MacDonald's *The Princess and the Goblin*. Whereas I had struggled and always felt uneasy about my competence when writing for a newspaper, and later magazines, sitting in front of a microphone with headphones on felt sort of right, sort of easy, sort of 'Yes, this is what I was supposed to do.' I had found it by accident.

III

In the mid-sixties I moved into a house in Montpelier Road, Brighton. Pete Townshend of the Who came and played the grand piano there after opening a tiny discotheque on Western Road called The Box, which was all decorated in silver. I too went through a silver year around that time. I made a bathroom silver, sprayed white knee-high boots silver, and wore a silver fur coat and silver plastic poppet beads as a necklace.

Montpelier Road is a long, sloping street which runs up from the seafront to the town centre, and the house was great to play in. It had five storeys, including a basement area that was so spooky that initially I was afraid to look in the ancient cupboards for fear of finding – literally – skeletons. The house was completely dilapidated and had therefore been cheap to buy, but I knew it had enormous potential. It was – is – a bow-fronted Victorian house, a Grade-2 listed building that had been turned into a rooming house with Yale locks on the inside doors, but it had all its original features intact, including the iron kitchen range and the marble fireplaces, which were coated in dark-brown paint. It was one of the few houses in the street which had remained one dwelling, all the others having been converted into flats. It needed a lot of work, but that was fun. I had psychedelic William Morris purple-and-blue wallpaper up the stairwells, and purple Wilton carpet on the unending staircases. Mike Love of the Beach Boys had got into transcendental meditation in Brighton and wanted to buy the house from me.

No one who lives within those four walls now will ever know what went on there. I quite like that. But in my time there it was a monument to partying. People I swear I've never met in my life still come up to me and say, 'I came to a party at your house in Brighton.' My only hope of identifying them is to ask, 'Which decade?' Having a jukebox certainly helped the parties along. There's a certain earthy, wraparound bass sound that emanates from jukeboxes which is not to be found on your expensive hi-fi systems. However, I ruined really valuable 'promo' copies of seven-inch singles, such as David Bowie's 'Space Oddity', by subjecting them to the grinding pressure of the jukebox needle.

Through the sixties and seventies people came and stayed and left, or came and stayed and stayed, either on the top floor or in the basement, which was gradually 'done up' as a guest suite. John and Monique Davidson started their fashion business J & M Davidson from 'the moat suite' in the basement (so called because of how frequently it flooded). 'JJ the DJ from LA', a friend of Roger Daltrey and his wife, Heather, came for a weekend because Roger thought Brighton would hold more allure for this distinguished broadcaster from California than the Daltreys' magnificent but remote mansion in East Sussex. JJ stayed for weeks. He went to Paris for the weekend to see Rod and Britt (Stewart and Ekland), then called a day later from Victoria Station in London saying, 'I miss you – I'm coming back to Brighton.' Mahin came from Esfahan in Iran to do a bit of au pairing, became one of my greatest friends, and was transformed into a radical art student. There were also Inga from Stavanger, Eva from Stockholm, Doris from Switzerland, French Annie and Susan Barnes, who had pulled my ad for a PA out of the wastepaper bin as an afterthought, and who ended up meeting her future husband, Jeremy Pascal, as she and I trained it back to Brighton after a Beach Boys gig.

All sorts came round later, during the seventies and early eighties. Eric Clapton became quite a close friend, along with Pattie Boyd/Harrison/Clapton, whom I'd known since the Beatles days. Being a mate of Eric carried penalties. You had to go to watch West Bromwich Albion with him, as well as deal with his very deadpan sense of humour and practical joking. I ended up staying at his place in Surrey after one of his big gigs – I think it was Blackbushe Airport, when Bob Dylan was also performing – and then propping up the bar with him at the pub at the bottom of his large garden the next morning. I had to drive to central London to do a live show for Radio 1 that day. Being late for a live broadcast is just not on the agenda. 'How long will it take me to get there from here?' I asked. 'Oooh, twenty minutes, maximum,' Eric said drily, knowing very well it would take me an hour and a half. Not that Eric was dry in other senses of the word at that time. He may have come off some harder drugs during this period, but he chopped out a good few lines at Montpelier Road, and drank a fair old bit. But then so did I. Imbibers tend to hang together, whether their poison be smack or Smirnoff. And, by the same token, when such users dry out, they then tend to avoid former cronies for fear of being led back into temptation. Quite understandably.

Apart from parties, Montpelier Road became an ideal

'all back to mine' venue for performers playing in Brighton, after the gig. Keith Moon roared in after a Who gig at Sussex University, left his driver, Dougal, in the kitchen, and roared off again into the night to cause mayhem wherever he could find it. This is what got Keith into so much trouble. As he so often pointed out, by the time *he* had finished work, where was there to go? His favourite cohort was Viv Stanshall of the Bonzo Dog Band (themselves frequent visitors at Montpelier Road). Ian McLagan and Kim Moon, Keith's ex-wife, once took so long to get ready for a fancy-dress party while they were staying in the downstairs guest suite that by the time they emerged up the stairs with stars in their eyes and spangles on their bodies nearly all the other guests had gone home. But they did look fucking amazing. Robert Fripp, the avant-garde guitarist from King Crimson, tried to summon up ghosts by lighting blue, silver and white candles in front of a mirror reputed to have been haunted by two young women in Regency dress. 'It's all very well you wanting to sit here all night summoning up spectres,' I said to him, 'but what if they won't go away again? I *live* here.' Robert was very into white magic, but my desire not to have ghostly guests prevailed on that occasion.

Then there was the benchmark Warner Bros party for the Faces. A friend of mine who worked at their record company was looking for somewhere to have an after-show party in Brighton for the then current 'wildest boys in rock', and suggested my place – the company would provide the food and drink. It went off surprisingly smoothly. All the guests, including John Peel, had been bussed down from London, and after they'd all eaten and drunk they got back on the bus and went home, leaving copious amounts of unconsumed alcohol. So, when my mate at Warner's asked if another band could have a party at my house, this time Curved Air, I said, 'No problem.' But of course this time there was, although it was not at all the fault of Curved Air. Hundreds of people showed up. This was in the days when my home had furniture and carpets, and wasn't just an empty house with bare floorboards. Now I know why people have 'security' on the door at their parties – otherwise whoever opens the front door just lets anyone in, as they did that night with the dozens of strangers who turned up. No one, including myself, knew who was invited and who wasn't. The event became a big PR affair. People flowed in through the front door, and the drinks flowed into their glasses and flowed out of the house by the bottleful. One geezer, who introduced himself as a visitor from Africa who'd heard the noise and music from the street and was curious to know what an English party was like, had simply wandered in, like everyone else uninvited. However, he wished to inform me that he was shocked by the sight of people taking away whole bottles of whisky. He was the most polite of all the guests and he was a gatecrasher! And about the nicest bloke there. Other people lolled all over my stairs holding out empty glasses and shouting, 'Get me a brandy.' Eventually my hostess instincts deserted me and I shouted back, 'Get it yourfuckingself.'

The next day I pulled back the heavy curtains in the first-floor drawing room to reveal the full horror of the previous night's festivities. Not only were there comatose bodies curled in corners and slumped unconscious under settees, not only were there empty bottles in the bath and broken glass strewn like fairy dust in a fine film on every surface – the normal expected debris from any half-happening rock 'n' roll party – but there were also cigarette ends stubbed, screwed and ground into the upholstery, and large dark brown burns seared into the floorboards, the walls, and the rugs, carpets, curtains and tables. Toppled bottles had poured their contents into widening dark red and brown stains under every chair and on each inch of carpet that had not already been burnt by fag ends. I phoned my friend at Warner Bros and in a shocked whisper told him the terrible news. 'No worries,' he said breezily. 'Get an estimate for the damage and we'll send you a cheque.' They did as well, though I was most anxious not to be seen paying a cheque for several thousand pounds from Warner Bros Records into my bank account, in case it was thought by Radio 1 to be payola.

Other Montpelier Road happenings included Dennis Waterman, Adam Ant, Amanda Donohue, Ian Dury, the Who, Stewart Copeland, Sting and Andy Summers and the rest of the Police entourage, long before even they had thought about asking me to accompany them around the world.

After the Curved Air party I had sworn never to have another one, but time heals . . .

IV

Local radio journalism was all well and good, but, based as I was outside London, with a small child and, most important of all from the BBC's point of view, *no degree*, I began to find it hard to move on. My interview in Southampton had given me the bug for TV work, and it was becoming apparent that, as pop music continued to burgeon, opportunities were beginning to present themselves for young people without the proper 'background' or experience to get on the box. Here again, chance was to play a part in my career.

One Sunday, some obscure instinct directed me to go and interview Dusty Springfield, who was playing at what was then the Essoldo in North Street, Brighton (now also a gaming hall). When I went backstage after Dusty's show, there was a woman sitting in the corner whom I'd been wanting to meet for some time. I'd become involved in part-managing a group called Peter and the Headlines. They had a deal with Decca and had made a record, and I was desperate to get them on *Ready Steady Go!*. The woman sitting in the corner was none other than Vicki Wickham, *RSG*'s editor. I'd actually applied for the presenter's job on her show, which went to Cathy McGowan. What I didn't know that evening was that Rediffusion were looking for a presenter for a sister programme, to be called *That's for Me*. I sent Vicki the Peter and the Headlines record and arranged to meet her in London. She told me that she wasn't that impressed by the band, but then, to my complete surprise, asked me if I was interested in doing a pilot for the new show.

No one told me that being a TV presenter was not, and never would be, a Proper Job. In 1964 or 1965 a thirteen-week series looked to be as good as a job for life, and it all appeared pretty straightforward. *That's for Me* was recorded in the same studio complex as *Ready Steady Go!*, with much the same crew and production staff. It had a highly innovative format, intercutting happening pop groups with clips from Busby Berkeley movies. Before it started, I was invited on to other TV shows made by Rediffusion; their press office organized interviews and photo sessions. Weird. I'd been used to doing interviews with celebrities, rather than being interviewed myself or photographed for magazines and newspapers. It all seemed like a bit of a joke; fun, nevertheless. Although this was supposed to be a TV request show, I had quite a considerable say in which bands got booked. I'd suggest Georgie Fame or the Yardbirds and, yo, there they would be in the studio.

The shows went out live, and there was no such thing as autocue, the great wonder of the twentieth century, whereby you can read your presentation script off a reflected paper roller that appears in the camera lens. My 'links' were straight off the cuff, unmemorized. Prepared, maybe, but delivered through simple terror rather than any kind of professionalism. For any show we'd be lucky to have one full-length camera rehearsal, giving a single chance to practise delivering one's lines.

I'd be fresh from Vidal Sassoon in Bond Street, where

I'd struck up a friendship with my then 'crimper', Allan McEowan (later to become TV producer of *Auf Wiedersehen, Pet*, a Hollywood mogul and husband of Tracey Ullman). Instead of listening to my indiscretions, he would tell me his.

In those days women in hairdressing salons were still shoved 'under the dryer' – a torture chamber resembling a huge hot metal beehive – for indefinite periods of time while the previous client was being 'combed out'. The crimper could leave you there for hours. An emotion somewhere between anger and panic would set in as I was marooned, under the dryer, fearful of being late for the camera rehearsal that preceded the weekly experience of doing a live, nationally networked TV show. 'This is not the *provinces* – get it *right*!' boomed the executive producer during one fluffed rehearsal. I'd never thought of myself as being 'provincial', so I took this as a huge personal slight, and from then on, I hope, became a better presenter.

Ludicrous as this may seem, it just didn't occur to me that being on TV made you 'famous'. 'You've just been recognized,' said the Beatles' press officer, Derek Taylor, to me as I walked down Kingsway with him towards the TV studio. Well, he was more used than I was to the experience of fame, owing to the Fab Four.

After the adrenalin rush of doing each programme, we would hit Soho for dinner and then go clubbing: the Ad Lib in Leicester Square, or the Scotch of St James off Berkeley Square, dancing to Motown music: Martha and the Vandellas' 'Dancing in the Street', the Velvelettes' 'Needle in a Haystack', the Supremes' 'Stop in the Name of Love'. Michael Caine would be sitting on a red velvet banquette the size of half of a first-class railway carriage, smiling benignly. Paul McCartney would sidle off the tiny

The family home in Ablon, France: my grandfather, left, my Dad, centre, and on the right my tall and elegant aunt, Florence, AKA June, AKA Friday.

My parents Basil and Celia on an unknown beach, before I was born.

Me at Kelvin Court clutching the cat, wearing the nearest thing to a tutu I ever possessed.

Above: We were all going to stay best friends for EVER. Lower Sixth Modern at Lady Eleanor Holles School. Me centre back, elsewhere Dumbo, Taddy and Mouse. Whatever happened to them?

Left: Only surviving picture of my bohemian days. Grubby raincoat, worn over Dad's shirt tied in front. Note contrast with my friend and fellow student Valerie Pitt, young elegance in pearls and white gloves – but we got on really well!

Me, Leslie and
Janice, Cap d'Antibes,
Côte D'Azur.

Me and Alex make
our modelling debut.
(*Helen Piers/Vivienne
Studios*)

Left:
Me – You sure
it's only done
10,000 miles?
Car salesman – You
bet your Courrèges
boots it has!

Below: The Mayor
of Worthing – no,
I can't remember
what HE was doing
on *Ready Steady Go!* –
Cathy McGowan,
Beau Brummell
and me.

Rehearsing in St James's Park, London, for my onslaught on the Royal Enclosure, Ascot, in jumpsuit and Kangol beret. (*Eric Harlow/Daily Mirror*)

Me and Mickey Dolenz of The Monkees. (*Harvey Mann/Daily Sketch*)

Keith Moon at Tara, his house in Chertsey, in front of THAT swimming pool.
Note lack of Rolls Royce. (*John Davidson*)

Lucy at probably her fourth outdoor festival that summer, with me and three unknown hippies.

Lucy and Alex on the steps of the house in Montpelier Road, Brighton.

Me in moody caftan style top
that I'd discovered in Tunisia.
(*Tony Barette/Daily Sketch*)

square parquet dance-floor and whisper to me, 'I saw you on TV tonight.' Hey, this was as interesting as tracking down murderers' ex-wives on housing estates such as Moulsecoomb or Whitehawk, behind the Brighton racecourse, for the *Brighton Evening Argus*.

Our show and the *Ready Steady Go!* mob were all part of the same gang, and I would often appear on *RSG*, as this was regarded as good 'cross-promotion' for our show. There was a great sense of camaraderie. Michael Lindsay-Hogg, the stylish and innovative director of *RSG*, did away with the idea of sets and used bare studio walls as a backdrop. It was a brilliantly original show. A whole generation tuned in on Friday nights. 'The Weekend Starts Here' was its slogan, and the Manfred Mann song 'Five, Four, Three, Two, One' would kick the show into action.

RSG was about music, dancing, fashion. And it was Vicki Wickham, who booked the acts, who single-handedly introduced Britain to the sound of Motown. I was just feet away from the Supremes, Stevie Wonder, and the Temptations as they performed on a tiny stage in the jam-packed *RSG* studio. The hand-picked, auditioned audience was at the mercy of the cameras, which would be *driven* across the studio floor like high-speed Chieftain tanks, and woe betide anyone who got in their way, or who became entangled and ensnared by the thick black cables snaking behind. Tight close-ups, unconventional camera angles, fast-cut vision mixing gave *RSG* its Look, the antithesis of glossy, big-production light-entertainment shows. And when the studio space ran out the action would move into a corridor, where Cathy McGowan might be found with three Rolling Stones and two members of the Dave Clark Five.

RSG turned the whole of the mid-sixties London pop

scene into a club. Dusty Springfield was semi-resident on the show, always lapsing into a loony Goon-type voice when she took over the role of guest interviewer. Sandie Shaw, with her shining sheet of hair and bewitching green eyes, was in the gang, as was the dry-witted, gangly Long John Baldry. Every week there seemed to be a whole new batch of fab new records made by ever fabber new pop stars. A sixteen-year-old Scottish redhead appeared from nowhere with a song called 'Shout', and Lulu was born. Twinkle, a teenager from the Surrey stockbroker belt, became an instant star with her motorcycle-tragedy song 'Terry'. And *RSG* created Britain's own Bob Dylan with a whispery-voiced, misty-eyed early hippie called Donovan Leitch and a song called 'Catch the Wind'.

It was the Biba period; Cathy McGowan was the main protégée of the designer Barbara Hulanicki, and we'd all wear new outfits every week. Dolly birds, we were called, most of us with long, sleek bobs; others, such as Marianne Faithfull and Patti Boyd, with longer, more flowing, blonde locks. As Cathy became 'Queen of the Mods', the Who exploded, almost literally, on to the mod scene. Their first TV appearance had been on *That's for Me*, not in person but on film – probably the first 'promo' shoot ever – directed by their managers Kit (son of classical conductor/composer Constant) Lambert and Chris (brother of actor Terence) Stamp. The group had just changed their name from the High Numbers and, of all the bands to appear on *RSG*, the Who made the greatest impact. There was a wild-eyed crazy intensity to all four of them. I arranged a late breakfast interview with them at a restaurant in Shepherd Market, Mayfair. They all talked together, they climbed all over the tables, and I think I ran out screaming. Ten years later I became fairly close friends with all of the Who, but at the start they all seemed quite as mad as their drummer, Keith Moon, later to be called 'Moon the Loon'. Once, after Keith's death, my daughter, Lucy, and I stayed with his widow, Kim, at Keith's bizarre and glorious house on the beach at Trancas Beach, Malibu, California, next door to Steve McQueen. For Lucy it was a great opportunity to ride horses and, together with Keith's daughter Mandy, she picked up a little of Keith's wickedness. As we adults sampled just about every one of those dark-glass-façaded restaurants along the Pacific Coast Highway between Trancas and Santa Monica, they found their own form of entertainment. In a classic Keith prank that was clearly embedded in her genes, Mandy, then eleven years old, with Lucy as her accomplice, was hitting the telephone and booking tables for six, eight or ten people under fictitious names at every eaterie from Malibu to Venice Beach. But I doubt she knew about the time when Keith, bored after a Who gig in Brighton, grabbed a phone, posed as a British Airways official, claimed that fog had grounded two thousand passengers, and booked every hotel room in the resort, then cruised up and down the seafront in his lilac Rolls-Royce, idly leaning out of the window and shouting to traffic cops, 'Know where I can find any birds?'

I got used to being chauffeured from Brighton to different parts of London or indeed Monte Carlo to be involved with TV 'specials' as well as the weekly *RSG* and *That's for Me* shows. The Glad Rag Ball at Wembley Arena of which I was a co-presenter had the headlining Rolling Stones performing 'Little Red Rooster' from a boxing ring in the centre of the audience. For the duration of the San Remo Song Festival in Italy, I commuted from the Hotel de Paris in Monaco. Paul Newman would be in the lift.

Then it all went horribly wrong. *That's for Me* was not the runaway success that *RSG* had become. After a thirteen-week run, the show was discontinued. But, not surprisingly, I was pretty well hooked on this TV-presenting lark, with its dressing up and hanging out. Up until this point I still had my 'credibility' (a word not yet in vogue) intact. I was a reasonably OK journalist and had done some quite respectable TV reporting and interviewing for other TV stations, but I now succumbed to the drug of being a 'presenter', to my cost in many ways, and therefore walked head first into my first bad 'career move'. I became a . . . bimbo TV game-show hostess.

The show was called *Sing a Song of Sixpence*, and my co-host was a distinguished silver-haired actor named Ronan O'Casey. Actually, he was most distinguished as being the dead body in the movie *Blow Up*, the corpse found in the corner of Greenwich Park on which the entire plot of the film centres. Ronan asked me if I would like to visit his flat to discuss our future co-presenting, and offered to give me some professional help. By this time I'd had a few dodgy run-ins with so-called grown-up blokes, and was very apprehensive. 'You're terrified of me,' he said, clearly amazed by my timidity. 'You're just a little girl.' I think he was right. I was happy enough hanging about with pop groups my own age, but serious grown-ups, especially men, really did intimidate me. Because of the 'ugly duckling' hang-up I'd had since the age of fourteen, I just didn't realize that I might be attractive. Sure, I went to a cool hairdresser and bought new clothes every week, but the low-esteem factor was still firmly in place.

However, I enjoyed the lifestyle, and by now I was heavily into sixties fashion. The late fifties had been dominated by American influences: jeans, T-shirts, tight waist belts, knee-length rock 'n' roll crinoline skirts with multi-layered crisp nylon petticoats like tulip-shaped tutus underneath. But now we had Mary Quant, Caroline Charles, Biba – unlimited numbers of London-based designers. But the bloke I picked on was a Parisian designer called André Courrèges. He created the trapeze dress with short skirt which, to me anyway, became the blueprint for the miniskirt. More important were the Courrèges boots: white leather, calf length, with toes cut out, slits at the top, and white leather bows on the front. I found faithful enough copies at Anello & Davide, the theatrical shoe- and boot-makers on the Charing Cross Road, and was determined that the white Courrèges boots were going to be my trademark on *Sing a Song of Sixpence*.

'Why', demanded a letter-writer to the (then) only ITV listings magazine, *TV Times*, 'does that girl wear the same pair of what look like surgical boots every week on TV? Hasn't she got any shoes?' My fashion statement hadn't got across to all and sundry. Nor had the show itself. The format was about tune-spotting, and one of my bimbo-TV-game-show-hostess chores was to add up the contestants' scores, which proved to be a terrifying ordeal. Chickens had come home to roost. How I had laughed at being allowed *not* to take maths as a compulsory subject when doing my O-levels, only to find that now I really needed it in the ludicrous context of a mindless TV game show. *Sing a Song of Sixpence* was the number-one hit TV show in Northern Ireland, but sadly nowhere else. It went, and with it my credibility. Hence my earlier comment – being a TV presenter is not a proper job. For the immediate future I was able to fall back on what was my proper job – being a journalist, of sorts. As the future was to prove, you are allowed at least one fuck-up, one step that takes you back before you can go forwards again.

Now might be an appropriate point to expound my 'You'll do, nipper' theory. This extends the 'being in the right place at the right time' syndrome. Basically, you have to hang in there at the right place, at the right time and be prepared to wait for *however* long it takes to get your break. You have to be at the front of the queue, the one who appears week after week, at an ungodly and unpaid hour, to make the tea, score the speed, work out how the DAT mini-disc machines work . . . One day there will be a hitch. A key person (a guitarist, a tape op., a DJ) will fail to show. Those in power panic. Your name springs to mind. 'You'll do, nipper you know what to do. *You* carry the show.' And you do. It's what you've been waiting for – .

In a sense that's what I had been doing, without realizing it, since my first audition for a regional BBC TV news programme in Southampton about three years previously. Television had never even occurred to me as a possible career beforehand. But I quite enjoyed the experience of being in front of the camera and, as it turned out, even more importantly, the microphone. Whereas journalism had always been an uphill struggle, inducing a feeling that I was just about keeping up with my colleagues but never shining, the microphone held no such fears. In fact, it felt so . . . natural. But broadcasting meant the BBC and nothing else. I was even more intimidated by the mighty British Broadcasting Corporation than I had been by Barney, the ex-military *Brighton Evening Argus* chief sub-editor, who never spoke to us reporters, only barked. But the BBC . . . How would I *ever* get to storm the gates of this particular bastion? Especially as my first 'showbiz agent', Bunny Lewis, took one look at me with my straggly hair and leather Beatle cap and pronounced, 'You'll *never* make it as a BBC presenter.' Cheers, mate. But this particular impasse was about to be broken by strange things happening – at sea. In 1964 illegal pirate pop radio was launched at an unsuspecting and swiftly ecstatic young audience – and that included me.

V

While the BBC was trying to cope with the revolution that pirate pop radio had brought about, there were serious changes going on within the music it was playing. Namely drugs. And even more namely lysergic acid diethylamide. Derek Taylor, having fallen out with Brian Epstein, left the Beatles office and headed for Los Angeles. There he discovered a band called the Byrds. He sent me a copy of their single, a cover of Bob Dylan's 'Mr Tambourine Man', and soon it became a number-one hit. The Byrds came to Britain. I was enslaved by the mournful lyrics and the twelve-string-guitar sound and went to every gig. The critics slaughtered them, said they couldn't sing and couldn't play, but I didn't care. The rather bizarre string of gigs that had been booked for them included Hove Town Hall. After the show I invited them back to my flat at Black Rock, Brighton. At one point I realized that the band's lead singer and guitarist, Roger McGuinn (then known as Jim McGuinn), who didn't say much at the best of times, had been gone a long time in the bathroom. I went to check if all was OK, to find him staring at the night sky over the South Downs out of the bathroom window. 'Y'know whaaat?' he drawled. 'Well, not really,' I replied. 'Whaaaal,' he went on, 'I think all politicians should be on LSD.' Now you have to remember that this was years before Britain converted to decimal currency, and therefore in common parlance 'LSD' meant 'pounds, shillings and pence'. I could not for the life of me think what this weird Californian was on about. I struggled through a twenty-minute discussion, trying to make sense of his apparently unfathomable statement. 'Ah,' I said, suddenly enlightened, 'what you're saying is that all politicians should be on LSD, so that they are in some way *sponsored* by their own governments, so that they cannot become corrupted, morally or financially.' McGuinn turned on me in horrified amazement. 'No, man,' he said. 'LSD is a *drug*!' That's how I found out about acid.

The Beatles had too, hence *Sergeant Pepper* and other acid-induced music which came to be called 'psychedelic'. But for all this wonderful mind-expanding that was apparently going on, all the weird colours and sensations, I'd heard as well about 'bad trips', people being terrified by monsters in their minds. What if my arachnaphobia became horribly exacerbated on acid? Huge purple spiders crawling through my brain? I swerved it. I have strong suspicions that I've been 'spiked' with acid on several occasions during the last few years, but nineties microdots are deemed a lot less powerful than the acid tabs of the late sixties.

The build-up to the psychedelic era had been brought about by the Beatles, as far as I was concerned anyway, and their contact with Americans who turned them on to acid. And it was to London that everyone now looked. It seems ludicrous today that Carnaby Street, an insignificant little backwater running parallel with Regent Street, should have become the centre of world fashion – a byway that for a while, and for the fast-thinking entrepreneurs who opened clothes shop there, was paved with gold. Flower power had taken hold, and I went along with it whole-heartedly. Along with the first wave of British hippies, I would roam the streets of London in mini-kaftans and granny shades, Indian bells and ropes of beads around my neck, handing flowers to bemused London policemen (whom we called 'the fuzz', of course) and uttering the obligatory words, 'Peace, man . . .', as I did so. I really did believe we could change the world. The Beatles' music had conquered the planet, and now it was up to the rest of us to spread their message. 'Make love, not war,' we pro-claimed. It was ludicrously naive, but I was swept up in the Beatles' philosophy with almost religious fervour.

There was a sweet innocence to our cause, which masked the real social revolution that was taking place in the United States, in middle-class America. Timothy Leary's slogan 'Tune in, turn on and drop out' was being taken seriously by young Americans, the first generation pre-pared to question the American Dream of a good job, prosperity and two cars in the garage. US teenagers had discovered the fun of smoking dope, making their own weird styles of music, and tripping. They were dropping out of school, college and the System in their hundreds of thousands, and suddenly the US government had a serious left-wing problem on its hands – exacerbated, of course, by bands like the Beatles becoming politically powerful and backing the draft dodgers, who saw no point in fighting the war in Vietnam. But, as pop stars became more and more outspoken as voices of this rebel generation, so the Estab-lishment began to crack down. The Beatles were busted continually in London for drug possession, and the Rolling Stones were imprisoned after the famed raid on Keith Richards' house, Redlands, near Chichester in West Sussex.

In so doing, the Establishment was driving a deeper wedge between itself and the hippie generation.

We could feel its consternation, and its outrage. Fathers who had fought World War II to ensure our freedom now saw a youth generation going to waste, embracing abandoned sex, illegal drugs and irresponsible behaviour. The music seemed to irritate the grown-ups particularly. 'What an awful din that "Yeah, yeah, yeah" Beatles stuff is,' they would grumble, and of course the Rolling Stones, who had been rejected by the BBC as possible broadcast musicians as early as 1963, were seen as even more appalling. The newspaper headline 'Would You Let Your Daughter . . . with a Rolling Stone?' hit home with deadly accuracy, echoing the fear of every parent of every teenage girl in Britain, the United States and all other territories that the Stones had terrorized. The fact that they swore openly and copiously, urinated publicly and had *long hair* made them the perfect *enfants terribles* – an image that their manager, Andrew Loog Oldham, and publicist, Leslie Perrin, had plotted to perfection. The growing links between pop musicians and political activists, anarchists and left-wing extremists had the Allied victors of World War II believing that they had bred a generation of Communists. Well, we were in a broad, idealistic sense.

Maybe the soaring opportunities of the sixties made us reject knuckling down to 'proper' nine-to-five jobs, wearing suits to work, settling down and having children. Well, I'd had a child, but I saw no reason why this should entail 'settling down' to a life of domesticity. Opportunities were there to be taken. As many of my friends had their own boutiques, I decided that I wanted one too. The fact that I knew nothing about the fashion business or the retail clothes trade did not, of course, deter me in the least.

I loudmouthed my plan in enough public places eventually to attract two professional schmutter businessmen who were prepared to go along with my scheme. I was to be the 'front' person for what became an enormously successful string of clothes shop called 'Snob'. Fortunately I was not responsible for the wholesale buying of the clothes we sold. I would go to fashion shows with the proper buyer, Shirley Hillman. I'd fall in love with every item modelled – till she advised caution because clothes must have 'hanger appeal'. I was really a glorified publicist, and Snob was not a real boutique in the sense of the avant-garde London shops I admired, which would sell original creations by up-and-coming talented designers. We just sold high-street merchandise, but with a lot of pizazz. We installed jukeboxes in the shops, which blared out the Lovin' Spoonful's 'Summer in the City' and my favourite Byrds tracks, as well as Sonny and Cher's 'I Got You Babe'. We decorated the old Victorian hatstands with feather boas and flowing scarves and bright plastic jewellery.

My role was to get the name Snob across in the media, and organize our own local fashion shows. This part I enjoyed immensely. The models were unpaid volunteers, and I'd dress them up in all our latest gear, swathe them in scarves, and hang jewellery from their every appendage. Not many of them shared my new found 'stylist's' enthusiasm, 'I'm not wearing *this*,' they would say contemptuously. I also played music during the shows and directed the models to *dance* down the catwalk.

Snob expanded very quickly, with branches on the south coast and in London. The subsequent two shops were to open simultaneously in the Medway towns of Chatham and Maidstone. I hit on the idea of a double opening party, hired a London double-decker bus, invited as many fashion journalists, gossip writers and pop stars as I had in my address book, filled the bus with drinks and food, and looked forward to a highly successful party night. No one turned up. No one. Except for the American cult singer, songwriter and friend of the Beatles, Harry Nilsson who got as far as the departure point on London's Embankment to apologise for not coming any further as he had another scene to go to. At least he turned up to *say* so. I was gutted. But then, on reflection, would *you* want to travel on a double-decker bus to either of the miserable dormitory towns of Chatham and Maidstone in your own time?

I had also embarked on doing publicity for Kangol. Their woolly flat hats were not at all in vogue at the time, and I found myself trying desperately to be photographed wearing one of these itchy and uncomfortable items, either gatecrashing the royal enclosure at Ascot or appearing on a TV show for the express purpose of being seen in a Kangol beret, and hoping that a whole generation would want to copy me. Mr Kangol (not his real name) was a grumpy septuagenarian Basque, the beret having originated in that region of Spain. He was not an easy man to satisfy, and at Kangol headquarters would crash his gnarled brown hand down on the highly polished boardroom table in fury when I had not fulfilled his demands in terms of column-inch coverage for his beloved headgear.

I began to realize that I was not cut out to be a fashion publicist at all. I parted company with Snob, having only ever been on a small retainer, and watched the two directors go on to become millionaires. But it was my choice. Fashion was fun, but my passion was music, and the two seemed to be pulling me in opposite directions. The rag trade really was still the rag trade it had always been, and a boutique was just a glorified clothes shop. The hippie culture was becoming horribly commercialized, with brash salesmen cashing in and selling plastic flowers, nylon kaftans and cheap 'Swinging London' T-shirts with badly printed Union Jacks on the front.

Having learned my lesson about the inherent insecurity of being a TV presenter, I relied once more on my skills as a journalist. I wrote a weekly column for *Honey* magazine, contributed to *FAB* magazine, and then became pop columnist for the national tabloid newspaper the *Daily Sketch*. In those pre-Murdoch days the tabloids were far more innocent than scandal sheets such as the *Sun* are today. I could happily compose features on my favourite pop stars, champion new talent, and write about whom I liked. This was principally because the editorial management team weren't in the least bit interested in pop music, but recognized the need to include it, much as every paper had its gardening column, or its daily horoscope. I did come in for torrents of abuse from more news-oriented and jaded journalists, who accused me of merely 'rewriting publicity handouts', but, insecure though I was in the tough, hard-drinking, cynical world of Fleet Street, these comments didn't particularly bother me because I knew they weren't true.

Music was diversifying in the most exciting ways at this time. The 'underground' movement was getting under way. I met a brand-new band called Pink Floyd at their first press conference at EMI's offices in Manchester Square, London, where they spoke elegantly and enthusiastically about their plans to play live shows where their instruments would be linked to an elaborate and sophisticated lighting system, which would *pulsate* colours pre-synchronized to specific notes in their music. Revolutionary! This kind of presentation has become *de rigueur* at every rock concert since, but Pink Floyd and other experimental bands such as Jefferson Airplane were inventing a new concept in terms of visual thrills in rock 'n' roll. 'Weird' became a new synonym for 'wonderful'.

Then the dazzling Marc Bolan appeared on the scene, and we walked fur-hatted together under the Christmas lights and through a blinding snowfall past Austin Reed and Hamley's in Regent Street as he unfolded his plans for Tyrannosaurus Rex (later to be abbreviated to T. Rex, as it was feared that radio DJs would not be able to pronounce the original name). There was also Kim Fowley, the inspired American eccentric behind Napoleon XIV's cult hit 'They're Coming to Take Me away Ha-Haaa!' (which incidentally featured on the B side of the record the same track backwards). Kim, now a deity sought out by lovers of obscure sixties pop, agreeing to meet only at out-of-the-way parking lots in West Los Angeles, would in the early days of underground London parade up and down the Aldwych, ranting. This is where I first met him, and he challenged me to come up with a word for him to turn into a full-length rant or poem. I think my word was 'wineglass' – inspiring enough for a three-minute rant which Kim performed oblivious of guests at the Waldorf Astoria, outside which hotel he held court.

Strange the people you met on the streets of London . . . Another was Jimmy Webb, writer of 'MacArthur Park', who was amazed at the length of London girls' legs and the shortness of their miniskirts, even on Savile Row. London seemed to be swarming with Americans, some dodging the draft, like Glenn Campbell – not the country singer, but someone who came looking for fame and fortune with his underground band the Misunderstood, and rather more successfully with the Walker Brothers. If anyone should have been called 'the misunderstood' it was *their* lead singer, Scott Walker. Blessed with breathtaking good looks, an unequalled vocal range and the moodiest personality since James Dean, Scott led the trio to immediate fame in Britain. But it was not the sort they wanted. The Walker Brothers suffered early on from TIDS – Teenage Idol Depression Syndrome. Scott particularly was an intense intellectual and (as his later recordings indicated) a follower of the Belgian existentialist writer Jacques Brel, yet the only acclaim the Walker Brothers were getting was from pubescent girl fans, in their thousands, screaming their heads off. Scott couldn't cope with this, and was apt to pull out of sell-out shows at the last minute, and go into hiding with his collar up, shades on and head down.

During one such incident, I was commandeered as a decoy to drive his white Mini Cooper S to a safe destination away from the marauding fans backstage at a Walker Brothers London gig to somewhere in what is now Docklands. I'd only just learned to drive, and was terrified that I'd crash a pop star's car on the first privileged opportunity I'd been given to be the getaway driver. After that, Scott, who for some strange reason believed that I lived alone in a huge mansion in Brighton, was given to calling me up from secret locations, mumbling down the phone in true Stanislavsky/Brando/Dean style, and then hanging up. The Walkers split soon afterwards, and Scott Walker really did go into hiding – until 1984, when he agreed to be interviewed for his comeback album. I was really curious as to where he'd been holed up all those years. Prague, maybe? Paris, Amsterdam, Berlin? 'No,' he said, 'I've been right here in London, in Notting Hill Gate, all the time. It's easy to disappear if you really want to.' And with that he vanished yet again.

So many citizens of the United States were coming to London to seek the recognition they had not found at home. P. J. Proby was another example, and Jimi Hendrix was dragged across the Atlantic to Britain by Geordie Chas Chandler of the Animals before his own country realized just how brilliant he was. But the fact that he came to London was significant. Until the Beatles 'cracked' America, no British pop performer had ever done so. I'd been brought up on Frank Sinatra, Elvis Presley and my father's adoration of Bing Crosby. But once the Beatles had established their prominence in the USA, Herman's Hermits followed, together with the Rolling Stones, the Who, the Kinks, Cream . . . 'We wouldn't have done it without the Beatles,' Mick Jagger told me. Perhaps England was turning out all these transatlantic stars purely because its geographical location was fashionable. It still seems to happen every decade or so.

In the summer of 1994 I expounded my bewilderment on this point to Ian Ralfini, who had been label boss of Warner Bros in London in the late sixties and early seventies – a hugely influential man, who had signed, among others, Van Morrison and the Faces to his label. 'There were', he said, 'just as many talented musicians in New Orleans at that time, but they just didn't get the recognition.'

Without being too aware of what I was doing, I was actually building up trust with the pop artistes which was to prove of lifelong worth. I had witnessed the Beatles' treatment of journalists – they were cooperative until crossed, whereupon they would not talk to you again, which I thought was fair enough. Years and years later, at a very showbizzy party hosted by Pamela Stephenson and Billy Connolly, George Harrison came up to me and said,

'You were very good to us.' As if the Beatles had needed
me! But I was never in the business of 'stitching people
up', simply because I wouldn't have wanted it done to me,
and also it was not in my nature to betray anyone. And,
on a practical level, I didn't want a reputation as an
untrustworthy journalist. The sub-editors who sweated
over incoming copy at the offices of the *Daily Sketch* had
no such qualms. If they had written an uncomplimentary
headline above one of my interviews, which I would of
course protest about, the subs would declaim airily, 'Oh,
they'll never remember,' whereas I knew that any bad
review or journalistic slag-off was etched in the brain of
its victim for ever.

At one time, while working for the *Sketch*, I did face an
ethical dilemma. The Beatles and their press officer – Derek
Taylor – trusted me, and expected me to keep their secrets.
I was spending a lot of time hanging out at Apple, the
Beatles' inner sanctum at 2 Savile Row. The 'hospitality'
was endless. The band's favourite drink was Scotch and
Coke – specifically J&B, which became the house brand.
And there were drugs in all shapes and sizes. We'd take
anything in pill form – uppers, downers; pink, yellow, blue
– with no idea of the pharmaceutical content. Possibly
some were harmless, but no one bothered to check. No
doubt this was irresponsible and potentially dangerous
behaviour, but none of us seemed to come to any harm.
The giant spliffs that were expertly rolled by the house
hippie, Richard di Lello, were extremely potent. (There
was no evidence, that I saw at any rate, of any heroin or
cocaine around the Beatles at that time.) In my stoned
state, Derek Taylor's office, with its white walls, white
leather settees and nodding plastic birds seemingly
drinking at a glass pond, became my universe. Just two

minutes away from Savile Row was Regent Street, with its red double-decker buses trundling up and down past brightly lit department stores, and just a step further away was Piccadilly Circus, with its flashing neon Coca-Cola sign. But sitting in the white world of Apple, listening to the latest Beatles or Mary Hopkin recording, totally off my head, nothing and nowhere else seemed to exist. Eventually I would *have* to leave, catch the train to Brighton and, smile beatifically at my family as they sat sedately around the TV at home.

The dilemma involved the fact that John Lennon was having a secret affair with a strange Japanese artist called Yoko Ono. I knew about it; the world, the press, didn't. I was trusted, a member of the inner sanctum, but I was also a journalist. If the story broke, as surely it eventually must, wouldn't I be blamed for leaking it? The more I was accepted and drawn into this clandestine situation, the more worryingly conspiratorial it became.

One afternoon John, Yoko, myself and various Apple people piled into John's white Rolls-Royce to visit Alexandra Palace, which John and Yoko wanted to recce as a possible venue for a concert or 'happening'. Ally Pally, once used by the BBC, was now a huge empty behemoth high on a hill in north London. The bar, however, was open. Yoko ordered Malvern water in her high-pitched, jingly-jangly Japanese voice. I was dead impressed. How sophisticated she seemed. I'd never heard anyone ordering a mineral water before, let alone one from a specific location.

The proposed happening did not happen. But John and Yoko continued their affair and I was becoming more agitated by the day, feeling that the story *had* to break. I felt, and not for the last time in the Beatles' presence, that

I was in not the right place at the right time, but rather the wrong place at the wrong time. It was actually a double dilemma: what if, when the truth *did* become public knowledge, the *Sketch* found out that I'd known about it all along, and could have – *should* have – given them a worldwide exclusive? Would I face instant dismissal and be drummed out of Fleet Street for ever? Which was I – journalist or groupie? Fortunately John and Yoko eventually came out and appeared in public together, and immediately the world's press all knew what was going on. It was a great relief to me. Subsequently they actively encouraged the press with their bag-ins and sit-ins and learned how to use the media to their advantage, although Yoko continued to arouse suspicion.

Maybe I was regarded as a 'soft' journalist, but at least I got interviews with almost anyone I wished to meet, and hopefully would be able to look them in the eye if we ever met again. Thus I was ushered into a first-floor Soho office to meet Jimi Hendrix. This superb musician had such a reputation as a wild sex maniac who would leap on you as soon as look at you that I was not prepared for the sheer courtesy with which he greeted me. He lit my cigarettes for me, and stopped to let me speak first if my questions and his answers overlapped. Off-stage Jimi Hendrix was a model of decorum.

While we're on the subject of dead pop stars, yes, I did meet Jim Morrison of the Doors, and, no, I wasn't particularly impressed by him. Granada TV were making a documentary about this band, who were holding court at some kind of quasi-intellectual gathering at the ICA in London. Morrison, moody and lip-curling, mooched about the room, saying nothing. I decided I must engage him in conversation. 'What do you feel about money, Jim?' I asked him. 'What do I feel about money?' he repeated, and reached for my lighter, which was sitting on a conveniently near table. 'This is what I feel about money,' he said, reaching into the breast pocket of his black leather jacket, pulling out a hundred-dollar bill, and setting fire to it. I thought he came over as rather a pretentious git.

VI

Until then, Britain had never known round-the-clock pop radio. I'd grown up listening to Radio Luxembourg, and the BBC had given us a degree of pop-music radio with the superb *Saturday Club* and other assorted pop items, but they were scattered in the weekly schedules of the Light Programme, which was hardly a youth-oriented network. Its presenters were pretty much BBC Establishment types like David Jacobs and Pete Murray. Only Alan 'Fluff' Freeman seemed a bit off the wall, but he also appeared to be a one-off.

This truly eccentric Australian told me that he'd only become involved with the BBC because, during a visit to Britain, he'd heard an announcer saying: 'And now, here is Frank Sinatra, on a gramophone record.' 'Well, fuck me,' Fluff had thought, 'of course it's a gramophone record; the BBC is hardly going to *fly* Frank in to sing *one* number. What these Brits need is a *disc jockey*.' The term just didn't sit comfortably with the hierarchy at Broadcasting House. The BBC had bred and nurtured its own strain of broadcasting performers. They spoke the Queen's English, with no regional accents, wore dinner jackets to read the radio news, and had names like Alvar Liddell. '*Disc jockey*'? How vulgar. How American.

Irish nutter Ronan O'Rahilly, whom I'd already met through a pop publicist, had told me about his wild romantic notion of beaming all-day pop music from an off-shore ship. I was near delirious when I saw Radio Caroline's ship go gliding past out in the English Channel from the vantage point of my seafront balcony.

The pirate ships, principally Radio Caroline, Ronan's station, and Radio London, pumping out pop music from the safety of international waters off the coast of Britain, were to have a devastating and lasting effect on the BBC. Not only was it the first time we'd heard pop records and commercials played continuously, it was also the first time we'd heard brash young voices between the records. Dave Cash, Kenny Everett, Simon Dee, Johnnie Walker and Tony Blackburn became instant media heroes – pirates of the airwaves, swashbuckling frequency-stealing bandits, daredevils of discdom. They were in publicity heaven. They didn't talk down to us like some poncy BBC bloke; they were our mates, riding on the high seas to bring us the top tunes, with the ever-thrilling notion that what they were doing was against the law and could be stopped at any time by a grim-faced gang of Customs men on a secret midnight boarding raid. Total romanticism. And for me total inspiration. Now I really knew what I wanted to do. Become a disc jockey. What better idea? I liked being in front of a microphone, loved pop music. Simple equation. Bingo! The fact that there did not appear to be a single female voice among these saucy sailors did not deter me in the slightest.

I had never experienced 'sexism', nor any discrimination in terms of anything I had ever wanted to do. Occasionally I had been dissuaded from covering some of the more gory criminal acts – such as bestiality – which

came before the magistrates when I was doing my necessary stint as a court reporter in Brighton, but other than
that nothing had ever been barred to me through my being
born female.

The dream of becoming a pirate disc jockey, however,
was a little far-fetched even for me. A little impractical,
also, as I was married with a child. But only a little far-
fetched. It had not occurred to me that being a DJ meant
being A Bloke. A Bloke with a Very Large Ego. It also did
not occur to me that DJs were all men because that was
the way they wanted it, and that they regarded themselves
as sex symbols exactly in the way male pop stars did.
Which is not to say that I did not like and admire them. I
wanted to *be* a DJ, *be* one of them, *be* one of the boys, as
I had been in all my previous jobs. And I believed I had
the right attributes for the job. I loved talking and playing
records. Surely there was nothing more to it than that?
Friends and colleagues were horrified at my latest
ambition. 'You? On a ship with all those blokes?' I thought
it would be great fun.

In 1967 the government stepped in, and the pirates,
having defied the law for several years, were finally run
ashore. As an appeasement, we pop-loving kids were to
be given our own legal music station, run by the BBC and
called Radio 1. In an act of unprecedented magnanimity,
the BBC even agreed to employ ex-pirate DJs on this
station, and they were consulted at the drawing-board
stage on the design of the customized studios to be built
to house this new phenomenon. It is my firm belief that
the custodians of the BBC never wanted an American-style
pop station cluttering up its frequencies and cheapening its
deserved worldwide reputation as the finest broadcaster in
the world. Setting up Radio 1 was a political sop to shut

70

up those who had protested at the pirate stations being silenced, and we all knew it.

Somehow the idea of a legal pop station wasn't nearly as appetizing as the cheerful naughtiness of the pirates. But it had other things going for it, to my mind anyway. With no commercial restraints, no vying for top ratings, Radio 1 could be the best radio station in the world. By not having to kowtow to advertisers, there need be no compromise, no opting for the lowest common denominator.

Radio 1 was launched in 1967, when British pop music was at its zenith. It was the year of the Summer of Love, of *Sergeant Pepper*, and the charts were overloaded with brilliant records. What I didn't know then, nor for many years afterwards, was that Radio 1 was launched by its original producers in an atmosphere of sheer paranoia. The first front-line management team knew that the governors of the BBC had adopted this wanton child unwillingly. Non-stop pop music, introduced by babbling DJs, *untrained* broadcasters, unscripted, *live*, ruining the Corporation's reputation? A terrible prospect. Well, perhaps it was a fad. Perhaps this 'pop-music' phase would pass, and with it Radio 1, hopefully swiftly and mercifully soon.

The one potential weapon that the originators of the station had at their command, and which they used constantly, was the power of numbers. If Radio 1 proved to be a *huge* success, in terms of audience figures, millions upon millions tuning in every day, then the Corporation cops would not be able to shut it down. Radio 1 had to prove from day one that in the public broadcasting sector there was a great demand for this so-called 'pop' music.

American-style jingles, recorded in Dallas, Texas, blasted out the station's identity and that of its DJs. And these DJs quickly became household names, becoming more famous than many of the artistes whose records they were playing. But the underlying paranoia remained. There was a relentless drive for more and more in terms of audience figures, more and more millions of listeners. And somewhere in this relentless pursuit of people came a gradual slide into the pit of populism. Playlists, banned lists . . . the pirates hadn't had these. And as the easy-come-easy-go wealth of Britain in the late sixties surged, so did record sales. Pop music had become not just fun any more, but big, big business. And Radio 1 was its largest and most effective shop window.

But in gaining its millions of listeners, if not enforcing a *lowest*-common-denominator policy, certainly there was a *lower*-common-denominator factor at work. This then became the Radio 1 Chip on the Shoulder. Few of the original line-up of producers had university backgrounds, unlike their peer group from the Home Service and the Third Programme. Radio 1 was made to feel the poor relative, the slightly thick and stupid relation, by those in the upper echelons of the Corporation. It was no one's fault. The guys who had the challenge of setting up and sustaining Radio 1 had come mostly from hands-on technical backgrounds – engineers, studio managers.

I was extremely shocked and surprised at the chauvinism displayed by Radio 1 in its first couple of years of existence, especially in the climate of growing acceptance in other areas of the media and the arts of 'women's lib'. I'd heard quite horrifying stories of senior producers launching their own private dinner-party entertainment by playing their guests audition tapes sent in by would-be female DJs. The tapes were rumoured to be of such a pathetic, unprofessional nature that they would be guaranteed to reduce the entire party to uncontrollable laughter, thus breaking any layer of social ice that might have settled on the evening's proceedings before the starter – melon balls, no doubt – was served.

Shamelessly, Radio 1, like the pirates, basked in its *Boy's Own* glory. 'No girl DJs for Radio 1,' its bosses would proclaim in print. 'Disc jockeys are husband substitutes!' the all-male team of disc jockeys would announce smugly. Seriously. I tried, and I tried and I tried, and found that for me the doors to Radio 1 were locked, bolted, barred, chained and shored up from within, the portcullis down and the drawbridge up. But *'why?'* I asked anyone connected to this Sanctuary of Sexism whom I could get to speak to. *Why? Why? Why?* I had proved I could hold my own as a news reporter, feature writer, TV presenter; I had proved myself as a capable radio journalist on other networks of the BBC. Why did getting a job as a Radio 1 DJ seem to require me also to own a dick? 'Er, well . . . um . . . a female DJ would alienate the listeners . . . A female voice just doesn't sound right on radio . . . A girl DJ would have no authority . . . wouldn't have the technical know-how . . . No experience . . .' And so, ludicrously, the lame excuses of the management went on and on. I lobbed salvos of protest at them in print and easily blew apart their spurious objections. Not that it made any difference. Blackburn, Emperor Rosko and the rest of the first wave of Radio 1 jocks still ruled their boys-only roost, and rejoiced in their locker-room humour, their simplistic jokes and their already hugely inflated egos. Ironically, I was popular among them, as they hoped I'd write about them and increase their fame. It was a curious part of the strategy of Radio Paranoia to build its DJs into star names. This had never been the case in any other English-speaking country which witnessed the phenomenon of the DJ. DJs did not become massive media stars in Australia. Nor in the United States (until Howard Stern), because even the largest pop stations there have never had the transmitter power or perhaps the logistical inclination to broadcast coast to coast. Perhaps it was the blanket national coverage of Radio 1 that needed its identity to be welded to that of its presenters, to ensure on-going popularity.

However, I was not done with it yet. I practised what I later preached to others in the 'locked-door' situation that I found myself in then, and prowled. Through my journalistic connections, I would occasionally find myself at a record-company reception, or playback launch of a new album, or live preview of a new band playing at the likes of Ronnie Scott's club, where a covert group of Radio 1 producers and the odd DJ would also be in attendance. They all seemed quite stand-offish and snooty, and didn't mix with the hoi polloi of journalists and professional liggers who always attended these freebie occasions. All except one. His name was Teddy Warwick – a small, smiling man in glasses, who had a distinctive habit of jingling his change in his pocket. He was a producer in charge of specialist and magazine programmes, and he alone among the Radio 1 hierarchy didn't dismiss me with a haughty scoff or just plain laugh out loud when I asked if I could have a go at being a DJ.

I began the 'You'll do, nipper' campaign in earnest, submitting to Radio 1's magazine programme *Scene and Heard* interviews with pop stars that I'd recorded on cassette on my own admittedly primitive tape recorder. Jeff Griffin worked on *Scene and Heard* as a young tape operator (or he might have been studio manager, but I didn't know the difference at that stage). He had an attractive chipped-front-tooth smile and a deadpan put-down style of 'wit'. When he said of my submitted tape, 'We can't possibly use this. The quality – it's *appalling!*', I just thought this was typical BBC arrogance. Later on – much later on – Jeff became a distinguished and principled producer and one of my best friends within the BBC. We worked together on a Friday-night Radio 1 show, which meant spending Friday afternoons in his office putting the final touches to the running order. These sessions became almost an ordeal as Jeff would make me laugh until I cried, usually with jokes at my expense, and I would think, '*And I'm getting paid for this!*' But by then I'd paid my dues.

Having my tape rejected meant I was no further on in my operation to penetrate Radio 1. I believe I actually got bored with the idea for a while (not that anyone reading this must ever abandon the 'You'll do, nipper' scheme until it has been brought to a triumphant conclusion), but then I was being diverted in other directions, namely Apple, where I was still getting stoned every night, listening to white-label promos of new Beatles records before anyone else had heard them, and offering any useful piece of advice I could think of regarding how to solve the Fab Four's increasing difficulties in staying together as a group. Also, a marvellous opportunity came up to get some more hands-on experience in radio away from the chauvinist brutes at Radio 1. The BBC had launched local radio stations in selected parts of Britain, and Brighton had its own brand-new station. Myself and two friends, Jeremy Pascal, now a quiz king of BBC TV, and Binky Baker, whom I later married, were given our own weekly programme, called *Pop Inside*. We used as a signature tune the same Booker T. track, which has since been used until this day to introduce live cricket coverage by BBC TV Sport.

Pop Inside was a bit like having our own fanzine. We had 'world-exclusive' interviews with Ringo Starr or Harry Nilsson (i.e. badly recorded tape spin-offs from newspaper or magazine features I or Jeremy had done elsewhere), and we would argue for hours about the three records we would be allowed to play in each weekly half-hour programme. We were paid two pounds between the three of us for each programme. It was enough to buy a bottle of Yugoslav Riesling and one round in the pub for us and the long-suffering producer, Phil Fothergill, who, as we argued, discussed, rewrote, re-recorded and agonized, would sit with his feet on a window sill shaking his mop of shiny, shaggy hair in disbelief at all this fervent time-wasting.

We were not allowed to broadcast *Pop Inside* live, and consequently there were endless retakes of 'fluffs' during the links. Inevitably, after a tiring seven- or ten-hour session in the studio, someone would forget to edit out a retake and we suffered on transmission the embarrassment of hearing one of us saying, 'Oh, sorry, do you want me to do that again?'

I've no idea if anyone apart from the three of us ever listened to *Pop Inside*, although we did our best to cover the local scene, with sessions from Brighton bands, reviews of gigs, and interviews with up-and-coming musicians from the surrounding area. None of which sat at all happily with the general format of Radio Brighton, which was more concerned with targeting the elders and pensioners of its catchment area. Which meant we were going nowhere in terms of making dazzling, ground-breaking and original programmes. With my usual naivety, I expected that, because we were working, in however ignominious a small area, for the British Broadcasting Corporation, this fact would be recognized and valued by producers at Broadcasting House. No fucking way! Anyone in local radio was treated with great derision as an absolute tosser, loser and amateur.

But, unbeknown to me, attitudes were changing inside the now, due to pollution, pale grey fortress of Broadcasting House in Portland Place, and even more so inside Egton House, the ugly, squat, 1960s architectural abomination next door, which housed the offices of Radio 1. The upper echelons of management were apparently beginning to shift rather uncomfortably in their boardroom seats at increasing criticism from the media about their didactic, chauvinist and sexist attitudes towards presenters, and particularly presenters on Radio 1. Changes in top-level management were being made. Among the newcomers was one Douglas Muggeridge, nephew of the TV sage Malcolm Muggeridge. It seemed that Douglas had rather more of a social conscience than his predecessors at Radio 1. He let it be known discreetly, via Derek Taylor, the Beatles' publicist, that the station was now positively looking for a female DJ. No doubt the pressure of public opinion was mounting – usefully. This is where the 'You'll do, nipper' tactic paid off. What potential female DJ did Derek Taylor know? Yours truly. And why? Because I had been hanging in there, hanging in everywhere for so long that my name was the first to come to mind. So I became the Nipper. I submitted a tape of *Pop Inside* to Radio 1, and was offered four trial programmes to go out on Sunday nights, along with other try-out DJs including Noel Edmonds, Gary Taylor, the blond-haired, deep-voiced bass player in a fashionable pop group of the time, the Herd, and a guy called Stevie Mericke from Birmingham. I was the only female, however.

So, at last – success. Well, a chance at least, and a foot in the door. I didn't expect to last more than a year. 'Do you know how to work a desk?' I was asked casually by Ray Harvey, my first assigned producer. '*Work* a *desk*'? What did that mean? I thought you just spoke into a microphone, your discs magically spun, and that was the sum total of being a Radio 1 DJ. This was where the term 'self-op' and its ominous overtones came in, along with a complete language of technical jargon that BBC technicians seemed to want to keep as secret as my father's Freemasonry book.

'Self-op', an abbreviation of 'self-operation', had, since the pirate days, become the key to being a successful DJ – and it was what constituted the difference from being an announcer. Announcers read scripts, with a studio team playing appropriate tapes and discs. A DJ of the pirate style would work the mixing desk himself, and, apart from an engineeer in the cubicle next door balancing the sound, was totally in control of the whole programme being broadcast. The gang of brash young men from the ships who now dominated a national BBC network had mastered this skill – and the attendant jargon. 'Carts', 'cans', 'pre-fade', 'talkback', 'pots', 'faders', 'ring mains', 'modulation', 'frequencies', 'segues', 'jingles', 'idents', 'handovers', 'hot-seat changeovers', 'remote starts' . . . all this was to me (and as I'm sure it was intended to be) intimidating. Almost immediately I developed a 'woman-driver' complex. I felt perfectly competent talking into the microphone, but not operating a five-foot-wide piece of technology.

Some of the engineers were even more sexist than the male DJs. I was given a crash course in operating the desk, and then felt too intimidated ever to ask again how any particular piece of equipment worked. Consequently, when I performed my first live show, I was utterly terrified, demoralized and totally lacking in confidence. This proved to be quite justified. The producer, Ray Harvey, and I had evolved a studio arrangement that was about as effective as Norwegians deciding they would all drive on the opposite side of the road but would introduce the change-over gradually. Ray and I were each to operate for part of the programme, but we hadn't really specified who would do what, and when. So, while my first-ever nationally broadcast programme was going out live, I decided to do something useful and pressed the stop button on one of the record decks, believing it to be the one that had been playing the previously broadcast record. It wasn't. It was playing the record that was being broadcast live at that instant. The stop buttons didn't have a particularly fast reaction time, so, instead of just stopping dead, the hapless disc wound itself down, inexorably slowly, to a groaning, agonizing finish. The producer was totally flummoxed, not knowing what I had done. What followed in the confusion was *eight seconds of dead air* – meaning eight seconds of silence when the mighty Radio 1 transmitters of the BBC all over Britain had nothing to transmit. A horrible, bottomless pit of silence, which of course to me felt more like eight years. More like an eternity. All that ran through my mind was my endless pleas to Radio 1 to 'Let me have a go', after which on the first show I'd committed this horrendous error. Then I remembered the mighty cock-up Simon Dee had made during his first-ever appearance on *Top of the Pops*, when he had announced all the wrong groups, at which he threw his cue cards up in the air and said, 'Oh well, they give a guy a chance and he blows it!' So I tried to laugh it off in similar style.

It actually took me years to gain the confidence I really needed to relax and start enjoying Radio 1 programmes. I never had any problem with the talkie bits, and I loved putting the shows together and listening to the music. It was a dream job, and it still is. But I did have a complex about 'driving the desk', as it's known. Every time I made a mistake by playing the wrong side of the record, or spun a disc at the wrong speed, I wanted the floor to open and swallow me up.

I was terribly aware that I had a lot to prove to my male peers, who had all come from pirate stations and had so much more experience than me. I was learning on the job, live on national radio, which would be unheard of today. It was truly terrifying, and the sexist attitude of the engineers didn't help. With the advent of New Laddism, the wheel turned full circle – it's certainly been my experience on the club circuit that there are very few women DJs, and that the job is still very much a male stronghold. But now there is a new breed of 'bird' DJs coming up, who will brook no bias.

Of course, despite my terror, I was delighted that the BBC had given me the opportunity. And I survived that first year, which I never expected to do.

VII

In the early seventies I was asked by BBC TV to present a documentary series called *Before the Event*. This series looked at the build-up to major British sporting events, such as the British motor-racing Grand Prix, or the Hennessy Gold Cup steeplechase.Whereas I'd never had any trouble ad libbing into a microphone, I found it to be a very different story delivering a documentary script to camera. Perhaps it's because radio broadcasting has the advantageous intimacy of a one-to-one conversation. Working with a film or video crew automatically piles the pressure on. There are nerveless 'in-vision' broadcasters who can deliver a film critique, a book review, a diatribe on the quality of Russian chess playing, apparently off the top of their head, *and* bring the piece to a close on a three-minute-twenty-second cue, but I'm not sure I'm one of them.

More than one programme in the series involved horses and horse people. In the early-morning mist beside Lake Windermere in the out-of-season, deserted Lake District I'd sit by the roadside writing linking scripts to explain the difference between a head lad and a travelling head lad et al., stepping neatly into my own trap of making the links so convoluted as to be impossible to remember once I was in front of the camera. I gradually learned that being a documentary TV reporter means having to deliver scripts totally ad lib, or trying to create a similar performance by half-remembering a very rough script, or learning one's own lines word perfect as an actor would. In the end I went for option three. And it seemed to me that one's popularity as part of a documentary team rose in direct relation to the least number of takes necessary to get each chunk of footage 'in the can' – preferably one, because this minimized the time until the director could call 'It's a wrap' and the crew could line up the first round in the nearest pub. As a TV presenter you are required not so much to be sensationally magnetic or fabulously attractive (although this helps) or have everyone cracking up with laughter at your relentless streams of epigrams as to be *reliable* – being able to work fast, efficiently, accurately, if necessary being able to repeat the same take word for word if it's needed for different camera angles. The presenter, the reporter, is just part of the machinery, not the star. At least that's my view of it.

Outside-location filming is fraught with unforeseen circumstances. Bad weather (obviously), bad light, innocent pedestrians walking into shot (I once interviewed Long John Baldry outside the Bottom Line Club in New York, his every answer being upstaged from just behind by an oblivious bloke struggling to unshackle his bicycle from a lamp-post), but most usually sound problems. Pneumatic road drills, I swear, have followed me for hundreds of miles from one location to the next. Then there is the phenomenon of the mysteriously appearing helicopter. Imagine. Everything is cool. The camera is running up to speed, the sound engineer in his double-weather-protection anorak is crouched over his DAT recorder, headphones

82

clamped across his ears, the director is happy. 'Right . . . camera turning over . . . up to speed? . . . then . . . ACTION!' A few seconds of perfect silence follows, and then from nowhere comes the unmistakable throbbing noise of an unseen helicopter's rotor blades thudding into the engineer's sound spectrum. 'Cut!' calls the director resignedly, and we wait until the Mystery Chopper, which haunts every camera crew even in the most distant locations, passes out of earshot.

Most of the problems attached to outside-location shooting are to do with sheer discomfort. You are always hung over from the night before's revelries in the hotel bar. In the instance of the Lake District shoot, I and Jill Roach, the young director on the series, realized that the world of steeplechasing and National Hunt jockeys is one of extremely heavy drinking and hospitality. Every employee of the stable seemed to feel it was their obligation to top up our drinks every alternate nanosecond. Also, we realized that the trainer Gordon Richards's employees regarded the two of us as being involved in this documentary purely as decoration, with no serious responsibilities to fulfil. But, as it was my first documentary series, all this was just part of the learning process.

Looking good in front of the camera also takes some achieving in the absence of an on-site make-up artist or a studio make-up room. If the shoot takes place during a frosty early morning your nose will appear to be bright red on the finished programme. This also happens if you are shooting in temperatures above 90°F in the Middle East, through sunburn. Facing the camera in strong winds is also extremely unflattering: your hair is flattened and swept back, and tears roll down your face, leaving your eyes red-rimmed and grimy black streaks of mascara down your cheeks. This happened to me when the new luminary film director, Iain Softly, had me deliver a TV piece from the roof of a multi-storey car park in a force-nine gale.

Directors will never take into account possible attacks of vertigo, either, when positioning you for a major straight-to-camera delivery. I've been stood on top of the Schlitz skyscraper in Milwaukee, on the edge of a steep bluff in Arica, Chile, surrounded by circling black and hungry-looking condors, balanced on the toes of the Sphinx in Egypt, and atop a crumbling, almost vertical hillside overlooking Kowloon. Ironically, on the one occasion when I tried to persuade a director to come and film a university tour which I was DJing, he refused, saying that not enough interesting filmable incidents happen on tour. The very first night of the next tour I took part in I spectacularly disappeared down a black hole where I thought a piece of staging was and crashed into a fire extinguisher some six feet below, bringing my DJ set to a rather unexpected and abrupt close, which would have looked amusing at least. It also robbed the planet of some possible archive footage of the then deeply un-fashionable headlining band Freur, with their crimped hair and red plastic stage suits, who were later to become two-thirds of the ultra-successful nineties house-music band Underworld.

Another hazard of documentary film-making is the sudden and unexpected onset of uncontrollable laughter, known in the theatre as 'corpsing'. It's probably brought on by some form of nervousness, and usually involves tripping up on the same word over and over again during one useless take after another. But shaking with mirth over some private joke doesn't make for very watchable television, and the humour of the situation begins to pall on the crew when one continues to be unable to reach the end of the take without fucking up. Sure, such incidents are the lifeblood of programmes like *It'll Be Alright on the Night*, but at the time when one of these attacks occurs one feels just a miserable amateur. My only advice, should you find yourself in this situation, is to think of the worst tragedy, the most appalling disaster, you've ever known about, or the most horrible thing that could happen to you, in order to get your straight face back.

Not that uncontrollable laughter is by any means the worst hazard of location filming or TV interviewing. It's actually probably the least bad. Reluctant or over-enthusiastic interviewees can be an enormous problem. Reluctant interviewees (and this applies to all forms of journalism and media interfacing) fall into several different categories, starting with the 'I don't want to do this interview at all, and I'm only sitting here opposite you because of movie-company/record-label pressure' type. The first I ever experienced in this category, surprisingly, was Sean Connery. I was a very junior reporter, it has to be admitted, and he'd just made his first James Bond picture. Either my interviewing technique was non-existent or he was bored by doing the rounds of the regional press, but he seemed to have *nothing* to say! Sean Connery – James Bond – with nothing to say! Perhaps it was the surroundings which failed to inspire him. Rather than meeting him in a down-town speakeasy in Leningrad, sipping vodka and dodging snipers at dawn, our rendezvous was . . . a Wimpy bar, drinking sludgy coffee at three in the afternoon. During one of many lulls in the conversation I was trying to maintain with a guy on the brink of a thirty-year career as one of Hollywood's greatest and consistently highest-paid stars, he picked up the matching cheap stainless-steel knife and fork from the Formica table in front of him. The two implements were sealed together in cellophane. 'They do this in the United States too,' uttered James Bond, flatly. 'Wrap up the knives and forks. As a hygiene measure. I've just been there.' And that is the entire extent of my memory of Sean Connery the interviewee.

Worse was to come. The late American singer Bobby Darin was not exactly in over-friendly mode when I was ushered into his suite at the Dorchester Hotel, London. As an innocent opening gambit, or so I thought, having espied his Harrods shopping bags strewn across the well-upholstered easy chairs, I asked him what he'd bought. 'None of your goddamn business,' he replied tersely, and this proved to be the longest phrase he uttered during my audience with him.

Neil Diamond also gave me a hard time on the first occasion I interviewed him in London, at probably the same hotel – probably the same suite. He told me that he'd been a 'latchkey' child, and when he had got married and fathered his own children he didn't want the same fate to befall them and therefore discouraged his wife from working. 'So what did she do before you were married?' I asked him. 'Oh, she was a hooker,' he said, which made his minders laugh – all three of them, sitting around him wearing black suits over their huge bodies, looking more like KGB men than a showbiz security team. Although years later I interviewed Neil Diamond at his office on Melrose in Los Angeles, when he could not have been more cooperative, this first meeting was doomed because, clearly, he had no wish to be interviewed. In this type of situation one's only hope as an interviewer is to hang on in there as long as possible and hope one's subject will thaw out. However, as an American superstar usually allots a pointless twenty minutes maximum per interview, it is usually a no-win situation. Maybe I've just been unlucky with Americans and actors.

Patience and tolerance really are vital virtues for media interviewers. On a TV interview programme called *One to One* which ran in the late eighties, I asked the rock singer Stevie Nicks a simple opening question about a pendant she was wearing around her neck, and her uninterrupted reply lasted a full eighteen minutes, filling practically a whole magazine of videotape. At around the same time I asked the controversial actor-director Steven Berkoff if he could give me a five-minute résumé of his production of *Salome* for a Radio 1 arts programme. He roared at me, 'A *résumé*? Of *five minutes*? I cannot sum up my work in *five minutes*. I do not talk in *soundbites*.' At which point he wheeled across his mirrored drawing room in full theatrical fury, and declaimed, 'I do *not* wish to do this interview.' An extremely ugly pause ensued. I considered getting up and walking out, which I guessed that he both did and did not wish me to do. I decided to call his bluff and chill Mr Berkoff out. I'd had a fair amount of experience of actors' and performers' 'temperament' by now. He was trying to out-Jagger Jagger, and I'd learned years before how to humour Mick in an interview. I changed the subject obliquely, and led Mr Berkoff into a general discussion about his current production, and let him bitch for as long as he wished about the lack of air-conditioning at the theatre, the lack of accommodation for his actors, and the lack of hospitality from the promoters of his play. After he'd grumbled and grouched till he'd run out of complaints, I gently raised towards his mouth the microphone I'd been clutching all the while and said, 'Shall we do this interview now?' He delivered a masterly performance on to my tape machine in one take, with no prompting or further questions from me at all.

Another method for the hapless interviewer when dealing with Difficult Customers, Awkward Bastards or just plain shy people, especially for broadcast media, is to put into practice what I call the Anti-Vacuum Effect. This principle works thus: you ask a question; the interviewee does not reply. What do you do? Ask another question? No. You say nothing either. Silence prevails. (This technique, I have to admit, is highly dangerous on *live* radio or TV.) By not rushing into the vacuum, the empty space, you are much more likely to force a reply out of your interviewee, though it can take nerves of steel to do it. The theory is that someone has to break the silence, and ideally it shouldn't be the interviewer. It may be that your subject *is* just shy, or is just carefully considering an answer to your question. Peter Gabriel has in my experience been a prime example of this type of interviewee, as is Bobby Gillespie of Primal Scream, the latter also having the unnerving interview habit of finally answering your last question when you are midway through asking the next one.

People who chime in an additional answer during the next question create a nightmare for film video and radio editors, since there is then no clean break to cut from one topic to another. This is why all audio and TV interviewers have to develop a habit of tight-lipped, vigorous nodding during interviews, which is totally unnatural in social conversation. The BBC threw up its hands in horror when I first submitted some of my self-produced cassette-recorded interviews. I had committed the cardinally naff sins of interjecting 'Mmm' and 'Oh, I see' and 'Oh, really' as well as 'How interesting!' throughout my subjects' answers.

Initially, I found the nodding discipline extremely hard to adapt to, as in my early days of interviewing for print media I had merely lifted the quotes that were relevant and ignored the rest. Also, I'd found that people were a lot more forthcoming if you gave something of yourself, some personal banter and chatter rather than the hard-nosed, written-in-stone rigid interrogation routine.

With extreme cases of Awkward Bastards and Difficult Customers I would resort in desperation to asking them their star sign – which always worked. Naturally the subject would protest that he (women are very rarely ABs or DCs) didn't believe in such nonsense as astrology and had no idea what his birth sign was. But once I'd prised the actual birth date from my subjects, they were, and still are, unbelievably susceptible to flattery and personal attention. 'Tenth of March? Ah, Pisces – very sensitive, very intuitive . . .' No one is not going to admit to these charming qualities.

VIII

Lucy Kalinka Tamara Celia Mair was born in the glory days of flower power. As everyone else was calling their children 'Saffron' and 'Lemon', I decided that my daughter would have a whole bunch of names, and then whichever one she liked best she could use as a first name. 'Lucy' was partly for my Russian friend Lusia, a great influence on my life, a fabulous woman who had escaped from Russia during the Revolution and been married several times, lastly to film director Gordon Parry. Nina, her youngest daughter, became a lifelong friend. Her eldest daughter, the actress Natasha Parry, had been named one of the ten most beautiful women in the world and was married to Peter Brook, the world's most distinguished theatre director. The other influence was the Beatles' song 'Lucy in the Sky with Diamonds'. John Lennon had told me that the song was not about LSD, as everyone thought, but about a picture his son Julian had brought home from school when the Lennons lived in Weybridge. 'This is Lucy in the sky with diamonds,' he had said. So I always knew that the song was about a child Julian was at school with, and that one day I would find her. And one day I did. 'Kalinka' was after the Russian Red Army song, which I thought was great, and I believed it would make a very good single name in lights if Lucy ever wanted to become a stripper. By the time she was old enough to know what a stripper was she was inexplicably horrified by the idea I should ever think of her being such a thing. Lusia was also horrified by 'Kalinka'. 'Darlink,' she would say, 'you can't call a child that. It means "red berry on tree".' So? 'Tamara' was Lusia's suggestion, inspired by Tamara Ustinov, Peter's daughter. 'Celia' was my mother's name. And 'Mair' was suggested by her father's side of the family, who were Welsh. To be honest, I don't think Lucy's ever been very keen on any of her names. When she's asked for her full name for official purposes she often can't remember it.

I never thought it would happen to me, so I was deliriously happy to have a daughter – partly, I confess, because I thought I could treat her like a doll and dress her up. For about the only time in my life that I can recall I had money, and I indulged myself, buying her clothes from Biba and Harrods. Then, proving at the age of one and a half that she was a grown woman, Lucy got hold of a pair of scissors and cut up her clothes – obviously a gesture of rebellion. Whereas Alex had been a very placid baby, Lucy was the complete opposite. I'm convinced that she came into this world an adult soul. Our mother and daughter roles were reversed – *we* were *Ab Fab* long before the TV series.

The *Before the Event* TV series was a welcome addition to my other activities, in no small way for financial reasons. The dawning of the seventies heralded not only the end of the Great Party that was the late sixties, but also the beginning of my financial problems. My first marriage ended shortly after the birth of Lucy, and I found myself with a large house signed over to me, but with two small

children to bring up. I began to build up a spiralling overdraft, which was to lead a scintillatingly sympathetic bank
manager to say to me, 'Working for the BBC is a luxury
you can't afford. In fact,' he added cheerfully, 'with your
overheads and financial commitments, really you can't
afford to live at all!' 'Cheers, mate,' I thought, and
wondered how I should phrase the suicide note to include
the word 'NatWest' before I slashed my wrists.

But to the outside world I was the golden 'girl in a
million' with the dream job. I wore outrageous pink-crêpe
flares, green glitter eyeshadow and metallic-coated fake
snakeskin platform shoes in a red, blue and silver stars-
and-stripes design, and got on with being Britain's only
female DJ. This did not just entail broadcasting. My peer
group, i.e. the boys on Radio 1, all seemed to be earning
far more than I was, by doing several public appearances
a week. Let us say that I did not take easily to the club
world during the seventies. Being a Radio 1 DJ club enter-
tainer seemed to involve not playing records but organizing
'Miss Wet T-shirt' competitions and snogging contests, and
encouraging the male punters to drop their trousers and
show off their Y-fronts or, worse, their bare bottoms. It
was holiday-camp-style entertainment. And, if you were
booked to appear as the star turn from Radio 1, you
were *expected* to turn up in a flash sports car. My Ford
Anglia and subsequent Morris Marina just didn't cut it in
this kind of macho milieu.

On arrival at the venue, one would be given a microphone on a long lead and would be expected to deliver, as
per the night's contract, an hour's worth of patter, make
endless sexually suggestive remarks to the crowd, sign
autographs in felt pen on girls' naked breasts and boys'
white sweaty backsides, and *give money away*! Yes, give

money away. Your own. Fistfuls of fivers, preferably. This was to prove that you were a Highly Successful Household Name, with more wedge than you knew what to do with. Radio 1's management encouraged its DJs to do these spin-offs, and would arm us with 'giveaways', – glorious promotional items such as Radio 1 pens, keyrings, car stickers, publicity photographs, badges, sweatshirts, headbands and calendars.

DJs were not expected to DJ during their appearances, or necessarily go anywhere near the decks. There would always be a resident operator ready to spin the discs for you. It did not seem to occur to the organizers of these events that one might just care a smidge about what was being played. Or that people might have paid money, expecting you to play the kind of music you played on the radio.

I loathed these events, not surprisingly. They were degrading and humiliating, and 'entertaining' people by throwing money at them seemed excruciating in its lack of taste. However, I needed the extra income from making public appearances. Desperately. But, because I would not resort to playing the smutty sexual-innuendo games, my club appearances – when I would far rather just have stayed behind the mixer and play records – were nearly always disastrous. I felt highly uncomfortable turning up and failing to 'perform' in the manner expected of a Radio 1 DJ – well, a male one anyway – and also faintly guilty that I wasn't earning my money, or living up to the expectations of the promoter. I was rarely rebooked at any of these venues, and I wasn't really surprised. I just wasn't cut out for this kind of 'live entertainment', which was aesthetically as inspiring as being a female stripagram at a stag night.

But at least I was being allowed to play more or less what I wanted on radio. I'd become heavily into 'prog rock', and found myself sharing a Wednesday night slot with the Scottish DJ Alan Black. We co-hosted a review slot under the banner of evening programmes called *Sounds of the Seventies*. Other DJs on different evenings were Bob Harris, the warm-hearted Stuart Henry and John Peel. It's unthinkable now, but often Alan, myself and legendary producer Bernie Andrews, having put the running order together, would spend the early part of Wednesday evenings in the BBC club *drinking alcohol* before we went on air. A degree of tripping over words then went on, but, amazingly, going on air pissed was never noticed by the management. I would not dream of taking any kind of intoxicant before a live broadcast nowadays, and nor have I done so for many years (though afterwards is a different story, of course).

Radio 1 then still enjoyed the luxury of being the only legal pop-music radio receivable in the UK, apart from Radio Luxembourg, which had waned in its influence after the launch of Radio 1. But the paranoia was still apparent in the offices, as was the constant pressure to bring in staggeringly high ratings.

I was still feeling extremely insecure about my position and popularity at Radio 1. I still felt I was the token woman – tolerated, but not necessarily appreciated. This sensation was confirmed for me by the then controller, Derek Chinnery, when he said quite airily and casually, 'Oh, we don't regard you as a DJ really. We only took you on because of your journalistic background.' Soon after that, swiftly and without warning, came the first Radio 1 Night of the Long Knives – the first of the pogroms, the bloodletting and wholesale sackings which were to become an almost regular feature in Radio 1 life, a real-life horror film, in later years.

Most rumours emanated from the open-plan office called Room 306 on the third floor of Egton House, Radio 1's home. Room 306 housed the radio production assistants who worked on evening and weekend programmes. Through the centre of this room, lined on either side by desks and typewriters, was a thoroughfare leading to the next floor. Along with the ladies' toilet just beyond the swing door, which was the most reliable source of information to be found anywhere within the BBC, it was an early information superhighway of fact, fiction, truth, myth, circumspection and complete lies. DJs Were About To Be Fired, so the story was being spread. But which ones? Many of those who had worked on *Sounds of the Seventies*, it transpired. Eeny, meeny, miny, mo . . . Who was going to get the push? Phrases like 'chill wind' and 'corridors of power' began to be bandied about. Paranoia levels were hitting a Richter level of 9.2. Not a day later the axe fell with a mighty clang and an eerie echo which seemed to be intoning in a doom-ridden boom, 'NOBODY IS INDISPENSABLE . . . cover your ass . . .' Overnight, Bob Harris, Stuart Henry and Alan Black were told that their contracts were not going to be renewed. It was a horrifying shock to them, and a horrifying lesson to me.

In one sense I'd been right to be so insecure as to believe in the sheer ruthless power of the BBC and its willingness to cut off any branch, any bough, that wasn't, in its corporate view, bearing fruit. But this was bewildering. There had been no murmur of criticism of *Sounds of the Seventies*, no word that the ratings had dropped, or that the audience wanted more Abba and less Allman Brothers. This was the first enactment in Radio 1's history of Edgar Allan Poe's 'The Pit and the Pendulum' in terms of DJ sudden death, though oft to be repeated. I felt the wind of the axe-laden pendulum whisking very close to my head.

The most horrible irony of this whole incident was that dear Stuart Henry had apparently had his contract terminated owing to his increasing tendency to slur his speech. This, it has been alleged many times, had caused the management to believe that Stuart had become an alcoholic. How could they have got it so grotesquely wrong? Stuart was battling against the beginnings of the lifelong scourge of multiple sclerosis. He was not going on air pissed, as I had sometimes irresponsibly done.

During those early years at Radio 1, whenever I'd been foolish enough in a social situation to admit to my chosen line of work, people's first question would inevitably be 'What's Tony Blackburn really like?' As the years went on, this was modified to 'What's Noel Edmonds really like?' Later on the names might be changed to Simon Bates, or Steve Wright or Chris Evans. The truth was we DJs rarely saw each other. And very little socializing ever seemed to take place. They were either too busy or disinclined to 'hang about after work' for a pint. There would be a surface camaraderie, but it only thinly disguised the rampant rivalry that always existed between the male DJs. As the only female, I had the luxury of being able to rise above and ignore the tension that always seemed to exist between them.

Deep-seated distrust, jealousy, paranoia, an insatiable lust for satisfaction of the ego, envy and white-knuckled insecurity were, of course, qualities that the management looked for and engendered in its jocks. Knowing that at any given moment there are several hundred thousand people lined up *waiting* to take your job, prepared to *kill* for your job, does not lead to a rosy glow of satisfaction and contentment. Every DJ on Radio 1 was as jittery and jumpy as a junkie waiting for a connection. And the management played on it. For those without a TV career in the offing, Radio 1 was the pinnacle. There were no lucrative commercial stations at that time to transfer to. The only way out was down. And ignominy.

After the first Night of the Long Knives I was informed that I would be taking over the *Dave Lee Travis Request Show* on Sunday afternoons. I thought it would be quite fun to continue calling it the *Dave Lee Travis Request Show*, even though I would be presenting it. Such flippancy was not well received. But I did see this new radio show as an opportunity to play some damn good tunes. The ever-wise Teddy Warwick said to me, 'You will get the requests you deserve, depending on what you play.' Meaning that if I played an endless stream of crap music people would ask for more of the same, but if I played quality music the audience would reciprocate by writing in with suggestions for . . . more quality music. It worked! After a very short while, letters arrived in shoals week by week requesting glorious, fab music.

By now, the mid-seventies, both my children were at school, so I decided that, in order to spend as much time with them at the weekend as possible, I would take them to work with me on Sundays, so that at least we could spend the journey there and back together. With a huge sense of responsibility about being on time for work, and not trusting British Rail, I would drive us from Brighton to Broadcasting House each Sunday lunchtime. Once I'd arrived at the studio, I would effectively tell them to get lost until I'd finished my show. It being a Sunday, they had complete freedom in Broadcasting House, running in and out of the newsroom, barging into unoccupied offices, ransacking conference rooms, riding up and down in the lifts, and being given conscience money by me to buy endless hamburgers and ice cream from the top-floor canteen. I had no idea what malfeasance occupied Alex and Lucy during the hours I was ensconced in front of the microphone. Nor did I want to. Some time later they made a small admission. The pair of them had held spitting contests from the sixth-floor fire-escape stairwell. What else went on I'll never know.

Musically I felt well on top of what was happening, although in retrospect, and compared with the almost weekly changing musical influences in the underground, it was not nearly as exciting as what is happening now. The seventies sound was in place, and I was into Mott the Hoople and early Queen, the Stones, Bowie and Rod. But most of all I loved the Who. I loved their danger, their unpredictability, their power, energy, excitement, emotion . . . and their *lights*! I don't think there has ever been a greater moment in live rock 'n' roll, for me anyway, than when at the end of a Who set the huge coordinated battery of stage lights would swoop out from the top of the rig, turning to *drench* the entire exalted audience in a blinding white effulgence as Daltrey roared into the microphone, which he held above his mouth as though he were about to give it a blowjob, 'We . . . won't . . . get . . . fooled . . . AGAIN!' Which he followed with an unearthly screech as Moon ran around the kit with his sticks until the ultimate shattering climax. It was like being in the front line in a war zone. There was the possibility that you might die from the sheer velocity of the Who, that they might just decide to turn heavy artillery fire on the audience and kill you as part of the performance. Not until the nineties, with the advent of the Prodigy, did another band come close to the sheer excitement and feeling of danger that the Who generated.

IX

It was a source of acute embarrassment to me that, among most of the people I knew, by the late seventies I was the only one who had Never Been to America. Finally, in 1977, with a gaggle of journalists who laughed openly and derisively when I admitted that this was my first flight to the New World, I was on my way to New York to interview the country star Don Williams. At that time he was quite hip, having been given many accolades in Britain by Eric Clapton, who was himself hip enough still to be known as 'God'.

I'll spare you my first impressions of New York – you've heard it all before, as indeed had I. Except in one respect. At that time the most impressive manner in which to arrive, or so I'd been led to believe, was by helicopter link from JFK to a landing pad atop the PanAm building on Vanderbilt Avenue in midtown Manhattan. I was disappointed when this means of transport failed to materialize, as our group had no reservation on the chopper trip, and I had to make my first entrance into NYC in a boring old limo. I checked into my hotel room, still a bit miffed that I'd missed the special chopper ride in, and switched on the TV. Every news channel was showing the same live pictures – of the very same helicopter I'd so much wanted to fly in, which had crash-landed on the roof of the PanAm building and was poised to topple over the edge of the skyscraper down on to the street hundreds of feet below. The rotor blade had already snapped off and spiralled down from the top of the building, killing a woman shopper as it hit the ground. What a welcome to New York! Have a nice day! After this horrific accident, the helicopter service from JFK was cancelled forthwith.

The incident had become but a dim memory until twelve or so years later, when I was sat face to face with Lou Reed in London for a TV interview that he had agreed to do in order to promote his latest album, *New York*. One of the most difficult aspects of TV interviews is how to conduct a conversation with the interviewee while the lights and sound are being set up, without covering any topic you wish to commit to film or video later. You need to build a rapport with your subject somehow, without him or her saying anything too interesting before the interview has begun. Lou looked about as enthusiastic about the prospect of doing the interview as he would if he'd just been given the death sentence. I gamely tried to warm him up with innocuous small talk. 'So, Lou, when did you arrive in London?'

'Yesterday.'

'How was your flight?'

'OK.'

'What's your hotel like?'

'Fine.'

OK, Mr Monosyllabic, so you're going to be hard work. Finally the camera was rolling and I could ask some proper questions. Lou's manner was that of a resigned traveller forced into making conversation with a person of limited intelligence he'd just met on a train. He explained patiently that recording an album in New York City could be hazardous. 'The very first day we started in the studio a manhole cover in the street outside – do you have those things here? [I nodded assent enthusiastically] – shot twelve feet in the air, just from the heat and the pressure from under the ground. New York', he added, 'is a dangerous place.'

At this point the helicopter incident popped into my head and I began to recount it. Lou nearly leapt out of his chair. 'You were *gonna be* on that flight? *You* were? On your first trip? Wow. I remember that whole thing.' He was almost agog. Not only was he almost agog, he was genuinely impressed by how close to being in a bizarre fatal accident I'd come on a maiden trip to his city of residence. After that the interview went swimmingly, and when it ended Lou said how much he'd enjoyed the experience and how it hadn't been like an interview at all, more like a conversation between friends. Funny what turns people on.

I felt extraordinarily at home in New York. It crossed my mind that if my mother had taken up Dr Scholl's offer, and had stayed and married in the USA, I might have been born on the other side of the Atlantic. It was just a strange feeling of familiarity that I experienced in the city, which brings out the best and the worst in me.

I fell in love, fearlessly, with the Big Apple, picked up on the energy on the streets, felt its friendliness, delighted in its delis. But horribly soon, as I was part of Don Williams's promotional tour, I was moved on to Nashville, Tennessee. The whole concept of the theme park, even before Dolly Parton's own Dollywood was conceived, must have been inspired by Nashville – a living, breathing tourist

102

attraction, year round, and around the clock. 'Music City USA,' it proclaims, brashly, with every street name, every hotel and bar and restaurant and clothing store, relentlessly reminding you that you are in close proximity to the Gran' Ole Opry and at the very epicentre of America's own music – country music. And its stars. Liverpool's enshrinement of the Beatles has caused the same shopping-mallification of the Mathew Street area, but at least the Fab Three, as they are now, are not on hand to be dragged out of their homes to greet visitors, as was the case, I found, with the Nashville stars.

Over a breakfast bowl of grits – apparently the South's romanticized version of cold tapioca, and a deep culinary disappointment – a true blue-eyed, weather-tanned Tennessean said sagely, 'Y'know why all our female country-music stars stay happily married?' It was obviously a rhetorical question. 'Bee-kawse', he went on, 'they all scrub their own floors.' I supposed that Tammy Wynette and her huge international hit 'D-I-V-O-R-C-E' was the exception that proved the rule. Or maybe Tammy hadn't scrubbed her own floor.

It was arranged that I should meet the country-music star Barbara Mandrell, and I was duly briefed that she had been recently remarried. To the same guy she had married the first time, who had apparently been a personal helicopter pilot to President Carter. I assumed they had split up and got back together. Barbara ushered me on to her tour bus, of which she was rightfully proud, and showed me all its luxurious fittings and fixtures – quite necessary, too, for someone who spent most of their life on the road. She was a gorgeously pretty woman, with blonde hair surrounding a heart-shaped face, like a fifties movie star. I tactfully broached the subject of her remarriage. Had it been an emotionally fraught reunion? Barbara looked a little confused at this. Then she enlightened me. 'Oh, gee, we never split up – we were just so in love that we rededicated. We had a preacher round to the house, a proper ceremony, wedding cake, champagne . . . I wore the gown I'd gotten married in . . . Unfortunately my husband couldn't get into his original uniform because he's put on a few pounds since . . .' 'Wait a minute,' my head was screaming. 'What was all this "rededicating" business?' Was this, I asked Barbara, a local Nashville custom? 'Oh no,' she said. 'But I saw it done on *The Waltons*, and I thought it was real cute.'

I had one other unusual experience in Tennessee. Someone in the travelling group of journalists decided we should take a day trip across the rolling green countryside to a tiny undistinguished hamlet called Lynchburg. Undistinguished except in one respect. Lynchburg, Tennessee, is the location of the distillery where in 1866 one Mr Jack Daniel first perfected his unique mellowing process, creating the now world-famous sour-mash whiskey. And such pride does the United States government have in this hallowed place that the distillery is entered in the National Register of Historic Places. Now I'm sure you're thinking what I thought on arrival in Lynchburg: a quick guided tour of the works, and then one would be presented with a free souvenir bottle of JD. Several hours of anticipation later, spent sending free postcards to one's loved ones at home and examining the filtering plants in minute detail, came the climax to the Jack Daniels tour. A charming Southern belle in pigtails and a frilly checked cotton frock paraded in front of us with an array of glasses. 'Ree-yal home-mayde lemon-ayde!' she proclaimed. Lynchburg, it emerged, is situated in a dry county. You can look, but you'd better not touch. There was one member of our party even more disgruntled than myself. This was the photographer Richard Young, not only a teetotaller, but a young man who was trying to build his reputation as a paparazzo, who found no one famous enough to photograph in Lynchburg. So we photographed him instead.

Before the expression 'compassion fatigue' set in, and probably because of it, Live Aid lifted the musical doldrums of the mid-eighties. The rather banal-worded 'Do They Know It's Christmas?' record had opened the charity floodgates. That special combination of pop music and poignant visual image which makes people dig deep in their pockets or go recklessly crazy with their credit card was just evolving. The interminable chart-topper, Bryan Adams's 'Everything I Do (I Do It For You)' is a perfect example of what I call 'greeting card lyrics'. Pop songs with gag-inducing cheap sentiments bought by people who can't express themselves emotionally. Bob Geldof had found that the combination of music and television was the most powerful media instrument to put across his desire to sort out the situation in Ethopia. The idea of the 'global jukebox' with alternating musical numbers bouncing across the Atlantic, city to city, London to Philadelphia from the stages of Wembley Stadium to the JFK in Philly was a truly exciting broadcasting prospect. It had never been done before, and neither BBC TV, nor Radio 1 or any of the North American counterparts had any idea if it would really work. There wasn't much of a rehearsal either. Although there was great alarm at Wembley during a tryout, the evening before the concert, of spinning the revolving stage. One entire band set-up of equipment and instruments went flying off in the general direction of

Neasden. The line-up for London looked, for its time, particularly strong. The Who, re-forming for the event, U2, Sting, Boy George, George Michael, Queen – and Prince Charles and Princess Diana as spectators in the Royal Box. Any and every rock act was pleading to take part. There were unquellable rumours that the surviving Beatles would get back together for the show with Julian Lennon taking his father's part. Julian told me afterwards that when Live Aid was broadcast he was just sitting at home watching it all unfold on television like everyone else, waiting for The Call That Never Came. The problem was America, and that's where the BBC sent me. Throughout the run-up to Live Aid there was this nagging doubt that the American side hadn't really 'got it'; that the Stateside concert would just be a giant recording artiste marketing exercise. The fact that the Wembley team, riggers, TV crews, caterers, musicians gave their services free, but their North American counterparts all got paid for their services said a lot. Quite a few British or British-based stars were assigned to play the Philadelphia stage in order to beef up the look of the running order there – Mick Jagger and Keith Richards, Eric Clapton, David Bowie – because there was a real doubt whether any American superstars would actually turn up. In the end Bob Dylan did, Michael Jackson and Bruce Springsteen didn't. I was disappointed not to be involved with the Wembley show as it was being run by the *Whistle Test* team and London was the core of the whole Live Aid buzz; but I couldn't really complain about being asked to be the BBC's only representative at the Philly Show. Well, little did I know . . .

The weekend kicked off to a bad start. The taxi which took me from the airport to the hotel in Philly had what looked suspiciously like a large bullet hole in the wind-screen and the driver informed me cheerfully that the hotel where I was to stay was the very hotel which had hosted the first outbreak of Legionnaires's Disease. I had a two-fold part in the Philadelphia Story 1985. One was to liaise with BBC TV, organizing interviews with the likes of Eric Clapton, Jagger and Chrissie Hynde, and the other was to take part in a US sourced worldwide radio broadcast of the entire Live Aid event. For this purpose I took a very fat file of research material; press releases, biographies and such and never have I been so grateful for a bit of forward thinking. The production team I was assigned were an extraordinary bunch of amateurs, who were fond of holding hands at unnecessary breakfast meetings and chanting: 'two . . . point . . . five . . . *billion* . . .' repeatedly. 'Two point five billion *what*?' I asked, perplexed. Potential listeners they told me reverentially.

However many did listen, they would have heard a lot of my voice 'filling' for up to twenty minutes at a time, while bands changed over on stage and there was no music to broadcast. This was where the research file had came in so handy. There were a lot of media lies told about Live Aid, many hopelessly optimistic or downright inaccurate figures as to numbers who heard or saw the show live. In many of the countries I visited later people told me they hadn't got the show 'live' at all, and in the Soviet Union they saw only snippets, months after the event.

The early part of the Philadelphia show wasn't broadcast – it didn't go global until later in the day. We watched two different monitors, one showing events on-stage locally, one transmitting from London. Suddenly, at midday, the two pictures became one. Although the temperature was in the eighties, I felt a shiver run down my spine. 'They've done it!' I thought. The global link up.

There were any number of technical problems. When the Who were playing in London, transmission was abruptly interrupted in Philadelphia – apparently helicopters were flying across the satellite beam, disrupting the signal. Then the Who lost power altogether, whereupon a great groan went up in Philadelphia. Someone had pulled out a lead bringing this unique worldwide broadcasting event to a temporary halt.

As always at these events, security passes were a major headache. In the middle of the afternoon my two BBC New York colleagues discovered that their passes had been abruptly downgraded – and they no longer had backstage access. Television colleagues would request me to get hold of Eric Clapton or the Stones or Chrissie Hynde before they went on-stage, but I was separated from my mini-team. Then, the whole area suddenly had to be cleared for Madonna to have a pee. Live Aid was really her great debut – she'd scarcely been heard of up to then – but when Madonna visited the Portaloo all the other performers had to piss off.

It was in Philadelphia that Simon Le Bon of Duran Duran introduced me to Yasmin. I ended up travelling back to New York with Simon, and he lay on his bed at Morgan's Hotel and drooled over magazine shots of this girl. I said, 'Simon, you've got to marry her.' And he did.

I'd made friends with one of the US broadcast team, Roxanne, and when the end of the proceedings was in sight and there was little more to do we had a bit of a chill at the side of the stage, from where we watched the final line-up of Bob Dylan, Mick Jagger, Keith Richards, Tina

Turner, Eric Clapton et al. In front of us were two young boys. When Roxanne asked them about their accreditation, they said, 'We haven't got any.' Rather in the manner of John McEnroe, she exclaimed, 'You cannot be serious! Where are your credentials?' They shrugged and told us, 'We hitched from New York. We knew someone with a catering pass, and they got us in. We brought head phones with us and pretended to be stage managers.' Whereupon they jumped out of their seats, went up-stage, and started hanging with the stars. I'd been through three days of hassle over the status of my pass, and here were two possible assassins, for all anybody knew, who'd breezed through all the security without so much as a challenge.

It had been a long day, starting at four in the morning, and I was exhausted by the time I got back to my hotel at four the next morning. But I still had to file a story for the *Daily Express*, for which I was writing a column. When I tried to make a collect call to London, the operator asked me for the name of the person I was calling. I said, 'It's not a name, it's a newspaper.' 'Sorry, ma'am,' I was told, 'you gotta have a name.' 'OK, OK,' I said, 'I would like to make a collect call to a Mr Daly X. Press.'

Later, when I was complaining to Chrissie Hynde about how early I'd had to get up and how tiring it had been, she said, 'Well, if you were a milkmaid, you'd have to do that every day. Who said life was going to be easy?'

If Live Aid had been difficult, Woodstock 2, in 1994, was hilariously appalling – positively, hopefully, the worst broadcasting experience of my life. Apart from the fact that it was a very male, macho, very rock affair, with acts like Henry Rollins and Aerosmith, the whole thing was a shambles, incredibly badly organised. The Orb, one of the few British acts appearing, had to break down the fences to get on to the site. We called it Auschwitz '94 afterwards. Radio 1 was to broadcast for eighteen hours live. Our studio was a pick-up truck, parked on the media highway among the flash trucks of the American heavyweights such as CNN and ABC, all sprouting an array of impressive satellite dishes. Ours had a driving cab at the front, and the rear area was about the size of a very small living room – the sort that would just accommodate a two-seater sofa, two chairs and a coffee table. At a pinch. It was not remotely designed to take in a TV monitor, a mobile mixing desk, two reel-to-reel tape machines and editing facilities, two cassette machines, two DAT players, two radio pre-senters (both Aries, with egos to match), two producers and an engineer. I spent the first afternoon inking the letters 'BBC' on a piece of card and taping it to our base to identify us.

Woodstock Pete, our hired engineer, worked fastidi-ously all day Thursday and Friday to get us 'powered up'. Miraculously, he would pull in lines of cable, like a fisherman hauling in a catch of eels, attach electrical leads that were seemingly just lying around on the ground to each other, and then grin triumphantly as small red and green lights on the mixing desk winked sexily back at us, indicating that we were, electronically anyway, in business. Woodstock Pete seemed to be something of a local cel-ebrity, as every ten minutes or so the door of our makeshift studio would be swung open by another acquaintance of his dropping by.

The organizers wouldn't let any other vehicles on-site. Yellow school buses were to operate on a twenty-four-hour basis, ferrying festival goers and crews from the site

to the giant car parks many miles away. Having worked
on pre-production till three a.m. on the day of broadcast
we left our truck to catch a bus to the car park, from
which we had a further forty-mile drive to our hotel.
There were no buses. The system had broken down. One
hundred thousand white middle-class kids milled about in
the pitch black. Next morning the police closed the high-
ways altogether. Getting back on site by car was a matter
of keep blagging, keep moving and sheer determination
born out of knowing we were on air in three hours. It was
then discovered that the stuff we'd recorded on DAT to
plug any gaps in the live transmission was flawed and
unusable. I scrambled up the grassy bank to the press area
and grabbed anyone who looked famous. 'Right,' I'd say
to Youssou N'Dour, 'you'll do. I need to talk to you' –
anything to get some interviews to fill airtime.

Passes were an inexplicable mystery. A pass might
admit one to areas 6 and 7, but there were no maps, so
no one had any idea where these areas were. I said to
one of the organizers, 'I'm surprised you haven't been to
Glastonbury to look at that.' She replied, 'Where?' She'd
never heard of it. At one point, a boy, maybe nineteen
years old, with sleek, shiny brown hair, wearing a white
cut-off T-shirt with the legend 'SID AND NANCY' on the
front, hovered outside our makeshift studio. 'My Mom
used to go out with Steven Tyler of Aerosmith. I'm sure
he'd remember me. 'D'you know where I might get an
Access All Areas pass?' he asked winsomely. 'A *what*?' I
screamed. 'An Access *where*?' By now I was well stressed.
'*All* areas? You must be fucking joking!' No one, but *no
one*, had an Access All Areas pass. No one I met had ever
seen one. I'd *still* like to see what a Woodstock '94 Access
All Areas pass looked like. Finally, after intensive research,

i.e. slogging all over the site, we discovered where areas 6 and 7 actually were. They were nowhere special, for sure. Intensive questioning, staring and gazing at other fortunate festival-goers revealed that there were other areas to be 'accessed'. One to eleven, actually. Maybe zero let you into the mud moshpit in front of the north stage.

I do wish all rock festivals would standardize, in some way, the ritual of the backstage pass (obviously with some idiosyncrasies, otherwise there would be mass forgeries on the scale of that carried out by the Happy Mondays at Glastonbury in 1990, when they allegedly 'simulated' two thousand passes for their best mates with an on-site colour photocopier). At present it seems to take the best part of a day to sort out whether your pass indicates that (a) you are totally worthless and won't even be welcome near the backstage Portaloos, (b) you're a music journalist with beer-tent access only, (c) you're doing the catering or (d) the merchandising, (e) you're an authorized drug dealer or (f) a friend of the band, (g) golly, you're *in* the band, or (h) you're the promoter. You spend precious hours, if not days, trying to ascertain if you're allowed backstage, back-backstage (i.e. into a hobnob-with-pop-star possibility area), into the inner sanctum (an array of Portakabins where hardly famous pop stars are allowed to hang out for one hour before and one hour after their set – proper rock stars have their own luxury two-tier buses and never hobnob backstage), or into the inner inner sanctum (viz., in the case of the Rolling Stones, you are allowed into Keith Richards and Ronnie Wood's guitar-tuning room).

You weren't allowed to take alcohol on site, or drugs, (though we did) even though the original Woodstock had been all about that kind of freedom. You had to buy tokens and exchange them for Woodstock Coke or Woodstock hamburgers – the whole thing was an enormous concessionary exercise. I don't think the Americans will try it again in a hurry.

X

In England, in the late seventies, the era of 'pomp' rock was in full swing, with appallingly long guitar solos at Yes concerts, Rick Wakeman doing ice shows, and Rod Stewart appearing on the stage of the Wembley Arena like a tiny, tartanned, overpriced dot from one's vantage point way up underneath the metal roof. Rock 'n' roll had become sop 'n' dough, self-serving and self-indulgent. The big names like the Rolling Stones and Alice Cooper put on bigger and more spectacular shows, shifted more units, and the record-company moguls were in heaven, controlling what had become a vast industry, and doing it their way – promoting the artistes they liked and were comfortable with. Something had to give, and something did.

A new generation of would-be pop stars found that the doors of the major record companies were as locked, bolted and barred to them as the BBC's doors had been to me. The music industry had reached a situation that occurs cyclically every few years, in which the big names get bigger and bigger and nobody else can get a look in.

Punk was a movement that needed to happen, and it was another example of Britain importing an American idea, making it our own, and then trying to sell it back to the States, as had happened with the Beatles and rhythm and blues. Malcolm McLaren had gone to New York and seen the New York Dolls, the archetypal punk band, an experience that inspired him to form the Sex Pistols. The Pistols, Siouxsie and the Banshees, the Jam, the Clash, the Stranglers, the Buzzcocks and the Adverts now took it upon themselves to storm the citadel.

I was knocked out by their music and its determination to blow away the pomposity that had taken over rock music at the time. I remember seeing the Clash early on and being wildly excited by them. This generation believed in a DIY approach to life – DIY fashion, DIY music. Anybody could form a band. You didn't need to be able to play – in fact it was better if you couldn't, or at least pretended you couldn't. Captain Sensible admitted that he had had to unlearn to play the guitar in order to join the Damned, and when I first saw the Stranglers I thought they were suspiciously good musicians. The Police later admitted to jumping on the bandwagon – Andy Summers had played guitar with sixties bands, Sting had been in a jazz group, and Stewart Copeland was a highly competent drummer.

The floodgates opened, the punks poured in, and, bewildered and frightened, the record companies signed contracts with people wearing bin-liners, who pierced their bodies, took speed and had no homes or money. The girls all looked like wonderful sluts, with fucked-up, back-combed beehive hair in any colour other than that they'd been born with – bright acid yellow or henna scarlet, Quink-ink blue or spider black – with black lipstick, black nail polish and enough black eyeliner to need a hundred-weight of crushed coal to achieve.

It was punk that was ultimately responsible for me getting a job as presenter of BBC TV's *The Old Grey Whistle*

Test. First called *Colour Me Pop*, then *Disco 2*, *Whistle Test* had, by the mid-seventies, become very well established, with Bob Harris (known as 'Whispering Bob', because of his quiet, intimate style of presentation, and a colleague of mine from Radio 1) as presenter. Bob was very much associated with the established bands of the time, principally American outfits such as the Steve Miller Band and Lynryd Skynyrd. When punk came along he decided that this new music wasn't for him – the New York Dolls had appeared on *Whistle Test*, and Bob had not been impressed. The crunch came when he was in a club with a friend of his and Sid Vicious, who was also there with a mate, asked why the Pistols had never been invited on the programme. The discussion deteriorated, and it ended up with Bob's friend getting glassed by Sid's mate and needing about 120 stitches in his face. Bob felt he couldn't carry on after that experience.

But it was clear that *Whistle Test* couldn't ignore the phenomenon of punk, and in 1978 I was asked if I'd like to take over as presenter. I'd already worked with the production team on other projects – notably a series of simulcasts, simultaneous live broadcasts on BBC Television and Radio – and because of the experience I already had as a TV presenter (and my radio background, seen as an advantage because I knew how to keep talking if anything went wrong) they believed I was the right person for the job. I ventured to ask politely if a dress allowance might be in order. 'We didn't have this trouble with Bob,' they said.

It turned out to be a baptism of fire. As the newcomer, I was in any case very nervous, feeling that Bob had made the programme his own, and my first show was just after Keith Moon had died. Keith had been a close friend – ten days before his death he'd said to me, 'I'd like you to write my life story, 'cos there's a lot of good pubs in Brighton.' I pointed out that if he wanted me to cooperate on a book he'd have to be serious, and we couldn't just go on a pub crawl. I saw him the night before he died, at a party at a bar in London called Peppermint Park organized by Paul McCartney for his annual Buddy Holly Week. Keith seemed a bit subdued for him, but it was still a bad shock the next day when the news filtered out; at first I thought it was a joke. Roger Daltrey told me that even at the funeral he expected Keith to jump out of the coffin and go, 'Ha ha, fooled you.' Roger appeared on my first *Whistle Test* to talk about Keith, and I remember him coming up with this wonderful mixed metaphor: 'The Who is like a table with four legs, and we've lost a leg, but we've made our bed, so we must lie on it.'

I held the *Whistle Test* production team in high regard. The producer was Mike Appleton, a big man with floppy hair, known to us as Biggles (because once at Euston Station he went off to buy me a ticket at which this enormous personal effort was rewarded with the remark: oh, look, 'Biggles Gets A Train Ticket'). Mike was usually a wonderfully unflappable individual. The only time he ever lost his temper with me was when we were filming together in India. He liked collecting old phonographs, and had decided that the back streets of Bombay would be a good place to find spare parts. I was teetering along behind him on ludicrously high heels with ankle straps, unable to match his pace through the pot holes and cracked uneven paving slabs.

Besides Mike there were Tom Corcoran, the wild Irish studio director, very good at his job, who wore tweed fishing hats and reminded me of Spike Milligan; Rosa

Rudnicka, production assistant; Autocue Susie (of whom more later); and Alma Player, researcher/archivist, a great eccentric and (appropriately, given her name) a great smoker. (Once, in Manchester, when the fire alarm went off in our hotel, Mike phoned Alma and said, 'Alsy, you've got to get out of your room, there's a fire on.' She said, 'Well, all right, darling, but I've got to have a cigarette first.')

The show was very smooth-running. People always ask me about the mad things that happened on *Whistle Test*, but in fact it was a very professionally run, well-oiled machine, not chaotic at all. It was rare for things to go wrong. As presenter, I was not individually that important – I was simply there as part of a team to do the links. I took pride in my ability to get it right first go, in just the same way as any of the technicians got it right first time. They were wonderful people to work with, and the atmosphere was pretty much the same as when I'd worked on the *Brighton Evening Argus* – it was a lot of fun as long as you got the job done. Mike had bypassed all the main BBC departments (*Whistle Test* came under the Presentations Department, which also did the news and weather, and, although this was later to change, not Arts or Current Affairs), so we escaped all the usual BBC politics.

Despite my early apprehension, the show was more nerve-racking for the bands than it was for me. *Whistle Test* was done 'as live', sometimes completely live – in other words, filming was done in one go, and we'd only stop and retake if there was a technical problem. If a band member broke a string during their performance, that was tough luck. For most bands it was their first TV experience, and they tended to be very nervous – not least because one appearance on *Whistle Test* could really launch an artiste in

118

a big way. I began to realize its power when people started coming up to me and saying, 'I saw April Wine on *Whistle Test* last night and went out and bought the album today.' I'd appreciated the power of Radio 1, for some time, but this was something else.

This was before pop videos became the norm, of course. If a band wasn't appearing live we'd accompany the music with bits of film – cut-up clips of Busby Berkeley musicals or black-and-white thirties movies, or a series of animations, many created by Philip Jenkinson. These were a strong feature of the show, in my view often overlooked in the past.

A number of the shows came from Manchester, and these were a lot more fun to do. If we were based in London the whole programme would be done in a day and we'd all just go home in the evening, whereas if we were filming in Manchester the entire crew would travel up, stay overnight, and go clubbing after the show. Shepperton Studios, then owned by the Who, was another regular venue. We used a big old sound stage – when they opened the doors (large enough to take the big sets for old feature films) it was freezing cold, and it always seemed to be during the winter that we were there. My dressing room had one bare light bulb hanging from the ceiling, a bit of broken mirror and one chair. There was a good atmosphere, though, as we all had to huddle together for warmth!

Every summer we'd go to California and interview bands nobody had ever heard of – most of whom were never heard of again – or to New York, where on one occasion I was due to interview Paul Simon. Although I'd known Simon and Garfunkel's music since they started, and was perfectly well aware that Paul Simon wrote all the songs for the duo, for some reason I worded a question badly, implying that they were a writing team. Paul got very uppity, and as a joke *I* got up and walked off the set. We left this incident in the finished film because we thought it was funny. When the film, was shown, *Melody Maker* tore me to shreds, for alleged lack of research.

Often American guests on *Whistle Test* would be accompanied by record-company representatives, anxious that their charges should have as many opportunities as possible to plug their latest album. I'd talk about everything else until the very last minute, just to wind them up. One overzealous British plugger was Judd Lander, who'd arranged for Jeff Beck to appear on the show. At the last minute Jeff decided he didn't want to do the interview. Nothing daunted, on the day of the show Judd stood outside Jeff's house playing the bagpipes, saying, 'I'm not going to stop until you come out and come to the TV studio.' Jeff finally agreed, on one condition – that while he was being interviewed Judd would walk across the set in front of the camera, naked, playing the bagpipes. Which he did. Deliberately, none of us batted an eyelid. I hoped casual viewers might suddenly sit bolt upright in their seats and say, 'Hang on a minute, am I going crazy, or did I just see . . .'

This was an interesting time musically, with people like Wreckless Eric and Ian Dury and the Blockheads starting out, and there were some memorable performances during my time on the show. I like to think I can claim some credit for helping Ian on his way. I asked him once in an interview at what point he felt he'd really become famous, and he said when I mentioned him in the *Daily Express*. Sweet! Finding somebody with talent like his and helping to spread the word is what keeps you going in the music world, what gives you the buzz.

One performance I particularly remember was from Public Image Limited, in a show taped in Manchester. After the programme I went over to the band and congratulated John Lydon on a very powerful performance. John replied with the characteristic snarl, 'Don't be so fucking *patronizing.*' It took me half an hour to convince him of my sincerity and John bought me drinks all night. 'You're my sort of woman,' he commented. We got on really well, and I asked him if he'd like to be a guest on my radio show. In that rather nasally, whiny voice of his, he said, 'They won't let me do it live. I'll have to pre-record it.' To my embarrassment, he was right – Radio 1 wouldn't let me have him on live. They were afraid he was going to swear. Some such incident occurs every few years – recently Liam Gallagher upset Radio 1 by using the C word, and the station received seventy-five complaints.

From their first appearance on *Whistle Test,* I got on well with Duran Duran, despite their drapes. Even at the height of their fame I could call them into Radio 1 for an unscheduled chat. At one point I spent a week with them on the island of Montserrat, now virtually destroyed by recent volcanic eruptions, where George Martin, the Beatles producer, had built a recording studio. The band was recording *Seven and the Ragged Tiger,* amid huge iguanas, black volcanic beaches, and bright red flowering trees. I was there on behalf of a magazine. Given the exotic but intimate locations available to us, I asked the magazine to send a cool photographer. Unfortunately the man they sent didn't get on with the band; in fact he thought they were a bunch of wankers. And his photographs of Duran Duran said as much. On the way home we stopped in Antigua, and I said to him, 'You haven't enjoyed it, have you? Why not? Where would you have rather been?' He replied, 'Northern Ireland.'

Duran Duran had the most avid fans, known as 'Duranies'. They all wore similar clothes, inside-out sweatshirts made by a company called Naf-Naf, all in pastel colours, pale greys and pale yellows. They'd stand outside Radio 1, and their intelligence network was extraordinary – they'd know exactly where each member of the band was at any given time: 'Simon's gone to see his mum in Pinner, Nick Rhodes is shopping in the King's Road with his girlfriend, and John Taylor's having a meeting with EMI.' There were certain expressions of devotion expected of the diehard Duranie. I was told, 'A true Duranie has got every Duran Duran record on CD, even if they don't own a CD player', and 'A true Duranie can't see one inch of their bedroom wall or ceiling because they've got it so covered in posters.' They'd write to me endlessly at Radio 1 – we're talking hundreds of letters a week here – requesting the band's records. It got to the point where I could spot their letters before I opened them – I simply recognized the style of handwriting. Endearingly, they always put their fan-club number at the bottom of the letter, under their name.

While I worked on *Whistle Test*, I was also doing a column for the *Daily Express*, as well as a new Radio 1 show called *Mailbag* on Wednesdays and another radio show on Fridays. I've often wondered since how I managed. The answer has to be that many of these commitments dovetailed. I met a lot of the recording artistes of the day through *Whistle Test*. If, say, Duran Duran were appearing on the show, I'd also interview them for my newspaper column, and then have them as guests on the Friday radio show.

Mailbag was great fun, and way ahead of its time. We'd invite Establishment figures such as politicians and civil servants on to the show, if necessary lying about our audience ratings, saying we had five million listeners, to entice them on. I'd be interviewing the Minister of Nuclear Procurement, say, and I'd address him by his first name, which would throw him completely, and ask him if he believed in God. Both of Margaret Thatcher's children appeared on this show as guests; Carol was the preferable of the two. French and Saunders, who were just starting out at the time, were also guests on *Mailbag*, in their newest guise as Duranies. I asked them what their fan-club numbers were. Dawn and Jennifer looked across the studio at me, aghast.

In Montserrat, Duran's John Taylor, who'd just been voted the world's most fanciable man, had pushed me into a swimming pool at about four in the morning, and I just happened to let this slip on air. One Duranie then, to me, perfectly summed up my relationship with my young female listeners, she wrote in; 'You should have pretended you were drowning, and then John Taylor could have given you the kiss of life!' The fans didn't see me a threat, more a big sister. One of the early objections to me becoming a Radio 1 DJ was that I would alienate women. Not with some deprecating wit, I don't!

In December 1980, in an incident that shocked the world, John Lennon was shot in New York. I heard the news when Lucy woke me to say that Richard Skinner, who was presenting *Newsbeat* on Radio 1, was on the phone asking if I had Paul McCartney's home number. *Whistle Test* had been due to fly to New York to film John two days later – I had already bought presents for Yoko and their son, Sean, to take with me. My colleague Andy Peebles had the dubious distinction of having conducted John's last-ever interview. He'd actually been flying home when John was shot – when he left New York John had alive; by the time he landed in London he was dead.

We decided to compile a *Whistle Test* tribute that day. It proved nearly impossible to get guests to come on the show – everyone was too shocked. At one point during transmission, when a piece of film was running, Mike Appleton came over to me and said, 'Paul's on the phone for you.' I thought, 'Paul who?' I went into the control room and Paul McCartney, who hitherto had refused to speak to anybody about John's death, said to me, 'You know how it was. Please say thank you on behalf of me and Ringo and George.' At that point it hit me – there were now only three Beatles! I had to go back in front of the camera and carry on with the show. I thought, 'I'm not going to crack up, I must hold this together.' It was really difficult, but somehow, when you have to, you do it.

Poor Autocue Susie (who, as her nickname suggests, worked the autocue for me) had come into the studio in a particularly cheerful mood that day. She was bouncing around asking if there was anything she could do to help. It transpired that she thought John was coming in to do an interview, and that was why we had been rummaging around looking for film clips. Eventually, in the middle of afternoon, I said to her, 'Susie, I think there's something maybe you don't know.' Having to tell her what had happened was one of the most difficult aspects of that day.

Later I remembered that when and John and Yoko had still been living in London, before they went to New York, at a time when they insisted on being called Johnandyoko, I'd been at Abbey Road studios with them, while John was mixing. For once Yoko sat outside the control room. Chillingly, as things turned out, she told me that she was very worried that she'd end up 'alone and shaking in a New York apartment'.

XI

The highlight of my four years with *Whistle Test* turned out to be making a world-tour documentary. The band concerned was the Police. I was initially very dubious about this project. They had dodgy credentials, to say the least. Their singer and bass player, Gordon Sumner, aka Sting (on account of the wasp-like look of a black-and-yellow striped sweater he was apparently wont to wear), was an ex-schoolteacher, and had played in a jazz band in Newcastle. Their guitarist, Andy Summers, had knocked around in the sixties with Hendrix et al., but had never really made a name for himself. The founder of the band was the drummer, Stewart Copeland, son of a CIA agent. They were three opportunists posing as punks – white peroxide-bottle blonds who had had their hair bleached for a TV commercial – and were, by their own admission, blatantly ripping off black Jamaican reggae. Sting had married a talented actress, Frances Tomelty, who passed on to him her influential theatrical agent, Pippa Markham. Thus he later found himself up for acting parts in such projects as the *Quadrophenia* movie.

Sting seemed to have the ability to knock out catchy pop tunes. I'd played the band's first couple of singles on Radio 1 and given them a favourable review in the *Daily*

Express, but at that stage I knew absolutely nothing about them. I'd suggested to Mike Appleton that they would be suitable for a slot on *Whistle Test*. Thus their TV debut was a *Whistle Test* recorded at the BBC's studios in Oxford Road, Manchester. The band and the BBC then asked me to be the presenter for their projected world-tour film. I turned them down flat. I wasn't prepared to commit to what I thought would be months and months away from home, and I had just begun a new Friday-night show on Radio 1. As it turned out, we shot the film in segments. The first leg was in Japan, and who should be hanging out backstage in the dressing room in Tokyo but my mates Sue and Jenny Maclean. Sue and Jenny were famous models at the time – wild, sexy twins, with whom I shared an affinity and the birth sign of Aries. So it seemed that a good time would be had by all.

The film's approach was light-hearted – there was no attempt to include a serious historical perspective, much to my initial horror. The director, Derek Burbidge, would simply point the camera at me and say, 'Right, talk to me.' It was ad-lib stylee, straight off the top of the head – no learning of lines, no scriptwriting, no cue boards. I guess it worked because it was just like working on radio. Derek made me laugh constantly, often by hanging a plastic chicken carcass or similar item below the lens. One night in Bombay, the crew tipped a bucket – and I mean a *bucket*-size bucket – of ice down the front of my dress. When I demanded of Derek why, he said, 'Because we like you.'

I'd never seen anything like the devotion of Japanese fans, though they behave the same way with any visiting foreign band. They'd follow us on the bullet train, find out where the band was, and book into the same hotel. I asked one girl how she could possibly afford to do this. She told me that her parents were paying – they thought she was on a cultural tour of Japan. I was taken to one side by a Japanese record-company employee who said quietly, 'Don't film her, she's the Shame of Japan.' 'All the more reason that we should,' I said loudly.

Japan seemed to me then a very conservative culture. Girl groupies *said* they were not allowed to give head, this practice being *said* to be illegal in Japan. Though quite how anyone else would *know* if the law was being upheld or not, so to speak, was quite beyond me. The Police were given the full treatment by the fans, presented with gifts – beautiful scrolls, eulogizing the three musicians in articulate English of perfect grammar. 'I suppose', said Sting loftily, 'I should spread my seed here. Trouble is, I just don't fancy 'em!' Irony, I suppose.

Despite the restrictions and the conservatism, I was fascinated by the dual themes of beauty and cruelty that seem to be at the root of Japanese culture – the beauty of the classical temples, the minimalism of Zen gardens; the cruelty of the Samurai tradition and the sadism of the typical daily output of cartoon shows on TV. I was also fascinated by the sense of honour, hospitality, generosity, pride; by the craven custom of trying to bow lower and deeper when introduced to a stranger, to show greater and greater respect.

From Japan we flew on to Hong Kong, for more band photo opportunities, rickshaw rides and dressing up in traditional costumes. After that the band and crew met up again in Bombay, where hardly any Western bands had played before. At the Taj Mahal Hotel in Bombay, Miles Copeland, the band's manager, had appropriated the Maharajah's Suite, which had a swing in it. Great footage opportunity, of course. After one night out partying I found myself sandwiched on the swing between Sting and Stewart with nothing to hold on to except their T-shirts or other outer garments, as Derek pushed the swing from behind, higher and higher towards the ceiling. We were all really pissed, and I'm amazed none of us fell off. Mind you, that wasn't nearly as dangerous as deciding some years later to climb the ladder rungs cemented into the wall at the back of the stage at the Brixton Academy and crawl horizontally across the proscenium arch about eighty foot above the stage, on E and in stilettos, with Schultzy. Schultzy was one of Primal Scream's tour managers, with special responsibility for Throb. His idea of waking Throb up in his hotel room, to catch a flight to the next gig, was to kick the door down.

The idea for the Police film was that in each country I would conduct a Major Interview with one of the band. I interviewed Sting on this swing. He took the opportunity to exhibit the usual rock 'n' roll tendency to exaggerate his working-class credentials. He began telling me about his father being a milkman. 'Hang on a minute,' I said. 'You told me before that he'd had his own dairy . . .' The three members of the band discussed sex continually, as a trio of young men fast becoming sex symbols would do. Banners would be draped over the balconies at their gigs begging, 'Fuck me Stuart' (*sic*).

The only available promoter in Bombay was the equivalent of the Townswomen's Guild, which normally hosted cultural events such as string-quartet concerts. It had certainly never put on a rock band before. Miles had gone on ahead and seen to it that the Police would have a far bigger impact than any other act that the loaded (in the financial sense) ladies had ever promoted before. But the priority was to get young fans in the locality to see the band, and not have the front few rows dominated by seventy-rupee ticket-holders – rich, middle-aged Parsees who might tap their beringed fingers politely but would not exactly help the show to rock. As it was, loose-haunched, swift-limbed young Indian boys jumped over all the expensive seats and the perfumed patrons and ligged it up the front pronto. Even European hippies from Goa showed up.

The band was understandably edgy about the gig, and Gordon Sumner's background as a schoolteacher was about to come in handier than ever before as he faced an audience who had probably never heard one of his songs before. 'SING!' he commanded from the primitive stage set up at one end of a basketball court. (The lighting was supplied by a solitary lamp on top of a pole.) 'Sing, "YAAY-YO."' This was presumably intended to ape the style of 'Wop-bam-a-lam-bam-a-wop-bam-a-loo', the no-particular language of American street-corner doo-wop rock 'n' roll. It was a gamble. He called. The audience responded, 'YAAAAY-YOH.' 'Now,' enjoined Sting into the microphone, 'sing, "YAYY-YAYY-YAYY-YAYY-YO." ' Obediently they complied: 'YAY-YAY-YAY-YAY-YO.' That was it: he had verbally seduced the audience, just as in the car on the way to the gig he admitted he had verbally seduced Paul Morley, the could-be-difficult journalist, who had come to India to interview him. Sting knew how to charm not only the ladies, but also the blokes.

The next stop was Egypt. At this point we split up. Andy Summers and Sting went ahead, 'to shag our wives at the airport' as they put it, while Stewart, the TV crew and I took a Gulfair flight, via Qatar. When we landed in Qatar, the aircrew told us that, owing to the lack of computer facilities in Bombay, our section was double-booked for the onward leg to Cairo. Apparently a sultan and his entourage were now waiting to board. And waiting to sit in our seats. We were then informed that if we didn't agree to move out of our seats we'd be arrested. I looked out of the cabin window. There was just sand, sand and sand as far as the eye could see. Being the only woman in our party, I thought being slung in the bints-only bit of the local slammer could possibly be less than a laugh. Stewart, sensing a piece of upcoming non-dissable-on-the-cutting-room-floor drama about to unfold, did the very worst thing he could have done. He got out his video camera. Immediately, and with much hissing, a gang armed with very serious expressions, chequered headcloths and machine-guns leapt into the cabin. And with much Arabic outrage they snatched the video mag out of Stewart's camera. Wasn't there something in Arab culture about stealing a person's soul if you captured their image in a photograph? Stewart Copeland, by the look of things, had just attempted to reclaim this people's entire religion. The situation was resolved when enough of our party moved back into Economy to make room for the sultan and his harem. I was curious to note that they bought the entire contents of the duty-free trolley – jeroboams of gin, and jerry cans of Guerlain.

We arrived in Cairo somewhat bedraggled, not just because of the Qatar quarrel but because Stewart, Mike Appleton and I had spent an extra day in India climbing a mountain near Poona to visit a temple carved out of rock. Stewart had bounded ahead like a giant schoolboy up the hundreds of wide, rough-hewn steps that wound round the mountainside. The heat was so intense I had a horrible fear of collapsing in a breathless heap as darkness fell on this remote, isolated and unlit terrain. But when I did finally trail my way to the mountaintop temple a guide was waiting to help pull me up the final few steps. Then came one of those magical moments that you know you will remember for life. Into the peace and silence of the mountaintop, floating upward, came the sounds of the village hundreds of feet below. Music, voices singing, laughing; the leaping and flashing of a hundred lantern flames; flickering, glowing orange fires; the sounds of cooking pots and pans being banged and stirred, the delicate tinkling of windbells, drifting upwards through the dark, sparkling heat. There it all was – the beauty, the vibrancy and the spirituality of India spread out beneath me in one swooping panorama. Bosh. I was happy, I was inspired. No place I'd been to on earth had affected me so much. Now I knew why Mike Appleton had wanted to come to India so much. (Actually, wandering along the wooded shady glades atop the Green Field at the Glastonbury Festival on the weekend after the summer solstice, the nearest real-life equivalent to Arcadia to me, off your nut at first light at around 5 a.m., looking down on a hundred thousand people partying their backpacks off, is the nearest approximation I can make.)

Egypt was a nightmare in terms of filming. It was Stewart's turn for the Major Interview, but as we set up in front of the Pyramids various rather brooding-looking blokes in billowing djellabas kept deliberately barging into shot. The requisite amount of baksheesh had apparently not been shelled out. The director finally erupted. He'd had a hard enough time of it in India trying to get all the camera equipment unimpounded, and convincing the immigration authorities that he was not actually trying to sell all his stuff for a vast profit but was making a film, which would not be possible without the use of cameras and their necessary accoutrements. Now in Giza, Egypt, beside one of the Seven Wonders of the World (which if they are allowed to crumble much more will be the former Wonders of the World, but there we are – there is, I'm informed, no word in Arabic for 'maintenance'), every guy on the strip wanted bribing. Quite for what I never discovered. To stay out of the shot, perhaps. To act as security, so that we could shoot some footage around the precious Sphinx and the Pyramids without being hindered by another team of unofficial officials. Kind of protection-style mafioso. Derek shouted at these unwelcome extras, 'Look, I *paid* the right officials *this morning* for permission to film here!' Sorry, mate, more baksheesh had to be forth-coming or they were going to ruin our sequence. Ah well, one has to accept people copping the odd coin of the realm where they see an opportunity. In the end Stewart and I just posed sitting on an ancient rock, the Sphinx in the background, and pretended we were tourists, while I asked him about his unusual childhood.

The Copeland brothers (Stewart, the drummer, Miles, the manager, and Ian, the band's agent) had all been brought up in the Middle East, in Beirut, where their father (also Miles) had been bureau chief for the CIA. Stewart claimed he grew up having no idea he was the son of a spy until his father wrote a book about it. As children, the Copelands played with Kim Philby's offspring and didn't become even remotely suspicious when one day they dis-appeared.

We decided on a night shoot, to try to shake off some unneeded bystanders, and formed our own strange caravan, the band and the crew riding horses and camels around the Pyramids, leads and chains chinking in the darkness, finding our way by moonlight. Now that the three Copeland brothers were reunited in their childhood environment, they indulged themselves embarrassingly, showing off their horse- and camel-riding expertise, swearing loudly in Arabic, and cavorting about all done up in long white robes like Peter O'Toole in *Lawrence of Arabia*; even Sting, usually the star of any Police dressing-up game, was upstaged.

I left the band in Athens, after the TV crew had dodged and ducked trying to avoid the tourists to make a memorable backdrop for Andy Summer's interview in the cool early morning among the olive groves beneath the Parthenon. In Greece the whole party was celebrating the luxury of being able to brush their teeth with tap water instead of bottled lemonade, as we had had to do in India. At the band's gig in Athens there had been a near-riot among the overexcited audience and an altercation with the chief of police – business as usual, in fact.

It was time to get off the merry-go-round and go home. And once back in the UK I thought, 'Why don't I do this – an around-the-world trip with different locations, a different band – *every* year?' No way. The Police film had been a miracle of financial juggling. It was never to happen again. To this day people like Grant Fleming – friend, photographer, raconteur and traveller, whom I dragged to Chile to see the solar eclipse in November 1994 – tell me that it was the Police tour film which inspired them to travel. There is no doubt that it was the highlight of my years on *Whistle Test*. And, if nothing else, I now had the urge and the confidence to want to explore as much of the rest of the world as possible.

XII

My quest to visit Russia had stemmed originally from my friend Lusia Parry's stories of her homeland before the Revolution of 1917. 'Darlink,' she would say, 'you must go and find the Fabergé eggs at L'Hermitage in St Petersburg.' What seemed a more practical proposal in 1987, a mere seventy years after the Revolution, was to visit Russia to meet a genre of rock musicians and to unearth a thriving underground rock scene unknown to the West, centred in Leningrad, as St Petersburg was at that time still called.

A young American entrepreneurial punk girl who called herself Joanna Stingray had discovered the Soviet music scene on a school trip to the USSR. When she returned to California, no one would believe her stories of Russian rock music, so she made another trip, smuggled tapes of Soviet rock music back to the United States, and released a compilation record, *Red Wave*, which finally reached my attention in London. Joanna provided me with all the contact names and phone numbers of the musicians and artistes she had met and recorded, so that I could make a BBC documentary about them.

The Cold War might then have been showing signs of thawing out, and the Iron Curtain was perhaps displaying metal fatigue, but the East–West barriers of suspicion and contradiction in ideology were still firmly in place. Glasnost and perestroika might have been the media buzzwords, but the Russians didn't seem any too enamoured of the way their leader, Mikhail Gorbachev, and his wife, Raisa, were conducting themselves in the international arena, while the guys at home were still queueing for bread. All the same, I was to be fairly astonished when a friendly, Armenian declaimed on a crowded tram trundling across Moscow, on discovering that I was English, 'Yorr Meesee Thetcha, she *strong*! Stronger than *one hundred men*!' The fact that Margaret Hilda was fundamentally opposed to Communism mattered to the Armenian not one iota. Her image said it all.

Once I set wheels in motion to make the trip to the USSR, my friend and colleague Carol Wilson, with whom I was attempting to write a TV series about the music business, declared her wish to come to Russia with me. Through the BBC, I had informed the Russian broadcasting authority, Gostelradio, of my imminent visit. But the last thing I wanted was a vetted official tour loaded with propaganda. Carol and I decided to go as part of a small anonymous tourist group. Once again the luck of the naive seemed to play into my hands as soon as we entered the Soviet Union.

Among my luggage I had brought in a large dossier issued by the BBC to foreign correspondents and broadcasters, containing maps, useful contact names and guidelines on general behaviour in the USSR. I had not bothered to read it before arriving in Russia. My immediate task on landing in Leningrad was to try to make contact with the rock musicians I was so anxious to meet. I buzzed like a crazily possessed insect into the very first Venus flytrap to open its pretty little jaws. Not wasting a moment of the bus journey taking our group from the airport, even before we had arrived in Leningrad itself, I leaned over the back of my seat and began chatting up two young Englishmen, students at Moscow University. Once I had established that they spoke Russian, and without a thought of any security risk, I told them exactly why Carol and I had come to Russia, whom we wanted to meet and the surreptitious nature of the whole exercise, and asked if they would help. Help us dial highly confidential private phone numbers; help us arrange secret assignations, and act as interpreters and translators during the interviews that I needed to set up, knowing not a word of useful Russian myself. The only two words I knew were *mietnik* (metronome) and *grabbli* (garden rake) – strange souvenirs of my days spent with Lusia! The two students readily agreed to do all they could to help. All too readily perhaps. Entering into further conversation with them, I discovered them to be deeply ideologically sound in terms of their sympathies towards the Soviet cause. Anyone else might have found this suspicious. But, hey, they were on our trip, Russian-speaking and eager to help. What a break!

I explained enthusiastically the skulduggery necessary to meet our musicians. That we must call them not from our hotel phones, which might be bugged, but only from public callboxes. And we were not to invite them to our hotel, but arrange to meet only at some innocuous public place. What a stroke of luck that these two young men seemed to have so few other pressing needs on this trip that they were able to devote almost all their time to help us contact the Leningrad underground rock fraternity!

Even continuously heavy grey skies and diaphanous sheets of summer rain could not dull the shimmering gold cupolas and pale primrose-and-white façades that domi-

137

nate Russia's most beautiful city. We dodged the rain around the magnificent squares, along the gracious canals, over the fine bridges spanning the Neva, and wove our way through side streets into cobbled, arched carriage yards, up winding dark stairs into the hidden homes of the country's most distinguished underground rock musicians and fervent fans. I was entranced. They were erudite. They talked about Lenin and the Beastie Boys, about Stalin and sampling. About their contempt for modern American pop icons such as Michael Jackson and Bruce Springsteen. 'They say Bruce Springsteen may come to Russia,' one musician commented. 'What's he going to sing to us? "Born in the USSR"?'

Seva Gakkel lived in a tiny but immaculate apartment, the walls hung with exotic foreign musical instruments, rather Parisian in its atmosphere. Seva – I savoured enunciating his name, See-ay-va – was cellist with Aqvarium, one of the USSR's best-known bands. With his dark shoulder-length hair and beard he looked quite Christ-like, and indeed he told me that he planned to become a monk later in life. He laid out tiny white china cups on a table in front of me. 'Please take tea,' he said. 'It is special. From Georgia.' For someone such as Seva, this was the most expansive gesture of hospitality he could make. He and his colleagues lived painfully frugally, taking lowly unskilled jobs such as janitors or furnace stokers in order to devote their energies to their music. Because this music, broadly rock or experimental, was not recognized as 'proper' by the state, none of them could become professional musicians. Friends and fellow artists and musicians trooped into Seva's apartment, and others I was taken to, always in secrecy and always from a different rendezvous point.

All the Russians I interviewed were far more open and

outspoken than I had imagined they would dare to be. And all of them emphasized that only a few months beforehand even meeting a foreign media person, let alone being interviewed, would have been out of the question. Even now they were putting themselves at risk, and I felt an enormous responsibility from the trust each one of them was putting in me. All were passionate about music and art, and incredibly well informed considering the lack of information available to them. I'd brought copies of *NME* and *Melody Maker* with me, the contents of which they devoured with immediate and avid curiosity, disappearing behind the pages for long, silent hours.

One guy told me that his entire knowledge of English had been inspired by the lyrics of Nick Cave and the Birthday Party. Sacha Kondrosov, a twenty-five-year-old worker at the Ministry of Higher Education, told me proudly, 'I was born on the same day, month and year as Dave Gahan, the lead singer of Depeche Mode, on 9 May 1962. Depeche Mode is my favourite group.' He then reeled off an impressively long list of all Depeche Mode's major concerts around the world, which he had managed to capture on smuggled videos and bootlegs and from foreign TV and satellite broadcasts. No mean feat for a Western Mode fan, but extraordinary for a Russian. Sacha's friend then chipped in, with a broad grin, 'My brother only knows two words in English: "sex" and "pistols"!' All the foreign groups they admired were as 'underground' as their own music. And, to a man, they were scathing in their criticism of Soviet censorship and repression.

Most of the former Eastern bloc countries have a reputation for churning out interminable numbers of inferior Western-style heavy-metal bands, but the musicians I met in Leningrad and later in Moscow were spectacularly talented, stunningly original players brimming with avant-garde concepts. Notably Sergei Africa, the enigmatic Sergey Kuryokhin of the extraordinarily innovative band Popular Mechanics, and the best known of them all, Boris Greben-shikov. Boris, a singer and songwriter, often described as the USSR's Bob Dylan, could sell out 10,000-capacity concerts ten nights in a row, yet he lived with his wife and child on the eighth floor of a school building, with no lift, no heating or hot water, and under constant threat of eviction. Every inch of wall on every storey of the cavernous stairwell that led up to his home was covered in idolatrous graffiti left by his fans. Here was an internationally famous man with none of the trappings associated with fame in the West. No personal fortune, limos, bodyguards or even privacy. All his fans could beat a path to his door, and many did. 'They knock on my door at two in the morning wanting to read their latest poetry to me,' he told me. 'What can I do? Sometimes I'm tired.'

I must admit to having been intrigued by Boris's situation, although 'intrigued' would hardly have described his own feelings, I'm sure. But it made me wonder how attractive the notion of stardom would have been to Hollywood folk without the money. How would Elizabeth Taylor or Rod Stewart have fared living in circumstances humbler than those of most of their fans? What if taking the leading role in a movie was no better paid or was held in no higher regard than working on a factory assembly line? In meeting Boris Grebenshikov and the other underground artistes, I had stumbled on the very antithesis of the tradition of Western-style show business. What price talent? What price popularity? In the world I've inhabited, chart positions, album sales and bums on seats have too often become the yardsticks by which an artiste is judged. But I found in Leningrad a different yardstick. Artistes such as Grebenshikov found it almost impossible to get their material recorded on the one 'official' record label, Melodiya, yet tapes of their music circulated through a vast underground network throughout the USSR. It was not unusual for Grebenshikov fans in Siberia to queue for eight hours at a time for a cassette of his songs.

Some three years later, when the Soviet regime collapsed, he and other Russian musicians eventually had the opportunity to seek wider recognition abroad. Indeed, I took Seva Gakkel to a rock concert at the Crystal Palace Bowl in south London some years after I had first met him in Leningrad. The Cure were the headline act. Just as the Russian underground rock artistes had no showbiz tradition, they also had no showbiz pretensions of the 'Darling, you were wonderful' variety. Just refreshing honesty. Seva gazed studiously at the Cure's performance for some time, from the far side of the lake that separates the audience from the stage at this particular venue, and then he announced to me, 'Now I am leaving.' I asked him why, and he replied, 'I do not like drum sound.'

However, such freedom to travel was no more than a fantasy to a Russian musician in 1987, as was the notion of the Communist state being utterly dismantled by the end of the decade. Sitting late one night in my hotel room in Leningrad, at the end of another evening session of interviews, Carol, my companion, asked to look at the as-yet-unread BBC dossier. After a few minutes' reading, she pointed, aghast, at the bold printed words on the page she held open. 'PLEASE REMOVE THIS SECTION BEFORE ENTERING THE USSR,' it said. Uh-oh. Too late. Far too late. Horrified, I quickly scanned the contents. These were warnings to foreign visitors such as ourselves about how

Communist agents would attempt to make contact with us. 'They will do so in a manner in which it will appear that *you* have made contact with *them*.' Well, it seemed I'd walked into that one, with both feet first. The students! I'd approached them right enough. It was obvious now, I realized, that they were plants. No wonder they had so much time on their hands to sit in on each interview, note down every telephone number, each name and address, and listen to each and every conversation and comment. I was appalled. How many gentle, trusting musicians had I put at risk by interviewing them in front of two people now confirmed in my mind as Soviet undercover agents?

Before I had a chance to voice my rising sense of panic, Carol silently pointed out another piece of information contained in the dossier. 'Hotel rooms in the Soviet Union are often equipped with infra-red cameras, which can photograph their contents, such as documents, in extremely low light.' Oh *no*! I looked furtively up at the ceiling of the hotel room, fully expecting to see the give-away sign of a red light winking away in the darkness, photographing successive pages of the BBC dossier as Carol and I turned them over. I felt wretched, as though I had compromised not only all the courageously honest musicians I had met, but also the entire BBC. What to do with the damned dossier? Flush the incriminating pages down the lavatory? Too dangerous. *Eat* them? I didn't fancy that. *Burn* them? But where? There was no fireplace in the room. And, anyhow, the amount of ash left by such a weighty tome would look horribly suspicious. I decided I'd just have to carry the dossier around with me until I got out of the country, and hope to God I wouldn't be searched. It could well be that the two students were not plants at all, in which case I unequivocally apologize to them, but it did seem a little odd that on leaving the Soviet Union I was allowed through customs quite unhindered and unquestioned, as though the authorities had enough tabs on what I'd been doing not to need to seize my interview tapes. Fortunately, as Seva and Boris surfaced in the UK some years later, I was able to assume that I had not dropped the other musicians right in it.

The tourist *groupa* now stopped over at Novgorod, between Leningrad and Moscow. This beautiful town, gracing both sides of a river bank, was dotted with twelfth-century churches and other ancient holy buildings, ringed with silver birch trees, and surrounded by soft mossy-green meadows. From beyond the river's bend, there appeared above cascading willows a midnight-blue cupola covered with gold-painted stars. This was fairy-tale Russia. And the reason we were there? Because Novgorod had been twinned with the English town of . . . Watford. Most of our tourist group were residents of Watford, and had requested to visit Novgorod as part of their Russian tour. On the evening of our arrival we were all invited to meet the local dignitaries. The chief of our group stood up and said, 'I am the captain of Watford Swimming Club. This' – and he indicated the woman beside him – 'is my wife, the swimming instructor, and we should like to offer an invitation to our very kind hosts, the people of Novgorod, to visit Watford.' This was too much for me. I had to run out of the municipal building screaming with laughter. Watford, being famous only for the fact that Elton John once took over its football team, and that it is a convenient stop-off town from the M1 motorway, has no basis on which to compare itself with Novgorod. No wide serene river, and a complete lack of cupolas. The idea of hundreds of Russians wandering aimlessly around Watford in search of medieval culture I found irresistibly funny. On my return to England I recounted this story on my radio show, and was rewarded by an official invitation by the mayor of Watford to visit the town. Hoist by my own petard, I was too embarrassed to reply.

Travelling from Novgorod to Moscow necessitated an all-night train journey. Our Russian tour organizer, Lydia, an attractive blonde and a painfully conscientious woman, was reduced nearly to tears when it transpired that our seats on the overnight express had been double-booked. She was stranded on Novgorod train station with her group, which consisted of the Watford swimming enthusiasts, an inordinately curious young male American student from Kentucky, whom Lydia was convinced was a CIA spy, a neurotic German woman suffering some sort of World War II guilt-trip-induced nervous breakdown, the two suspected KGB plants, and Carol and myself. And all our luggage. From Lydia's point of view, this was a fuck-up on a grand scale. A simple change of plan, whereby we could stay in Novgorod an extra night and catch a train to Moscow the next day, was just not possible. We had on our hands a bureaucratic crisis, big-time. Mistakes, overbookings, such as this were just not meant to happen. This was *serioizny*. Lydia, we learned, might lose her job over it.

After many huddled consultations standing over suitcases on the station platform, it was decided, incredibly, that we should all just *jump* on the next towering deep-green-painted train to make a stop at the station, and hope for the best. By no means good Party behaviour. Not rule-book procedure. Unscheduled, unplanned, and unapproved.

A train, pulled by a gloriously decorated scarlet locomotive, which I was sadly but strongly advised not to photograph, steamed into Novgorod. We jumped on, and I fell in love. At last I was on a Russian train! There were great silver samovars of steaming tea at the end of each carriage, looped lace curtains at the windows, and plants draped from windowboxes in each compartment. Pure *Dr Zhivago*! (Though, having said that, when I took Lusia Parry to see *Dr Zhivago*, she laughed hollowly all the way through the scene of dancing refugees fleeing Russia by train, and commented, 'Darlink, I was on a train like that. There was no dancing. Complete darkness. For three days. All I had to amuse my three young sisters on the journey was a live crayfish. Also, men kept trying to rape us.')

As the train took off, I didn't know where we were going and I didn't really care. I met only friendliness from Russian fellow travellers, and many toasts were drunk with strangers swigging from bottles of vodka and sipping hot black tea from tall glasses grasped in ornate silver metal holders. Then, at the dead of night, our group was suddenly ordered off the train. Out we tumbled into the darkness of a totally unknown railway station. It was lonely and desolate, yet inexplicably the waiting room was full of bleak-faced men smoking enough strong Russian cigarettes to create a thick blue pall across this mysterious and totally unscheduled rendezvous. None of us, Lydia included, knew where we were – perhaps uncomfortably close to a secret military airfield, or a nuclear-missile plant. We were apparently to leap aboard any other train that stopped, in the hope that it would take us to Moscow.

Regularly, as we stood hopefully in small groups by the track, another giant locomotive, pulling a train of twelve or more carriages, would appear out of the black night, its single bright lamp focused on the shiny track in front, and roar past the station without stopping. These trains travelled in both directions, and all of them seemed packed with passengers. Where could so many people be *going*, at such a speed in the dead of night?

Finally one of these ghostly expresses pulled to a stop at our Mysteryograd station, and we clambered on board, dragging our luggage in frenzied panic, not knowing when the train would take off again. My only regret was that I had not kidnapped the stunning young blond who had helped me get my baggage aboard at Novgorod. In doing so he had given me the sexiest wink I'd ever experienced. I should have brought him back to England – I could have turned him into a pop pin-up in a matter of weeks.

Through the rest of the night's journey, which did eventually take us to our destination in Moscow, I was far too excited and elated to sleep. I was mesmerized, gazing out of the window at moonlit goods yards, then dark empty platforms, and hearing the loud and then fading station bells toll to acknowledge the passing of our night train over steppes and plains and past villages of the country I had wanted so much to visit. The idea of being on a mystery train to a mystery destination fulfilled all my dreams of Russia. Journey's end was something of an anticlimax. Moscow was mosquito-ridden and warm, and the queue to visit Lenin's tomb snaked at deceptive length around Red Square. In exactly the manner of the zigzag lines for rides at Disneyland, so the opposite ideology had the same method of conning its visitors into joining a queue they would never have embarked upon had they known how long it was. Soldiers openly held each other's hands in the square, and I got told off for talking in the tomb. I was hardly going to wake Lenin up!

A year and a half later I returned to Moscow, now with

146

eight inches of snow on the ground, as a guest at a Soviet rock festival. And what a difference I witnessed in terms of lifestyle and privilege. On my first trip the accommodation had been sparse, the rooms clean but shabby, the food modest, and not a lot of it. Simple country fare, with tomatoes and cucumbers as part of every meal. Now I was treated to endless supplies of caviar, champagne and vodka. Especially vodka. The cheerful organizers of the festival insisted that the vodka was drunk neat (anyone trying to weaken it with a mixer was branded a lightweight), the first rounds being poured out well before midday, and the last of many raised-glass toasts being downed around five in the morning. So just how did these guys appear to live so well, when the rest of the population struggled with eternal 'deficit'? 'Easy,' said one of these jovial, hospitable festival organizers. 'You just become a Communist Party member. That opens all the doors you want.'

XIII

There was something of a hiatus in the mid-eighties. It is during such lulls that people say to themselves, or, if they happen to be taxi drivers, to their captive clients, 'I must be getting old. I can't stand this stuff in the charts. It's not like it used to be.' Well, of course it isn't like it used to be. That's the whole point. Not so much that the music's new and deliberately seeking to exclude all but the young, but that it's different. It has to evolve, to change. Mick Jagger grasped one half of this concept very early on in his career, reflecting, when he lived at Harley House on the Marylebone Road, 'Pop music is only of interest to most people before they get into a serious relationship, buy a flat and so on. It's less important after that.' This was during the course of a conversation about the Small Faces. 'Don't you fancy them?' he said in that cod camp drawl. 'You must be getting owwwld.' Obviously Mick also shrewdly grasped that it's the music of their youth that folk will pay an arm and a leg to see re-enacted at Wembley Stadium or the JFK in Philadelphia for the rest of their lives. When these lulls happen, I've learned that you have to hang on in there and wait for something new to come along.

Punk had exploded on to the scene in the mid-seventies and had now reached the end of its ten-year cycle. What would come next? As it goes, a great and secret adventure was being hatched. Acid house. A generation had gone under the wire, created its own currency, its own good time, its own wild, hedonistic tunes – Scarlet Fantastic's 'No Memory', the end-of-the-night, arms-in-the-air rave anthem: 'No memory . . . no memory . . . no memory . . . Ha! ha! ha! ha! . . . we just don't give a damn, 'cos we are free . . . standing here in the pouring rain . . . another sunrise . . . Ha! ha! ha!'

Acid house had its origins in a variety of different sources – the hip-hop and rap music of the New York Projects, the house disco music of Chicago and Detroit, the underground garage music that sprang out of the gay bars of New York, in which the concept of remixing tracks and producing twelve-inch dance versions became popular, and the Balearic beat that originated in Ibiza.

Ibiza had always been known as a Bohemian hangout. I'd first been there when I was expecting Alex. I remember walking along the beach, seven-months pregnant, wearing a peculiar black-and-white gingham affair that was almost like a clown's outfit – a bathing suit with ruffles around the tops of the legs. I've never seen anything like it before or since. There were all these weird English expatriates about – odd-looking, rangy, scantilly-clad characters who reminded me of the people I used to hang about with in Brighton. They'd invite me to cocktail parties, and my enduring memory of these events is that there'd be about three bottles of very cheap wine standing around, in at least one of which would be a fly floating upside down, its legs still flapping wildly.

I returned to Ibiza in the mid-eighties, before the whole Balearic beat movement kicked off, and went to the Ku Club, a fabulous place with a swimming pool in the middle.

I was staying with a friend, and ended up taking some medical students along to the club with me. None of them had any money; I had just enough to get us all in. They all went off dancing, leaving me on my own with enough loose change to buy one drink. Cheers, you wankers. (Ironically the last time I visited the Ku, now called Privilege, was to broadcast live for Radio 1 from there in 1998, following Norman Cook on to the decks.) This was a Manumission night – the club famous for its live sex shows. With exotic dress, transvestite trapezists, and freaky fire eaters. I felt like I was taking part in the last party on the last night before the fall of the Roman Empire. Suddenly I got it. Why Ibiza IS. Because of the clash and rush of cultures – Greek, German, Roman, Spanish, Moorish, French. They had to congregate *somewhere* in the Med. I was DJing at a party which had been going on for a thousand years.

Essentially Balearic beat was all about good-time holiday music, played by DJs like Danny Rampling, now with Radio 1. When the holidaymakers returned home in the mid-eighties they wanted to keep the good-time holiday spirit going. People began to have parties in places that weren't licensed clubs, and the rave scene was born (although in fact 'rave' as a term was common enough in the fifties, used to describe the beach parties held in places like Brighton and Margate, and the mods and rockers also referred to raves in the sixties).

These were the grim Thatcher years, when young people felt they simply didn't have any opportunities. Not once did she ever appear to offer one crumb, offer one small piece of hope to the long-term unemployed. While the Thatcher government claimed to be all for enterprise, firm control was strictly part of the package. This generation found its own way – and established their own culture with its own currency – MDMA, or Ecstasy. For fifteen quid you could get totally off your nut on a white Dove or a red-and-black Dennis the Menace capsule, or there were pink crunchy pills or tiny bright green ones. You didn't need alcohol, it sort of detracted from the effect actually. All you needed was a bottle or two of handbag sized Volvic or similar mineral water. You didn't need to go to a licensed club that would charge you to get in – you simply had a party in a field. Suddenly an entire network was created in which information about gigs was spread by mobile phone and over the airwaves on pirate radio stations. People would meet up in petrol stations around the M25 and head off into the night. I'm infinitely proud that it was in Blackburn, Lancashire, home of my forefathers, where some of the early top raves happened, though I was too far away to go.

Once again this was DIY culture, shooting off on its own extraordinary tangent, and the government was powerless to do anything about it. A whole generation that was supposed to be going to pubs and clubs and drinking lots of (taxed) lager was holding illegal parties in fields, drinking water, and taking a drug that was creating a multi-million-pound industry that the government couldn't touch. It was a true underground culture, and it broke all the rules. You didn't need a band any more – you could make a record on a computer in your bedroom. You didn't even need a record company – having recorded your track, you simply pressed up five hundred twelve-inch copies on vinyl. And this at a time when the major record companies were launching extensive advertising campaigns encouraging the piteous punter to ditch his old Pink Floyd *Dark Side of the Moon* vinyl LP for a CD which would never jump or get scratched, and would of course sound like it had been reprocessed in a germ-free laboratory!

Those who go in for conspiracy theories suggest that the people who had a commercial interest in all this – brewers, mainly – went to the government and said, 'You've got to stop these acid-house parties, people taking Ecstasy and not drinking any alcohol – it's ruining us,' and hence the Criminal Justice Act was born. Needless to say, the act was never enforced properly, since one of the criteria for banning a get-together was the playing of music with a 'repetitive beat'. How do you define a repetitive beat? After all, Mozart has a repetitive beat. So does Elgar. Were they going to stop the Proms at the Albert Hall?

Up until now I had still been miserably doing the rounds of Radio 1 guest-DJ appearances on the pre-acid-house club scene. I'd descended to inventing an awful cabaret routine in which I made myself hats with dreadlocks threaded with ribbons, like those worn by Boy George, and would invite people on-stage to wear them while they sang along to 'Karma Chameleon' – an early form of karaoke, I guess – after which I awarded prizes. Or I'd come up with silly quizzes with unanswerable questions like 'How much money does Paul McCartney have in the bank right now?', or make people wear Ronald Reagan and Margaret Thatcher masks while I threw custard pies in their faces. The pies, which of course are made not of custard but of highly expensive (if you buy a lot of them) tins of foam, always ended up on my face and clogging up my hair. I couldn't complain. It had been my idea in the first place.

I'd always fight to play my own records at these clubs, which they thought very odd and simply weren't used to. It was a difficult time. I wasn't cut out for cabaret work and didn't enjoy it at all. So why did I do it? Why do you think? Overdraft repayments. Fortunately soap stars were beginning to replace Radio 1 DJs as an attraction at these venues – which, after all, had had years of Noel Edmonds, Dave Lee Travis and Simon Bates. I was once put on with Leslie Grantham, the *EastEnders* star, and was amazed by his reception. He was mobbed by hordes of screaming women, all shouting, 'Can I have your baby.'

It was clear, when acid house started, that it would transform the club scene. Whereas the punks had been very angry and negative towards anything that had gone before, this new lot were totally open-minded and accepting of other generations. Ecstasy culture wasn't just about hugging people but involved a genuine openness, with no aggression. Football hooliganism stopped – there was hugging on the terraces and no violence, although nobody seemed to twig the real reason for this at the time.

I became very involved in the scene in Brighton. I used to go to a pub on Saturday lunchtimes, and met a man there who was a biochemist. I asked him what he thought of Ecstasy. 'Perfect,' he said. 'A perfect blend of uppers and downers.' I thought, 'If you say so, mate – you're the expert!' One day John Peel came up to me at Radio 1 and said, 'Can I ask you a very personal question? Have you been taking Ecstasy?' I responded, guardedly, 'Why are you asking?', and he said, 'I can hear it in the music you're playing.'

I started DJing at the Zap Club in Brighton, in their Friday-night chill-out slot. The resident DJ there told me that mixing was all to do with confidence and coordination. Oh no! The two qualities I most spectacularly lack! It seemed to me that you had to be a musician to mix well, and indeed lots of ex-musicians suddenly came out of the woodwork and became successful DJs, effectively using their decks as instruments. If I'd possessed good coordination I'd have become a musician myself, but I could never play left- and right-hand piano at the same time. The new young fanatical breed of DJ practised mixing, in their bedrooms, for months. I had a lot of respect for this amount of dedication. I got asked to DJ in the VIP Area at the Brixton Academy, at an Orb gig. The ex-punk DJ Kris Needs was doing the same. I told him how nervous I was, not being able to mix. He said, 'Don't worry, neither can I. It's the new thing in New York, not mixing. You let one record stop and then you play the next one.' Blimey, why hadn't I thought of that?

The scene evolved around certain key clubs, such as Spectrum and Shoom, in London and a key group of DJs, who were now becoming mythological in status, at least to me – Andrew Weatherall, Danny Rampling and Paul Oakenfold. Andrew Weatherall even had lookalikes turning up at gigs! Not that he was impressed by this. Quite the reverse. He had his long curly locks cut off, then promoters of his gigs were confronted by punters demanding their money back because they didn't believe this bloke with the skinhead haircut was actually Andrew Weatherall at all.

DJs never spoke – in fact they didn't even have a microphone – so there was no longer any of that horrible 'Hello, how you all doing?' cabaret nonsense I'd been putting myself through. On one occasion, by now emulating Andrew Weatherall and his ilk, I did a gig at a University of Cardiff college. It seemed weird to me to be a Radio 1 DJ and not to speak, but I realized that it would be totally uncool to utter a single word. A young man came up to me during this gig and shouted (as you have to above the noise in order to be heard), 'Haven't you got any *real* music, played on *real* instruments by *real* musicians?' As I had been a strong follower of electronic music since its inception, I felt really irritated by this young man's sanctimonious attitude and just replied archly, 'No.'

I'd started to play acid-house tracks on my request show, but by now I was really banging the drum at Radio 1, saying, 'Look, this music is epoch-making, and it's not being reflected by this station.' Acid house changed the whole beat of pop music, the most fundamental shift since rock. Again, Britain had taken a development in American house music and made it sound home-grown, just as it had in nicking rhythm and blues from the United States in the sixties, although this time it was to take ten years to break it back to the States, which proved very resistant to acid house – until the Chemical Brothers got a Grammy. I went to a New Year's Eve so-called 'rave' in LA in 1990. The Valley girls drew up in their purring Toyotas, wearing long satin evening gloves, and yawled, 'Where's the parr-deee?' They simply didn't get it. Throughout the rest of the world, however, acid house took off in a big way, mainly because of its DIY element – anyone could do it. It became an all-embracing culture, affecting fashion, graphics and eventually literature and film, – viz, to start with, Irvine Welsh's *Trainspotting*.

Three of the most influential bands were the Happy Mondays, Stone Roses and Primal Scream. The Scream were a Scots band who'd come to live in Brighton, apart from London-ensconced Andrew Innes, because Alan McGee, the owner of Creation Records (and the man who was later to discover Oasis), moved south to escape his protégés – all of whom promptly followed him, so he says! Their singer was Bobby Gillespie, formerly drummer with the Jesus and Mary Chain, and they had initially been known as a jangly, highly literate pop band. My son, Alex, was a friend, later to become their manager. I met them about the time they released 'Loaded', a key track in the change from guitar-based music to acid house. Primal Scream had been hanging out in clubs, had met Andrew Weatherall, and asked him whether he'd like to remix 'Loaded'. (It was becoming common practice to remix an existing pop tune, to give it a different twirl for club use, which gave rise to a whole new underground culture.) Andrew was a self-confessed 'virgin' as a remixer, but once he'd had a tentative go he told the band, 'Look, what I'd really like to do is strip everything down and take the track to pieces.' They said, 'Go ahead, do it.' The result was beautiful, and established that it was possible to put together punk funk soul acid electro beats and please *everyone*.

The music changed swiftly, so the major record companies found they couldn't market stuff in the way they market, say, a Celine Dion album, where everything is planned a year ahead. As a result, independent labels began to flourish again. Although I'd been well accepted by the acid-house generation – I think they were surprised by my enthusiasm rather than anything else – it took me a while to persuade small companies to send me advance copies of their releases to play on the radio. I was happy to buy copies, but the problem was tracking them down. Small labels couldn't and still can't afford a massive mail-out to uninterested DJs and radio stations. They produce only five hundred or so pressings, and when these sell out there are no more. I became (and still am) hooked on receiving white labels with press releases declaiming 'One of ten copies only'. Now you can press up your own 'slate' of a tune or a mix on vinyl, and be the only person in the world to possess and play it. In the late eighties and early nineties, little of this material reached CD, or if it did it would hang around for literally two or three years on vinyl before belatedly becoming a hit on CD, as happened with the KLF, the Orb and 808 State, among many others.

It was a magic time. I could hardly believe that such a massive, heart-stoppingly thrilling revolution was whirling all around me, and that, although I'd been so involved in the maelstrom of the sixties acid-power people, and to a degree the punks, here I was surrounded by such excitement yet again. Obviously I had to ask myself and trusted friends some very serious questions, which included the words 'mutton', 'lamb', 'bandwagon' and 'jumping'.

As was to be expected, commercial interests quickly saw that a lot of money was to be made out of ten thousand people turning up in a field. With the prospect of £20 admission charges, plus a drug concession worth £15 or so for a tab of Ecstasy or cheap acid, it wasn't long before the money guys muscled in, and suddenly the whole thing was no longer underground. Nonetheless, I still believe it was an incredibly healthy movement. Personally, I feel reborn through it. People say to me, 'Surely you don't like this stuff,' and I tell them I couldn't lie about it, couldn't have become so involved without being obsessed by the music. I've become a trainspotter, and I'm proud of it.

XIV

After my stint at the Zap Club in Brighton, I got really carried away and started my *own* club. That is to say my own club 'night'. This is what one did in the late eighties and early nineties – take over an existing venue and host one's own evening. The club owner would take all the money handed over at the bar, but you as host could have the door takings. I threw myself into this latest project with my usual wild, reckless enthusiasm.

The club was situated in Ship Street, Brighton, an old, narrow wind tunnel of a street leading to the seafront, with Georgian bay windows jutting from upper floors over the pavement. I was to have Wednesday nights there, at the invitation of a guy I knew as 'Dreadlocks Michael', then a key figure on the Brighton club scene. Getting guest DJs to play was no problem. What you had to do was get the paying punters in. I went through the usual rigmarole of producing flyers – the handbills given out to every clubber staggering along the street, starry-eyed and boggle-minded, to encourage them to go to *your* night – which were then a growing area of graphic art.

My night was called 'Mass'. The name was the idea of James, an advertising man and a fellow London-to-Brighton commuter. I liked the religious connotations, and ran with it all the way. Carlos the fantastic Spaniard, the man behind the Lanterna Magika light show, who had worked with Boy George and the like in early acid-house days, offered to do the visuals. We marched deadpan into a specialist shop in Kemp Town which sold religious accoutrements. Huge posters of the Madonna, lurid pictures of Christ on the cross, those red-glass night-light holders I remembered from Catholic masses . . . we bought up the lot. 'For a school play, is it?' asked the shop assistant. We could hardly tell her that we were going to take these religious images, slap them all over with psychedelic pink, green and yellow dayglo colours, and cover the walls of a nightclub with them. Ever seen the Virgin Mary's halo shining under ultra-violet lighting? Wicked!

I was in my element. I was blagging special lighting rigs, had new techno-pop artistes such as, aptly enough, Messiah doing 'live' personal appearances of their latest record, and got television coverage, features in newspapers and plugs on the new Pete Tong show on Radio 1. Friends would help me design the artwork for the flyers, and then the Radio 1 photocopier would come into its own. Part of the club ritual is to 'go flying', but it's none too narcotically exciting standing outside someone else's club doling out these handbills advertising one's own club night. Not a great laugh hanging around till two or three in the morning in a dark street in the pouring rain, seeing your precious work hurled cruelly and dismissively, unread, into the gutter. But it had to be done. The club licensees couldn't really care less what you did or didn't do to promote a club night, as long as you filled the place and packed the bar.

Not everyone was as confident as myself about the imminent success of my club night. For one thing there was the carpet in the bar. It was tartan. It was awful. 'Club'll never work, not with that carpet there,' said the many sages who came to the first night – and who, of course, were on the guest list and didn't pay to get in. Which was everyone who did come, except about seven people.

I was convinced Mass would be a huge success, with punters queuing round the block, because I was able to publicize it, because of its unique look, and because Brighton has a huge population of young people – two whole universities full of students, as well as an art college, a college of technology, and vast swarms of foreign students, always hanging around the town clutching their bags from EF, the organization that made au pairs and Louise Woodward famous. I was convinced . . .

Me and the guest DJs played the first known tune by the Prodigy, a number called – irony intended? I don't know – 'Charly'; stuff by Ariel, who became the Chemical Brothers; 'Don't Fight It, Feel It', the blue-labelled Andrew Weatherall 'scat mix' of the Primal Scream track. Mass had a cool dance floor, a large bar area (pleasant enough if you didn't look down at your feet or the carpet too often), and a chill-out zone with a large video screen where we'd run old episodes of *The Magic Roundabout* and *Koyaanisqatsi*, the trippy American Indian ecological film with music by Philip Glass.

Mass failed spectacularly. Partly because it was put on midweek in midwinter, a time of year when students, after the first few seductive weeks of term, find themselves skint. I hadn't taken heed of what I should have known after years of experience at students' unions. What students want is free entry, totty, and cheap, if not entirely free, beer. There was no way I could compete with huge venues like The Event, just two streets away on the seafront, which could pack in 1,800 people. The music policy at such a place would perhaps be questionable, but its doors were open to all the cheap-drinks promotions going.

I enjoyed the experience of Mass enormously, even though I did throw money at it. I'd do it again given half the chance. As it happens, there's a nice little downstairs club on the Portobello Road that's screaming for a lo-fi hip-hop funky sound on a Sunday night . . .

After the incredibly socially significant advent of acid house in the late eighties, the early nineties to me certainly meant parties – parties in warehouses, or any empty space where people could dance and do drugs. It was a regular scam to blag the keys to an empty house off an estate agent and then move in the DJ, the decks, the PA, some lights, and off you would go. I even let it go on in my own house!

As the eighties progressed there had been fewer guests, fewer parties there. My relationship with my second husband whom I'd married some ten years before had been drastically deteriorating, and on 1 October 1990 I left the house and him. Chris Smith and Jane Gibson, friends who lived nearby, had said, 'Come and stay with us for a couple of weeks till you sort yourself out.' I stayed, in their spare room, for two years. But, despite the emotional fatigue I was going through, I found a new freedom, a new lease of life, through music, and in particular through acid house, which initially I had been introduced to largely by my son. Although Alex and Lucy had been taken to festivals and rock 'n' roll venues from infancy, as a child Alex had not seemed to take much interest in music. Football was his passion. But with the advent of acid house he found his muse. With the help of Heavenly Records' Jeff Barratt, he set himself up as an agent, with a tiny one-room office in Clerkenwell, the now-fashionable EC1 area of London. His first clients were the reggae band African Headcharge, the Orb and St Etienne – artistes whom no one at the then Michael Jackson-obsessed Radio 1 had ever heard of.

Meanwhile Britain was in decline again. None of the young people I now knew in Brighton had jobs. Nor were there any prospects. The Tories ruled with an iron hand. They seemed so contemptuous, arrogant, unfeeling, oppressive, uncaring about young people. Greed seemed to be all they were perpetrating. They were breeding a sub-genus of hideous people, the yuppies, as I was discovering at first hand. I was now hosting a Sunday lunchtime programme on GLR, the groovy new BBC radio station for London, which involved playing records, talking to guests and running a phone-in. I discovered that I really enjoyed phone-ins. There was no 'delay' or panic button, everything was live, so if a caller swore or committed slander there was not a lot I could do. On this show the London yuppies found me and I found them. I would bait them. 'Which do like more: having sex or making money?' 'Making money,' came the constant reply. I was shocked.

GLR had been started by Matthew Bannister and Trevor Dann, who were later to take over the running of Radio 1. For the first time I was involved in a radio station from its inception, and my pioneering spirit really took to the quest of pulling in new listeners, yuppies or not.

By late 1992 the house at Montpelier Road was finally vacated by my former partner and I moved back there. Alex held a 'liberation party', at which the Orb DJed in the living room. Then there was the 'six-day party', not dissimilar in terms of onslaught to the Six Day War in the sixties. Sixty thousand pounds' worth of lights were set up in the drawing room on the first floor, in another room on the ground floor and in the basement. Montpelier Road was alive again. The police arrived to make official complaints about the noise and went away again. Or so I was told – I certainly wasn't going to answer the front door. Now we had paid bouncers on the door, U2's barman in the kitchen, and once again people I didn't know streaming in and out and up and down the five flights of stairs. The whole event had to be stage-managed. Everyone got a bit edgy when the lights and the lighting man were delayed by five hours. Andrew Weatherall arrived with his DJ box, an entire day and a night late. Bandulu had to cope with a seriously out-of-it Punch and Judy puppet show in the middle of their set. Kris Needs, the DJ, arrived with the Aylesbury posse, a serious set of partyers. On day two, in the mid-afternoon, when everyone was asleep, the Aylesbury posse took a walk to the beach and left the front door wide open. Day three was the beginning of the weekend, and there were still new guests arriving – the band Flowered Up, for instance. The party's centre of gravity moved from floor to floor, with huddles of people semi-comatose in a corner of the basement, or in my bed. I went to London to do my Radio 1 show, came back to Brighton, and found people still partying into the fourth and fifth day. Suppliers came and went, there were trips to the off-licence for top-ups and crisps, and a new set of DJs would come along and play a different set. The bloke came to take the lights away on the sixth day, by which time just the hardliners were left.

This was really to be the swansong, the last party at Montpelier Road. Soon the house would be sold. It was no longer viable for me to live there. By this time I had partially moved to London. For more than a year I had been looking for a crash pad, a room of my own in a London house where I could stay maybe one day a week, or three times a fortnight. Nothing could have been more of a contrast to the faded Victorian opulence of Montpelier Road, Brighton, than my new abode. A three-storeyed flat in a hideous sixties-built tower block, on a notorious crack estate, it faced on to Westbourne Park Underground station in west London. But it was very, very funky. I'd been introduced to the flat by a young record-company PR called Sarah Lowe. Over the next four years Sarah was the only constant in an ever-changing set of flat-sharers. We had starving musicians who would hide in the wardrobe when the landlady came to collect the rent. There were motor-bike-mad Cheeky in advertising and Lucas the heart-throb cycle courier, and there was a baby conceived and born to flatmate Sam and her boyfriend Danny, drummer in Shane McGowan's band the Popes; there were also twins born to Lucy and Will Pepper, he of Thee Hypnotics and Hurricane # One. They all – well, not all at once! – lived in a glorified cupboard in the basement which Sarah called 'the luurve tunnel'.

When my compilation album *Annie on One* was released on Heavenly Deconstruction Records in the mid-nineties, to my utmost astonishment it won huge critical acclaim, owing to the fastidious work of Martin, Robin, Tash, Chloe and Jeff, the staff at Heavenly. I was now being acknowledged by the growing underground dance press, DJing all over the UK, and gradually I realized that I just didn't have time to go back to Brighton any more. It was a sad wrench, but the pressure of work dictated that I live in London. But before I finally relinquished Montpelier Road, after I had moved out, there was one final request. Primal Scream wanted to hold an end-of-tour party there. I knew they were going to ask me, and I knew I'd give in. Even though it was going to be emotionally painful to go back to the now-empty house one more time, I just couldn't say no to them. So once more the house was filled with music, total strangers squeezed past me on the stairwells, the police came to complain about the noise, and Bobby Gillespie danced with me and persuaded me to drink a lot more champagne than I normally would. I cried a lot that night. But it was a good party from what I don't remember of it.

The Scream on this occasion left at dawn and repaired to a suite they'd hired at the Grand Hotel. This was no coincidence. The Grand was the very hotel – and I had heard the bomb explode – where the IRA had very nearly succeeded in blowing up the whole Thatcher government a few years before. When it was fully daylight they posed for a picture for photographer Grant Fleming, leaning over the balcony with a Confederate flag dangling over the edge and fluttering in the coastal breeze. It's a well-known photograph of the band. If you ever see it, you'll know it was taken after the last-ever party at Montpelier Road.

There was one final, telling, touch. A friend who still had keys said he would go back to the house the next day to make sure there was no incriminating evidence left behind. What he did find, wedged behind some wooden panelling, was a very small blue leather-bound diary of mine, from when I'd been a teenager. I opened a page at random. The first entry read, 'Went to a party. Got home at 5 a.m.' Mmm.

The day after this last Montpelier Road party I woke up at ten in the evening, to discover several urgent phone messages requesting me to call Matthew Bannister, the controller of Radio 1. God, it must be serious. He didn't normally just call you up for an idle chat. Even the day after the day after that party I was in no state to talk to the boss. What to do? In the end I had to own up to him, and mumbled very incoherently, 'I can't talk, Matthew. I am so shot to pieces I just cannot even speak.' Fine words indeed coming from a so-called professional broadcaster! He was very understanding. He was calling not to fire me, as I was half-expecting, but to offer me a new slot on Radio 1. Which, as they used to say on *The Fast Show*, was nice.

XV

Some time late in 1987 I was invited to the BBC to a 'working' lunch – a euphemistic term meaning sitting around a plate of sandwiches, some bottles of mineral water and a few glasses of dubious plonk – on this occasion to discuss John Peel's forthcoming visit to Russia. I had discovered that not only was John a star among the music-hungry fans in the Soviet Union, he was positively *venerated*. I urged him to go and visit. Now the discussion was turning to 'No, they don't have many bath plugs' and 'Yes, take as many pre-recorded music cassettes with you as possible.' Suddenly Stuart Grundy, my then executive producer, said, 'We need someone to go to Baghdad.' Immediately, without thinking about it at all, I replied, 'I'll go.'

I knew nothing of Baghdad, neither which country it was in, nor its politics. But the very name conjured up pictures of flying carpets, Scheherazade and the *Thousand and One Nights*. My then Radio 1 colleague Steve Wright, at the height of his *Steve Wright in the Afternoon* success (and one of whose catchphrases at the time was 'This is radio, this isn't *brain surgery!*', a phrase I was to sing mockingly back to him later), soon heard about this plan. 'Are you *mad*?' he said. 'Don't you know Baghdad is in Iraq,

167

and they're at *war*!' Well, maybe so, but I couldn't imagine that the BBC and the British Council, who had initiated the invitation, would send me on a fatally dangerous mission. Although just why the British Council wanted to send a British radio DJ to a war zone in the Middle East was never made clear. What I did not know then was that the fearless British Council thought nothing of sending an English string quartet to play in Beirut at the height of the civil war there, the bemused musicians being escorted across the strife-stricken city in screaming convoy by armed militiamen.

I'd had a passing interest in this part of the world ever since, for three years, between 1966 and 1970, a young Persian girl had lived in my house in Brighton. She had arrived a demure teenager to learn English, much of which she picked up from watching TV, and most bizarrely from Marx Brothers movies, which would have her screaming with laughter. I learned a little about her culture, and greatly enjoyed the presents her parents sent from Iran, of pistachios and Turkish Delight, Afghan sheepskin coats, Persian rugs and enamelled vases, which all arrived in 'parcels' made of plain white cloth. She had told me then that her brother was living in West Germany, in exile, plotting to overthrow the shah. And this is the underlying reason why, even now, so many years later, I think it unwise to reveal her name. When her father summoned her back to Iran, she returned home to find Ayatollah Khomeini running the country as a new Islamic republic, the shah having been deposed. Perhaps ignorantly, perhaps naively, I had done my best to 'liberate' this young girl, encouraged her to take up Western attitudes, go to rock concerts, go to art college, go wild. Now it seemed she must don the chador and live the life of a fundamentalist.

I still feel guilty that she had had a taste of life in the late 'swinging' sixties of Britain, and was then made to return to a life of almost unbelievable repression.

In 1988 Iraq was still at war with Iran – a scrap that had lasted eight years and was at that time called the Gulf War, not be to confused with the later hundred-hour effort featuring Exocets and F-111s instigated by President Bush after Iraq had invaded Kuwait. The Iran–Iraq war centred on the ownership or domination of a strip of water at the north of the Persian Gulf called the Shatt al'Arab. Once my trip to Baghdad was confirmed, I began to scan the newspapers for more information. News stories that read 'Civilian Casualties in Baghdad' caused me considerable alarm. 'No worries,' said the British Council breezily – 'just a spring offensive. It will all die down when the weather gets too hot again for them to fight each other . . .' By the time my visit was in its final planning stages, Iran and Iraq had reached a ceasefire agreement, ending a war that had cost $350 billion and more than 150,000 lives, and had achieved no significant territorial gains. Both sides believed they had won. The conflict had been one that the super-powers had desperately not wanted to escalate with full-scale intervention, yet desperately needed to contain, and at the same time almost every arms-producing country of the world was secretly selling lucrative weaponry, Irangate style, to both sides.

The third international Babylon Festival was in the offing – Babylon being about an hour's drive from Baghdad – and this was thought to be an event worth taking in during my visit. But then disquieting stories began to filter through. Iraq, clearly confident that it would win the war with Iran, had ordered a huge victory arch from an English foundry, several *years* before the ceasefire. This, in the

form of crossed swords, was to be erected above one of
Baghdad's main thoroughfares. Clasping the handle of each
sword was a giant hand, modelled from the very hand of
President Saddam Hussein. And decorating each hand, in
the form of huge round tassels, were groups of helmets
taken from dead Iranian soldiers, their decapitated heads
still inside.

It had struck me as rather odd even before I left London
that my entry visa, obtained from the Iraqi Centre of
Tourism in Tottenham Court Road, was issued only at the
very last minute, on the day of departure. When the Gulf
War proper kicked in, this innocent-looking building shut
up shop very quickly, housing as it reputedly did many of
the London-based Iraqi foreign agents.

I still had no real idea about the political regime or
what to expect when I got there. A BBC news reporter
who had filed none-too-favourable reports from Iraq told
me that she had had some very worrying phone calls to
her home number, she supposed from Iraqi agents in
Britain. Then I was told bewilderingly, 'Don't wear white
trousers or people will throw stones at you.' I was beginning to be seriously freaked. How should I dress, then? A
reassuring telex came back from the British Council's man
in Baghdad, Peter Elborne. 'Just dress as a DJ,' it said. So
I did. I boarded the flight for Baghdad wearing tight black
leggings and an acid-orange jacket. By now I was so
stressed out and just plain terrified of what I'd got myself
into that I became totally wrecked on the journey. I don't
even remember arriving in Baghdad, only that around
midnight I was dipping my toes in Peter Elborne's pool,
relieved to have finally arrived. Being of more or less
diplomatic status, he made no comment about my obviously inebriated state.

But even in my pissed-up condition on the plane, I had made a very useful contact and friend among the passengers. He was a British expat working in Iraq, and he tipped me off to the fact that all telephones were tapped, and to beware of the 'kermits', the coded term the British people working in Iraq used for Saddam's secret police – they wore green!

Baghdad itself was a curious mixture of grey tower blocks on the city's outskirts, wide palm-fringed boulevards, and aquamarine-tiled mosques. Moscow meets Vegas, minus the neon. I was booked into the Ishtar Sheraton Hotel, itself worth a treatise on modern Middle Eastern grossed-out architecture. The high-speed glass-sided lift was a huge buzz in itself. Having reached the top of the central atrium, it then burst into the open air and sped up the outside of the hotel's skyscraper tower, a white-knuckle ride that took in breathtaking views of the River Tigris snaking its ancient way across the city. My room was disquietingly right next door to the Presidential Suite. I wondered if I would bump into Mr Hussein coming out of the lift, or a visiting Colonel Gaddafi popping down the corridor to the ice machine.

Actually I was already feeling the heavy breath of intimidation, and a strong dose of paranoia was beginning to take effect. I found myself *whispering* into the microphone of my tape recorder at the dead of night, alone in my room. Not that I had anything particularly incriminating to report; it was more the feeling of not knowing the rules.

Everywhere in Baghdad, on almost every street corner, were huge portraits of Saddam Hussein. There was no-form of advertising, no signs flashing Coca-Cola or Budweiser, no posters or slogans, just The President, dominating everything. There were pictures of Saddam the

Soldier in full battledress, Saddam the Dad, the loving father posing with his children, Saddam the Concerned, the patriarchal head of state. He must have spent so much time posing for artists and photographers it was a wonder that he had time to be a dictator as well. As he seemed to be going for the blanket-coverage Michael Jackson-type pop-star image, I was amazed to discover that it was illegal to take photographs of any of these giant representations, which would have done the Sunset Boulevard movie-poster hoardings in Hollywood proud. 'But *why*?' I asked, bewildered that a guy so obviously into promoting himself would deny a punter a photo opportunity. 'Because', I was told, 'you might be ridiculing him.' Similarly, it was an offence to wrap a pair of your shoes in a newspaper containing Saddam Hussein's likeness. This apparently showed an unacceptable lack of respect.

The theme of the Babylon Festival that year was 'From Nebuchadnezzar to Saddam Hussein'. During the lengthy speeches at the opening ceremony – delivered, of course, in Arabic – the audience would every few minutes break into what seemed to be spontaneous applause. Peter Elborne explained to me, 'It is compulsory to clap every time the president's name is mentioned.' 'Blimey,' I thought. 'Thank goodness Margaret Thatcher never cottoned on to *that* idea!'

Apart from having been tipped off about phone tapping and hotel bugging, I realized that I knew virtually nothing about this part of the Middle East, its current political situation, its ethics or its etiquette. Sitting in the back of the British consul's car on the way to Babylon for the first time, I held my SLR Nikon camera up to the window to try to capture a particularly spectacular sunset over the Tigris. 'You must not *do* that,' hissed the British consul.

172

'There's a gun emplacement where you're pointing that camera!' Tsk. How was I to know?

Babylon itself proved full of surprises, too. Firstly there was absolutely no sign of one of the reputed Seven Wonders of the World, the Hanging Gardens. Not a trace. Not even a hanging basket. And nothing much to indicate that here was the Cradle of Civilization, where cuneiform writing on tablets had first been developed. In fact the most famous building I was shown around in Babylon, the Ishtar Gate, looked disquietingly brand-spanking-new. And it is, comparatively. The original gate building, its walls decorated with distinctive animal patterns of bulls and dragons in relief on the ancient brickwork, is just visible above ground. Built atop that is a half-size reproduction, looking about as authentic a historic monument as one made of blue Lego bricks. But the Processional Way, where we sat on wicker chairs, next to genuine American tourists, did have a feel about it as ancient as that of the Appian Way in Rome.

The opening ceremony was an impressive affair, featuring youths in loincloths adopting rugged poses on hilltops around the city, brandishing flaming torches against the night. As the ceremony reached its climax, to fanfares of drums and lutes and trumpets, what appeared to be two huge balloons, with the face of King Nebuchadnezzar depicted on one and the current president's face on the other, rose up and collided in the sky in a rather undignified manner which I don't think was quite intended. And despite persistent rumours, rather like those flying about Philadelphia during Live Aid that Bruce Springsteen *would* make a last-minute surprise appearance, the top geezer, the top VIP – the President – did not show. I was most disappointed. Which quite shocked me. Was I falling under the spell of this dictator superstardom vibe already?

On the return trip to Baghdad I was severely jolted back to the reality of the regime in Iraq. A young Englishman took me to one side and whispered, 'When you go home you must speak out about what is going on here.' He then went on to tell me that he was employed teaching English to Iranian prisoners of war. He said the POW camp where he worked was 'a show camp. It is purely for propaganda. The government fly in foreign journalists to show how well the Iraqis treat their prisoners, but as soon as the journalists have left, the prisoners are beaten up again. And most of them are not soldiers, just boys – goatherds.' Even more disquieting was the young man's belief that, once Iran and Iraq had repatriated their prisoners of war, both sides would execute their homecoming soldiers, believing them to have been brainwashed by the other side. I had no reason to doubt this story, but how was I to authenticate it?

Remembering my Brighton house guest, I was pleased to discover that the Ba'ath socialist regime in Iraq in fact allows women (the young ones at least) to wear what they want – Western-style dress or traditional and college-age girls are encouraged to reach a high level of education and go on to careers in traditional male occupations such as mining and engineering. But this is not so surprising, perhaps, in view of the thousands of young men's lives sacrificed during the war.

The British Council sent me off to meet students, whom I duly interviewed, looking, as always, for interesting developments in youth culture. As it turned out, there weren't any. No raves had reached Iraq, nor any acid-house parties. I just didn't *dare* ask them if they took any drugs. But the young Iraqis did enjoy discos, and one of my duties during my stay in Baghdad was to be guest DJ at the Scheherazade Club, situated within the Ishtar Sheraton, for a special student event. The resident DJ was an affable enough albino called Freddy, who spoke a small amount of English, with an extraordinary accent that I can only describe as Arabic with a strong, inexplicably Australian twang. He was completely incomprehensible.

As is usual with clubs and discos the world over, the lighting in the DJ booth was pupil-enlargingly minimal, so I could not read the labels on the records, nor could I understand a word of Freddy's explanation of how to work the decks or the mixer, which looked like nothing I'd ever seen before. He introduced me over the PA as 'Mrs Nightingale from The BBC One', at which I gave up all pretence of exercising any disc-jockeying skills and let him play the records. Curiously, the biggest floor-filler of the night was a tune by our very own Rick Astley, from Newton-le-Willows, Lancashire. The strangest elements of British culture have a way of penetrating the darkest recesses of foreign climes.

A British indie band called Hurrah, hailing from Newcastle, had been invited by the British Council to play at the Babylon Festival. They seemed as bemused as I was when we met for lunch at the home of the British ambassador, Terence Clark, in a lush suburb of Baghdad called Mansour. 'Terry' was laid-back and charming, and I was fascinated, never having met a high-ranking diplomat in a war zone before. Almost immediately I picked up the etiquette: do *not* openly criticize the Iraqi regime, do not ask overtly political or embarrassing questions. Unfortunately the next time I was to see Terry he presented a very different image, shakily delivering a stark message to Britain on the television news which put over the brutality of the Iraqi government in circumstances that no amount of diplomacy or goodwill could possibly hide.

However, this occasion was happily and thoroughly absorbing, and I savoured the experience of a British embassy staff in operation in a politically delicate part of the world. We were served Pimm's as a pre-lunch drink – how *perfectly* apt, I thought giddily, after the second – then Chablis with the main course of curried chicken and green beans in tomato sauce, served on a long mahogany table, glinting with polished silver and purple linen napkins matching the bougainvillea floral table setting. Then the pièce de résistance: the dessert, that delicacy, brown bread ice cream. What a coup! What a coupe! In Baghdad! So this was how the world was run. In fact I was about to find out just what a novice I was when it came to Middle East diplomacy and etiquette.

Although the British Council had organized a full and intensive itinerary, I found myself with one free early evening, and sat in the bar of the Ishtar Sheraton for only a short while before I was engaged in conversation. To one side of me had come to sit a flamboyant Jordanian, in a navy-blue, Western-cut suit, anxious to practise his English, and with him the rotund, Buddah-like figure of his friend, a Saudi Arabian, who wore pure white robes and plain white keffiyeh (headdress), with a black band around his temples to secure it. 'I had a girlfriend in England once,' said the Jordanian jovially to me. 'She called me "the Jordanian Bastard"! Will you give her a call when you get back to England?'

Anxious to switch the conversation to a less unsettling topic, I picked up and admired a large string of amber beads which one of the two Arabs had set down on the low brass-topped table that was positioned between us. This was a wrong move. Very wrong. The two men conferred for a moment, and then the Jordanian Bastard, with a wave of his hand, declaimed: 'It is yours!' How I wished, during the next few moments, that someone had explained to me beforehand that Arab etiquette demands that if a person admires an object belonging to another it must be presented to the admirer, as a gift. My conversational gambit had backfired, badly. My initial reaction, anyway, was to say, 'Oh, thank you, but I couldn't possibly.'

The amber beads belonged, it transpired, to the Saudi, who did not speak any English. 'You *must* accept the necklace,' the Jordanian intoned, *sotto voce*, to me. 'My friend will be very offended if you do not.' Something in my subconscious stirred at the word 'offended'. Whether from *Lawrence of Arabia* or from some real-life incident that had occurred when I had met and become friends with Arabs in Tunisia years beforehand, I knew that to give offence was a serious matter indeed. So I accepted the necklace, as gracefully as possible, picking it up and concentrating on the luminosity of the beads. To my horror, the Jordanian Bastard's next words to me were 'It's worth eight thousand dollars.' Then he added helpfully, indicating his Saudi friend, 'He's very rich.' There was another brief conference between the two men. The Jordanian Bastard emerged from it saying to me, 'My friend thinks you are very nice.'

I was recovering my composure. 'Thank your friend very much for his compliment,' I replied. The next salvo totally threw me. 'My friend', said the Jordanian, 'would like to know what you think of . . . his eyes!' Whew! I suddenly felt in urgent need of an instruction manual. 'Um, tell your friend his eyes are . . . erm . . . very pleasant.'

177

I was playing for time here. This was turning into a diplomatic ping-pong game, and I was lucky to be holding at thirty all. 'My friend would like you to *describe* his eyes.' 'I think', I said in as measured tone as possible, 'that your friend has very *warm*, very *sympathetic* eyes,' not daring actually to make contact with the brown half-moons which gazed almost lugubriously from the folds in the Buddah face. Forty–thirty to me. Then the killer serve: 'My friend would like you to go out to dinner with him tonight.' Deuce. 'I'm so sorry, but I have a previous engagement tonight.' Advantage Nightingale. 'In that case, what about tomorrow night?' Back to deuce. 'Alas, tomorrow night I have another engagement also.' 'My friend', said the Jordanian very pointedly, 'will be very offended if you will not have dinner with him.'

I was cornered. I had accepted the necklace, but I wasn't playing the game. I was thinking that as an independent Englishwoman I was not going to be bought for a row of beads, but at the same time I realized that there was a serious loss-of-face predicament looming for my Saudi admirer. Some form of compromise on my part was called for. 'Perhaps', I suggested, 'we could meet for drinks early tomorrow evening?' This seemed to mollify the Saudi somewhat. I then feigned tiredness, swept the necklace up from the table, and made for my room. 'What's your room number?' asked the Jordanian Bastard. I demurred from giving him this information, but within a minute of my reaching my room he was on the phone. 'The necklace . . .' he began. 'There is a pendant attached to it which belongs to my friend's family. He needs to remove it, and then he will return the necklace to you tomorrow morning. May I collect it from your room now?' He took the necklace and, not unexpectedly, I did not see either of them again. But honour had been restored, and loss of face had been avoided. I had learned an important lesson. Or thought I had.

The next day the British Council's driver, Amal, who had been put at my disposal, detoured down a side street in Baghdad, saying he wished to introduce me to his wife and small daughter. His wife was wearing large, colourful earrings, which quite spontaneously I began to make admiring gestures at. Promptly she began to remove the earrings from her pierced ears, and I thought, 'No, I've done it again.' 'Thank you, thank you, but no, look, I have no holes in my ears,' I said, demonstrating my whole, unsullied lobes.

At lunch with the British ambassador I had been introduced to Roger Matthews, a young English archaeologist who had been excavating throughout the war years in Iraq. He had invited me to the site where he was working, near Kish, one of the most ancient kingships of Babylonia. Away from the babble of Baghdad, the silence there in the desert, broken only by the buzz of an occasional fly, was majestic. Hardly a whiff of wind rustled the green palm groves, the only vegetation that could survive in the long-abandoned, hard-baked dry riverbed of the Euphrates. The heat, around 104°F, hit me like a punch in the face. When Roger, a cool, handsome Oxford man, invited me to walk across the open terrain to explore the mound he was planning to excavate, I thought it very possible that I would collapse and die embarrassingly right in front of him.

Fortunately I quickly became too fascinated by what lay at my feet to snuff it at that point. Strewn all over the ground were moon-shaped pot shards and big green decorated chunks of ceramic fragments, none of them,

Roger calmly explained to me, dating from later than 2800 BC. That's two thousand eight hundred years BC! Just lying about on the ground! The remnants of one of the earliest civilizations ever discovered. I felt awestruck, and avaricious. 'Can I nick one of these pot rims?' I asked Roger. 'No,' came the firm reply.

Nothing in this area, which had been a region of Mesopotamia, had changed, other than as a result of natural erosion, in nearly five thousand years. Cuneiform tablets, showing the day-to-day life of Sumerians and the earliest forms of shopping lists and inventories, had been found near the site, and also evidence of chariot ruts, indicating that it was in this area that the wheel had first been developed. As someone who had always longed to take part in any sort of archaeological dig, being at one of the world's most ancient sites brought most extraordinary feelings of exhilaration and desolation. Roger's mound was nothing more than a slight rise in this hot, crumbly, crunchy ground. Yet underneath it he believed he would find the remains of a huge house, its outside walls measuring at least ninety metres. There was a poignancy about finding the remnants of this ancient civilization silted up and lying abandoned in cracked fragments in this silent desert. I've always experienced a terrible melancholy at any ancient site I've visited: Carthage in North Africa, Athens, Rome. It's the desolation of broken monuments, the blind, blank stare of statues, their hands and feet and elbows missing and their glory all gone.

However, I was to witness a modern legend in the making amid the warring peoples of Iraq and Iran when I returned to Baghdad. I was taken to a hospital to meet the president of the Women's Union of Iraq, who was in the later stages of pregnancy. She was also in her later middle years, and explained that she had had several children already, and had not planned to have any more, until the Iranians had bombed a children's hospital in Iraq. Now, she said, she was giving birth to a child as an act of 'revenge', and that all children born in Iraq for the two years following the month of July 1988 would be celebrated as special 'revenge' against the Iranians children, and would be given special ID and privileges. The entire concept had an almost biblical feel about it, so much in the flamboyant Saddam style, like his self-proclaimed 'mother of all battles' which was later to ensue against the American forces in the Gulf War. Similarly, the president had apparently also toyed with a Hollywood Old Testament epic-style solution to the Iran–Iraq war, by planning to divert the path of the River Tigris several miles inland into Iraqi-held territory, thus gaining possession of the Shatt al'Arab and proclaiming this remarkably fortuitous event to be 'an act of God'. What a brilliant scam!

Not surprisingly, most of the people I was 'allowed' to meet and interview in Iraq all thought the president a pussy cat. If you'd had the misfortune to lose a son, a brother or a husband during the war, then his martyrdom was rewarded by Saddam Hussein with the gift of a Brazilian-made VW Passat to the surviving family. Cars don't come cheap in this part of the Middle East.

It was the ambassadorial staff who arranged for me to meet an eminent young Iraqi neurosurgeon who was also a disc jockey. I had to meet this person if only to tell my then colleague at Radio 1, Steve Wright. The guy in question was an earnest, hard-working doctor who got to DJ on the English-speaking Baghdad FM. He invited me to be interviewed on his radio show, but first he asked if I would like to accompany him during his rounds at the hospital where he was working. Normally I would never have willingly done a ward round with any medical acquaintance, but, hell, this was Baghdad.

The ward was much more harrowing than I'd expected – full of wide-eyed children with dressings and bandages wound in a primitive fashion around their heads, victims of bullets shot into the air by happy Iraqis celebrating their victory in the Iran–Iraq war, not considering that what goes up must come down. It was estimated that during the eight-year war more casualties were caused by 'friendly fire' bullets raining down on the heads of civilians in the streets of Baghdad than were caused by Iranian missiles, most of which didn't have the range to reach Baghdad anyway. The doctor unwound the bandages for me to inspect the wounds. In some cases the bullet would still be lodged in the victim's head. The children, coated with liniment, were curled foetally in their cots, huge black eyes looking out of frightened faces. The doctor deemed most of them too ill to survive. The worst, saddest Saddam own goal imaginable.

For me even to be allowed into the studios of Baghdad FM was a near-miracle, as the station was housed within the city's main military complex. There was much studying of my ID by the guards, much scrutiny of my papers, and much smiling, reassuring and direct, honest-to-Allah eye contact from me. Eventually I was allowed into the studio. I am obsessed with radio studios, and it is always a feeling of triumph to make a broadcast from the smallest shack, the most modest broadcast set-up, no matter where, be it Barbados or Bucharest. Perhaps it's part of the DJ's ego trip, but it's a strange and wonderful feeling knowing that your small, individual voice goes out into the ether, across the desert, and reaches someone at the oil well, the oasis . . . who knows what or where.

The neurosurgeon had me as his guest during a two-hour show, talking me through my favourite records – those of them I'd been able to find in Baghdad FM's 'library'. This comprised shelf after shelf of battered-sleeved vinyl albums, mostly imports from a strange mélange of countries. 'Where did you get them all from?' I asked the doctor. This was the only question he refused to answer. They must all have been smuggled in. On one of the shelves I found a copy of *Zenyatta Mondatta* by the Police, and pointed out to the doctor my photograph on the back cover, taken in Kyoto, Japan. I wasn't being flash – it was just a way of convincing him that I really was a DJ too. Especially as I had requested as one of my favourites 'Ghost Town' by the Specials. 'Actually,' said the neurosurgeon, 'I think you'll find that the correct name of the artist who performed that track was the Special Aka.' Which was absolutely the case.

Even at that time in Baghdad there were stories that Saddam was amassing nerve gas and silos of nuclear warheads. What I didn't know then was that Saddam regarded journalists as spies, which of course they are! I'd been allowed into the country as a DJ; the Iraqis didn't know about my journalistic background. Then Daphne Parish, an Irish nurse working in Baghdad, was arrested with the *Daily Mail* journalist Farzad Bazoft for spying. The two of them had apparently gone out into the Iraqi hinterland for a jolly afternoon drive, looking for missile sites. As you would. As I would have done. Out of curiosity.

The West still did not realize the unequivocal nature of the vengeance meted out by Saddam to anyone suspected of spying. The nurse was imprisoned, and later released.

But the journalist, when the British government requested that he be sent home, promptly was. In a box, having been hanged in a particularly slow and primitive way. The previously relaxed and genial ambassador, Terry Clark, now looked ashen as he delivered Saddam's curt message to British television viewers. 'You wanted your journalist back, here he is.' I could have, probably would have, walked innocently into the same trap. I would have regarded looking for missile sites rather like going on an outing to search for corn crop circles in Wiltshire. It was again a matter of not knowing the rules. As my father would no doubt have put it, 'gormless' naivety does not always serve as adequate protection.

I still wanted to encounter the fairy-tale aspect, the magic-carpet side, of Baghdad, if it was possible – and to capture it on tape for some as yet unspecified radio programme. Carrying a microphone and tape recorder around in this sensitive city was a nerve-racking business in itself; however, during one of my conversations with other guests at the bar of the Ishtar Sheraton, I persuaded a new-found Arabic acquaintance to relate the story of the *Thousand and One Nights* into the microphone. 'Well,' he began enthusiastically and colourfully, 'there wass thiss man, he wass married to thisss woman, and he was bluddy bastard.' I rather liked what I thought was going to turn into a highly colloquial version of the fable, but the background noise level in the bar was unacceptably high. I suggested that we should record the piece in my room. The storyteller suggested we go to his suite, which he was sharing with, I believe, two other males. I didn't think twice about this; I had done dozens of interviews in hotel rooms, in different cities, on different continents. Not, though, previously in the Middle East.

There were three other guests in the room, and the atmosphere was friendly and relaxed. One of the three gave me his business card, and I put it in my small black shoulder bag. The three men had their own bar in the suite, and asked if I wanted a drink. What happened next has taken me years to understand. I had never heard then of Rohypnol, now called 'the date-rape drug'. It's colourless and tasteless, and was certainly undetectable in the drink I was given. The next thing I knew I was falling forward, a dead weight, like a tree in a storm. I felt one of the guys grabbing me, and I struggled to fend him off, but I was totally powerless and blacked out. I had no further recollection until I was back in my room, next door to the Presidential Suite, calling room service on the phone because I couldn't find my key. I didn't feel drunk, or hung-over, but the previous few hours were a complete blank. I realized I must have my key, otherwise I would not have been able to get back into my room, and eventually I found it under the bed. I looked in my bag. The business card had gone. The rest of my belongings and clothes were in place, except for my knickers. And, although I remembered the guy grabbing me, I wasn't sore or bruised, so I'm pretty sure I hadn't been raped. But I felt furiously angry and embarrassed and bewildered. It was not until late 1997, when reports hit the British papers of the effects of 'roofies', that I realized that my drink had been spiked. Not your most recreational drug, I'd say. And I hope whoever took my underwear as a souvenir really appreciated it.

XVI

In the winter of 1989 I flew to Jersey with a journalist friend, Hugh Fielder, who had invited me to be his co-judge at a Channel Islands rock contest. His wife is Romanian, and Hugh and I spent the journey discussing the recent events in Europe – the Berlin Wall being opened up, the swift collapse of Communism in so many countries. 'But it will never happen in Romania,' said Hugh emphatically. 'Not while the Ceauşescu regime is in force.' A few weeks later I, along with the rest of the Western world, watched the Christmas Revolution in Romania unfolding live on TV from Bucharest. Horrifying pictures of gunfire, shelling, students crushed under the tanks, and one young man I especially remember risking his life by pushing his face into the camera lens and pleading to the outside world, 'Please, please don't let the Securitate kill us!'

I sat at home watching this, tears rolling down my face, feeling helpless and frustrated. A day later Ceauşescu was dead. Romania was free of its hideous dictator, and of the terrifying regime that had banned free speech for twenty-two years.

One would not necessarily have thought that the banning of rock music would have been high on the resentment agenda of the Romanians, who had suffered so much other deprivation. But as the media weighed in to investigate and document life behind Romania's closed frontiers, more and more young people came forward to be interviewed and expressed their acute desire to be able to listen to some noisy rock 'n' roll. 'This', I thought, 'calls for the British Council.'

I contacted a rock-agent friend, and other interested parties joined in a frantic scramble to put together a rock tour of Romania, backed by the British Council and its ever-helpful Edward Craxton. Exactly eight weeks after the revolution a contingent of British musicians, road crew, journalists and photographers landed, the first Westerners to do so since the revolution, in Timişoara, Romania, near the then Yugoslav border. This operation alone had caused near chaos. Our hastily arranged trip meant that three bands, plus their fifty-plus flight cases of equipment, had to be put on a skiers' charter flight that was due to land at Bucharest. The rock 'n' rollers' check-in at Heathrow and the unscheduled landing at Timişoara caused a five-hour delay to the flight, at which the skiers looked livid. (Mind you, not half as livid as when the same dishevelled bunch turned up again on their return flight!)

The 'Rock for Romania' gang was a strange bunch even in rock 'n' roll terms. There was Jesus Jones – new 'hot hip-hop acid rock' as they called themselves, baseball caps on backwards, sponsored white designer wear, and their own UV lighting; there was Skin Games, a Major Label Signing, with a cool and conscientious blonde lead singer named Wendy Page . . . and then there was Crazyhead. Crazyhead comprised singer 'Sex God' Anderson, Pork-beast, Fast Dick, drummer Rob Vomit and Kev Reverb, who did everything. He also drank anything, and every-thing, and once in Transylvania began to come up with one-liners such as 'What do you call a dictator with asthma? – Vlad the Inhaler.'

My role in all this was to act as MC and, as always, keep a tape recorder running for the inevitable documentary of the tour. For three rock 'n' roll bands, five hours' delay at an airport meant the inevitable – hitting the bar heavily and doing some immediate and serious bonding. But even with such a disparate group it was obvious that everyone was on this trip for the right reason. It was not about promotion or marketing or making money or getting a lot of good press. It was about three bands playing their hearts out to what turned out to be the most appreciative audiences anyone had ever experienced.

Not only had rock music been banned in Romania, but so had any music sung in English. We found a people starved of rock culture, which came as a surprise to me, having been to Russia, where, despite a Communist regime, rock fans were a lot more clued up. We arrived in Timişoara to discover a country that had been literally locked away from the outside world.

The group checked into the hotel at night and congregated for a late supper in an extraordinary dining room that looked as though it had not been decorated since before World War II. And it probably hadn't been. There were tall, upright, red plush chairs around large white-clothed tables, and dotted around the lofty-ceilinged room were what appeared to be real trees, with twenty-foot-high blackened branches winking white fairy lights.

The next morning, a Sunday, we assembled in the main square of Timişoara, and the full impact of recent events began to hit us all. It was here that the revolution that brought down Ceauşescu had started, fuelled by the proximity and availability of TV news pictures of events in the outside world beamed from Yugoslavia. It was here in this square during a demonstration on 17 December 1989 that at least 124 people, and possibly many more than that, including women and children, had been mown down by Securitate bullets, their bodies apparently being dumped in a nearby canal – here, where a cathedral service could now be held, freely, and the dead remembered in the most poignant manner. The entire centre of the square (actually an oblong shape, not dissimilar to Wenceslas Square in Prague) had become a huge shrine. Often wrapped in cellophane against the weather, photographs of those who had died in the massacre, which had lit the fuse for the revolution, were pinned on wreaths made from Christmas-tree branches. Eight-week-old bouquets of now-dead carnations remained untouched; newer wreaths were adorned with fresh cyclamen. At every other minute another sombre-faced Romanian would move forward out of the silent assembled gathering and bend to light another slim yellow candle on a growing ziggurat of wax. The silence was deafening. The public grief was heart-rending. The Rock for Romania party was, for the moment, jokeless, out of awe and respect for the situation we found ourselves in.

That afternoon I was taken to meet a group of drama students. They gave me thick black coffee you could stand a spoon up in, and told me, 'Eight weeks ago this could not have happened. We would not have been allowed to talk to a foreigner, let alone invite you into our home.' They told me how one person in four in Romania was supposedly an informer, so possibly your best friend was in the Securitate. 'We were terrified even to *think*.' Even so, they risked their young lives by staging allegorical theatrical pieces criticizing the state, albeit obliquely. 'But in

189

the end,' said their passionate, black-haired director, 'the revolution happened because we had nothing left to lose.'

I felt humbled by my ignorance about Romania during Ceauşescu's regime. But that is what he had intended – there was to be no outside Western interference in his rule of terror. It would appear that the incursion of foreign media and information brought about his downfall. Satellite pictures respect no political boundaries, and, once young Romania saw what the rest of the world had to offer, Ceauşescu's attempts to keep his people isolated were doomed. To the west of the country, in Timişoara, Romanians were picking up Yugoslav TV pictures; to the north and east, TV from Russia. In order to stem the flow on this early form of information superhighway, Ceauşescu had installed in millions of Romanian homes a one-channel-only TV service, featuring his own propaganda, and hours of his speech-led council meetings. 'It was so boring no one watched!' said the exuberant Romanians one after another, each on a huge freedom buzz, finally able to criticize the regime, and to a foreigner, without fear of arrest.

It seemed that Ceauşescu had lost the plot by believing in his own publicity and his own popularity. On his final pre-Christmas balcony appearance, he could not believe that the crowd in the main square in Bucharest were actually *booing* him. He could corral them with ignorance no longer. Ceauşescu was defeated by technology, and by the courage of a people who had had enough.

Everyone I met wanted to talk endlessly about the repression they had suffered. For Angela, a drama student, it was the subject of abortion above all that she wanted to speak out about. Abortion had been illegal, carrying a penalty of three years' imprisonment for anyone who had

190

First publicity shot for Radio One. I had to live with this image for years. (*BBC*)

John Peel and I sternly looking into the future and contemplating our long-term commitment to Radio One, which neither of us envisaged then.
(*Don Smith/Radio Times*)

Me and Paul McCartney at a London TV studio.
(*Thames Television*)

The Police dressing up in Egypt, in front of real pyramid and genuine camel.

'There ain't 'arf been some clever bastards . . .' Me with the author of that immortal line, Ian Dury.

I've never ever seen a band play . . . on the bandstand at Brighton seafront, but it's a great location.

Above: Me, Jess Hallett, Emily Hughes, Alex and Bobby Gillespie on a party mission in Brighton.

Right: Me and Throb AFTER a party in Brighton. (*Anita Young*)

St Petersburg, Russia. Taking tea with Seva Gakkel and Boris Grebenchikov. Left to right: possible spy, myself, Boris, Carol Wilson, possible spy, Seva.

Me skiing in Transylvania. Note Count Dracula spectating in top right-hand corner.

Putre, Chile, 1994. Left, Phil Kay uncharacteristically raising a drink to his lips. Centre, cameraman predicting I'd burst into tears when the eclipse reached totality. Me, disbelieving, right. (*Grant Fleming*)

Me in situ at Radio One at the time of the *Annie On One* compilation release. (*Martin Goodacre/Retna*)

DJ Adam Freeland and me
on the Active/Doc Marten
British tour, Brighton, 1998.
(*Piers Allardyce*)

The Night of *Les Sorcières Rouges*, serious Sicilian partying.
I'm holding SOMETHING aloft, top left.

one carried out. But contraception was also illegal, including use of the pill. Most women did resort to abortion, and risked death or imprisonment in so doing, as they dared not go to hospital if complications set in. (Ceauşescu's regime insisted that every Romanian woman bear five children, and anyone not bearing enough Romanian fruit would be subjected to a gynaecological examination. Every month. Not unlike the 'baby police' I'd heard about in the similar military dictatorship in Baghdad.)

Some months later the scandal of Romanian orphans and the barbaric way they were treated was to hit the world's media, and I was to witness it first hand, but now, in the post-revolution euphoria, that ugliest aspect of the regime had not yet come to light. There were just the merest hints of the cause of such a scandal, Angela's anger being a clue I did not pick up on at the time. Banned contraception and abortion in a Communist state – it was not surprising that this should result in thousands of unwanted children.

Other people I met directed their venom directly at the dead dictator. He had, in his later years, apparently tried to clean up the image of Transylvania's infamous ruler Vlad the Impaler by renaming him 'the Warrior Prince' – indeed, Vlad's very phyzog appeared on the labels of Romania's export-vodka bottles. Vlad's distinguished name came about through his method of maintaining his own tyrannical rule – by impaling his captives on sharp-pointed stout sticks inserted into the anus, causing unthinkably painful death. The victims would be left staked out on the borders of Vlad's territories, causing any challenging army to flee in utter terror at the thought of an unsuccessful skirmish with Vlad and his men. Vlad and Mrs Impaler were apparently enthusiastic practising vampires, drinking the blood of young children in order to preserve eternal youth. 'Ceauşescu did that too,' I was told on several occasions by Romanians, who understandably would not put their own names to this piece of information. Evidence, I was told, was found during the autopsy after his execution. Although an elderly man, he had 'the skin of a young boy. Smooth, unlined and unwrinkled.' Fact or folklore, such gory stories were bound to be told in a land where free speech had been at a premium for so long. Certainly there was much graffiti scrawled about the main streets of Bucharest proclaiming *'Ceauşescu Vampiry'*.

The curiosity of all of us and our interest in this fascinating country were unquestionable. The hotel bar in Timişoara in itself was an object of desire and bewilderment. Set off by a garish glass backdrop, it had on display shelves of brand-name bottles of alcohol which would be deemed a respectable stock by any bar in the West. Except that this bar didn't actually *serve* any such drinks. The bottles were purely an enticing decoration. Above the bar was an array of large decorated clock faces, all showing different times, and above each a city name – MOSCOW, BEIJING, PARIS, BUCHAREST. But, even allowing for time-zone differences, there was no way it could be 11.02 p.m. in Moscow and 8.49 a.m. in Beijing.

The first gig of the tour was to be held at a sports hall in Timişoara. The gig had almost been cancelled because the chief of police was concerned that, as so many fans had congregated outside the venue without tickets, they might storm the building and cause a mass riot. He was appeased, the show went ahead, and wishing to contribute to the proceedings in any small way I could, I volunteered to introduce each of the British bands from the stage. In Romanian. Knowing nothing of the language, I decided that the only way to do this would be to write down my introductions in English, speak them out loud to one of our five interpreters, Oura, have her translate my words into Romanian, and then write down again her translation my own form of phonetics. Thus an extract from my 'script' was scrawled in ballpoint, 'SPEREM QUE OSA VE PLACKER MOOSIKA PECARE AMADOOSO CAR UNE TRIBOOT PENTRU VOI TOTSZ PRESENTZ KOOT SHE PEI CHE DISPARUTZ . . .' The Romanian audience thought this was hilarious, and laughed their heads off. I couldn't blame them.

Jesus Jones went on stage with their self-styled 'acid rock', which all of us knew would be a type of music never before heard in Romania. And undoubtedly their bizarre, frantic stage antics would be something never before seen, to say nothing of the eerie effect of ultra-violet lighting on their all-white-clad bodies. Halfway through their set the audience started chanting 'JEE-ZUS, JEE-ZUS.' The band finished their act and came off convinced that the audience had been shouting 'Get OFF, get OFF.' In fact the young fans had been wildly impressed. They then went into over-drive over Crazyhead, who played the sort of heads-down, no-nonsense, timeless rock 'n' roll which the entire audience could get into. After which Wendy Page, with her high boots and long blonde hair, became the necessary rock chick glamour babe of the night.

Then Kev Reverb hit on the perfect finale. All three bands would come back on stage together to perform Neil Young's 'Keep On Rocking in the Free World', most fitting for the occasion. That did it. The audience swarmed on to the stage, the security people shrugged their shoulders, and the artistes and the audience embraced and laughed in a confused emotional throng. Afterwards the bands were euphoric, buzzing off their heads, staring into space, reeling with adrenalin rush. The only way to come down was to party.

Then began what was to become a nightly ritual in Romania after every gig. Namely a game loosely titled 'In the Style of . . .', from which no one was exempt. One might be asked to sing 'Smoke on the Water' in the style of Napalm Death. I was assigned 'Chirpy Chirpy Cheep Cheep' in the style of Kate Bush. Possibly the most difficult challenge fell to Jesus Jones singer Mike Edwards: 'Free Nelson Mandela' in the style of Douglas Hurd.

While our two drivers took two truckloads of equipment on a ten-hour overnight drive through the Carpathian Mountains to Bucharest, meeting unlit trucks coming in the opposite direction as well as the hazard of hay carts with no lights on, the rest of us flew to the Romanian capital. Getting out of bullet-riddled Bucharest Airport proved an experience of unexplained delay. Anderson from Crazyhead crashed out on a wooden bench, using his duty-free plastic bag containing a bottle of Jack Daniel's and two bottles of Romanian champagne as a pillow. Inevitably the bag smashed to the ground and the contents slowly flowed across the airport floor. Anderson woke, surveyed the scene, looked distractedly depressed, and went back to sleep. The use of straws was considered. The rest of Crazyhead were studying a sign which included a list in English of goods prohibited from import into Romania, which included the phrase 'NO PSYCHOTROPIC DRUGS'. Adopting this term, Fast Dick now became Fast Psychotropic Dick.

In Bucharest the sense of drama produced by the recent

revolution was even stronger. Another huge shrine in the main square, more yellow candles burning, more wreaths – here decorated with posies of fresh snowdrops – gutted blackened buildings, boarded-up windows, foot-wide shell holes, and the glass in every street lamp totally shot away. Strongest of all the images was the blue, red and yellow Romanian flag flying high over public buildings, the communist insignia wrenched out of its centre, leaving a gaping hole in the middle. Everywhere people asked us, 'How much do you know about what happened here? How much do you know about the revolution?' At a press conference I joined the artistes to answer questions. I told the Romanian press how I'd cried as I watched the terrified students appealing for help on live British TV. 'Thank you for your tears,' said one of the journalists, with extra-ordinary grace.

Rita Goldenburg, one of the interpreters assigned to our party, told us her story. She was then a twenty-one-year-old biochemistry student, all of five foot two, and a slender girl. She had been demonstrating in the square with her fellow students when she was arrested by the Securitate, taken to a makeshift women's prison, and stripped of all her possessions. The only information she could gather was that she and the other inmates would be executed the following day. But the next day it was Ceau-şescu who was shot. Rita, still wonderfully and wildly defiant eight weeks later, said, 'He tried to *run away*. He proved in the end that he was nothing but a *coward*.' I'd never heard anyone speak with such contempt.

After their triumph, the Romanians' main concerns were to have real political change, and free elections. Also that, having finally been attracted during their struggle, the attention of the world's media should not now fade away. 'Please don't let the world forget about us,' said one after another. 'We paid such a heavy price for our freedom.' More horrific than any of the shelled buildings was the sight of Ceauşescu's hideous 7,500-room new palace, almost finished but never lived in, a bleak mongrel cross between Buckingham Palace, the Reichstag and the KGB headquarters in Moscow. Entire communities in Bucharest had been razed to make room for this showpiece. Now it stood silent and shunned by the Romanian population. It was the most horrible, obscene building I've ever seen.

After more wild emotional concert scenes in Bucharest, Rock for Romania was now to cross into Transylvania for the last gig of the tour, in Braşov, a mountainous city and ski resort. The daytime bus trip proved to be breathtaking. Snow-covered peaks, waterfalls, low-roofed Hansel and Gretel houses, horse-drawn carts carrying local military around the treacherous hairpin bends, a hammer and sickle above a cemetery, and then a shining silver cross high on a mountaintop. This was the Grimms' fairy tales come true, like finding a land that had not been seen by any outsider for a hundred years. As we entered Transylvania, Kev Reverb made his way up and down our bus giving all the passengers a welcoming bite on the neck.

After the final gig in Brasov, we were to visit a local nightclub, before a night drive back over the mountains to Bucharest. The Rock for Romania bands, now understandably blind drunk, totally bemused the nightclub audience by storming the stage and performing appalling renditions of old Velvet Underground songs.

Coach surfing might have been a reasonably hazardless sport on a flat autobahn across Germany, but in sub-zero temperatures at the dead of night across the Transylvanian mountains it was sheer lunacy. Deafening sound systems appeared, courtesy of Jesus Jones, and upside-down bodies of half-clad men swung uncontrollably from one side of the bus to the other before crashing with a sickening thump to the floor, which was awash with spilt beer and littered with rolling empty champagne bottles. Ever trying to be the professional, I spent half the night endeavouring to get the thoughts and impressions of Rebecca Thompson, one of the three tour managers, on to tape, while ducking to avoid the bodies. The perfect cool English rose, with blonde hair and a peaches-and-cream complexion, Rebecca was quite unfazed by the manic behaviour going on around us. *'Is this the maddest situation you've ever had to deal with?'* I screamed at her above the pounding house music and alarming thudding sounds as another bundle of muscle and bone came flying down from the roof and hit the upholstery of the bus seats. 'Well, no,' she replied thoughtfully. 'I did once have a lot of trouble trying to get money out of a promoter in Portsmouth.' *'Portsmouth?'* I yelled back at her, incredulously. 'We're in the middle of Transylvania, about to be fatally flattened by two tons of drunken rock 'n' roll revellers, and you talk to me about Portsmouth?'

No one seemed to remember much after that. I woke up, not for the last time in my life, unsure which country I was in. Always a sign of a good party. I was on a bus, but for some hungover, deluded reason I thought I was back in England on an airport bus out of Heathrow. As it turned out we were still in Romania, having somehow survived the trip back to Bucharest without loss of life or limb. Another five-hour delay ensued before our journey home, during which Crazyhead, camped out in the middle of Bucharest Airport floor, and much to the conster-nation of the British skiing party we'd annoyed on the outbound flight, unconcernedly stripped off all their clothes.

When I finally did reach England, and really was waiting for an airport bus out of Heathrow, an American woman en route from Vienna struck up a conversation with me, saying she had to make a detour on her journey back to the USA to buy her son a T-shirt from the Hard Rock Café in London, and asking me where it was. Then she enquired where I had been. Having told her Romania, I expected that she would show some interest. Not a flicker. 'Do you know what has happened there?' I asked her. She shook her head. 'Do you not know about the revolution? Do you not know how many people sacrificed their lives to get rid of the dictator Ceauşescu?' She replied placidly, 'Where I come from [obviously Dicksville, Idaho] we like to, you know . . .' She made a gesture, cupping her hands together as if she were making a ball of dough. ' . . . keep ourselves to ourselves.' I thought of all the Romanian people I'd met who had asked how much of their struggle the rest of us had seen, and to whom the answer was so important, and how often these people had reiterated, 'Please don't let the world forget about us.' And here was Mrs Middle America frankly not giving a damn.

A year later I returned to Romania, and again to Braşov in Transylvania. By now the full horror of the treatment of Romanian orphans, victims of the odious repression there, had become known to the world. Carol Sarler, an English journalist and TV producer, had been put in charge of organizing help for some of these children through a newly set-up charity funded by London's comedy community. Financial help, nursing, toys and children's clothes had flooded into the country. But what Carol showed me was the blunt truth of the situation. Toys and teddy bears had been pinned to the walls of the particular orphanage that her charity had adopted. Lavish gifts from abroad decorated the corridors, but had not been given to the children to play with. 'Play' was altogether a luxury not afforded to these abandoned infants. Year-old children who could stand up were lined up in iron-framed cots and just banged their heads continually on the bars. On the top floor of the orphanage was the Aids ward, full of beautiful black-eyed babies not expected to live more than a few months.

Just how these infants had contracted Aids was the hardest fact of all to take in. It had stemmed from Romania's black past and vampiric obsession with blood as a life-giving or healing force. Sick children were given blood transfusions as a traditional medical treatment. Tragically and in ignorance, children were being injected with Aids-contaminated blood, now thought to have come from paid sailor blood donors in the Black Sea port of Constanţa. Once this appalling practice had been identified, clearly it would be prohibited, permanently, and there would be no more new cases of Aids among Romanian children. But, yet unbelievably, this turned out not to happen, and more new cases of Aids were being diagnosed among the infant population. Carol Sarler's fury understandably knew no bounds when, on this trip, she found out why. The reason was born of even more staggering ignorance. Despite the massive medical donations from the West, including hypodermic syringes, indigenous staff at children's hospitals and orphanages, so accustomed to shortages of drugs and medical equipment, were treating infants reusing syringes, despite being told that used needles would be Aids carriers.

Carol took me to the Aids ward. Most of the children

looked healthy enough, and it was almost impossible to comprehend that they had such a cruel death sentence hanging over them. But, locked in their bare cot cages, the children had an unearthly, forlorn look – one baby boy especially. I remarked upon him to Carol, who urged me to pick him up. When I did so, this tiny creature immediately locked his small arms around my neck and clung on to me with extraordinary strength, as though literally for dear life. I had never before experienced another human being's desperation and longing expressed through such raw physical contact, and never have since. When, inevitably, I had to put him down, the child's cries of anguish, anger, abandonment and deep despair were unlike any child's cry I had ever heard. And they will always haunt me.

XVII

Some time in May 1994, at a daytime music gig on the beach in Brighton, on a Saturday, a well-travelled female acquaintance, Sam Matthews, informed me about the solar eclipse that was to happen on 3 November 1994. It would be best viewed in South America. Something told me that I had to be there. Some magnetic force had drawn me into its field, then and there. I had no choice.

I had no idea what a solar eclipse would look like, but ever since I could remember I had gone out of the door at night, looked at the stars and the velvet night sky, wondered about time and space, and started thinking and worrying about infinity. When did time begin? Where did space begin? Where would it end? What is beyond our universe? How could stars wink at you when they were already dead? Are there people out there, or maybe intelligent moss, or fish, or clouds? What is intelligence? Do we believe the physicists who talk about the improbability of life on Mars because of the temperature and the gases and the winds?

No way. I've never believed in physics as fact, only as theory. When I was taught at school that you could change the magnetic field of a bar magnet from north to south, with all the molecules getting up and turning round, I thought, 'Bollocks.' Well, probably not exactly that word, as a fifteen-year-old being taught by Miss Bannister, sister of Roger Bannister, the bloke who had just run the first four-minute mile. Even she couldn't convince me. The magic of the moon and the stars for me had nothing to do with physics. I can even remember having to draw diagrams relating to eclipses, the moon covering the sun. But it meant nothing. Until 1994.

Research initially proved difficult. Word was out that there was to be some massive rave somewhere on the eclipse path. The problem was finding out where. It seemed a totally underground, word-of-mouth affair. I had the idea of making a TV documentary, but how could I persuade a TV company to sink a load of wedge into . . . well, a rumour? Weeks of negative vibes and of people indicating that they thought I was screwy just to think of trying to locate the rave went by. But the idea of going just wouldn't leave me. I called the British Council in Lima, Peru. 'BBC London speaking,' I said. 'I believe there's going to be a bit of a party to celebrate the solar eclipse. Know anything about it?' 'Oh my God,' the man said. 'We've got enough of a drug problem as it is.'

June, July and August came and went, and I was still none the wiser, but becoming more and more obsessed with viewing the eclipse and, more importantly, getting it on film or video. Then I had a breakthrough. Sam had managed to get hold of a glossy travel brochure with the heading 'Solar Eclipse Expedition to Peru – Guest Lecturer Patrick Moore'. The words 'Expedition' and 'Patrick Moore' filled me with excitement. So there was a plan after all! And the involvement of Britain's most famous astronomer was just the stamp of authenticity I needed to convince those who held the purse-strings that I was not entirely daft. The brochure was filled with tantalizing details of the eclipse area: Machu Picchu, the lost city of the Incas; Lake Titicaca, the highest navigable lake in the world, the wonder of the Andes mountains.

There were also details concerning 'totality', i.e. the time when the moon would completely cover the sun, and 'cloud cover possibility', which at that stage I had no idea were of such importance. Gradually more information on paper came into my hands, mostly from astronomical publications – details of the exact time and location of the eclipse, which was to sweep across northern South America on the morning of 3 November; maps showing where the least cloud cover was likely to be, and the best spot from which to view totality.

There was still no word as to where the rave party might be. Then it occurred to me that the stoned, blissed-out and fast-growing audience of my new Radio 1 show, *Chill-out Zone*, were the very people who were most likely to know its location, the most likely people to be *going* to the rave. I appealed for information over the airwaves – and immediately a response came through. A certain Fifi called to say that there would be a party in Cuzco, Peru, a sort of shamanistic gathering to celebrate a *lunar* eclipse, although the date *was* in November. Confusing. I called the British consulate in Lima. I was told I needed to speak to Roger Delgado. I rang him up. A woman speaking only Spanish answered the phone.

'*Señor Delgado, por favor?*' I asked.

'*No está,*' she replied. '*Lima.*'

'*Número teléfono?*' I asked, struggling.

'*Cuatro dos ocho cinco . . .*' she rattled off, and I was lost.

A fax came through later detailing events surrounding the eclipse period in Peru, including a rock festival, 'Rock en los Andes', supposedly sponsored by both Coca-Cola *and* Pepsi Cola, which on reflection seemed unlikely, and a meeting of 'Quackers', which possibly meant either Quakers or people interested in earthquakes. There was also to be a conference of psychoanalysts in Peru at around the same time. But still no mention of a rave. I felt I was seriously losing the plot. Even in my least obsessive moments I realized one could not expect a film crew to run around an unspecified part of South America looking for a party, without knowing even what *country* it was going to be held in. And for all the talk of Cuzco being Party Central, it wasn't even on the eclipse path.

Then another breakthrough. Another fax came in, this time from Frankfurt, Germany, detailing an eclipse party featuring around fifty DJs from the USA, Britain, Germany and other parts of Europe. But this was to be held not in Peru, but in Chile. At a place called Arica, a coastal town in the north of the country, and as it turned out much closer to the centre of the eclipse path than either Machu Picchu or Cuzco in Peru.

My feelings of elation and vindication were short-lived. I called a British record label whose artists Autechre had been listed in the Arica line-up. 'Nope,' said Warp Records, 'it's all fallen through. The sponsorship deal which was going to pay for the DJs to go has been cancelled.'

So, one step forward, two steps back. I called Katya, whose name had appeared on the fax, in Frankfurt. She sounded utterly distraught. DJs from all over the world had contacted her, offering to appear at the rave. But when the sponsorship deal had collapsed, and with it the free flights to South America, most of them had backed out. But she was still determined that an event would happen to celebrate the eclipse in Arica.

But I was no closer to achieving my aim of getting a crew to film the event. I had pursued Granada TV in Manchester, believing that with their long-held reputation of turning out innovative programmes the company would share my enthusiasm. No way. My faxes including diagrams about cloud cover possibilities and the best locations from which to view totality went unanswered. Time was running out. The eclipse was now only three weeks away.

Then the action moved, unexpectedly, to Scotland. I had been recording a brief interview 'up the line' from a studio at Broadcasting House to Glasgow for an imminent radio documentary about Creation Records, home to Primal Scream, the Jesus and Mary Chain, and more recently Oasis. At the end of the interview I poured out my heart and my frustration regarding the eclipse to the Scottish radio producer Stuart Cruikshank. Then he produced the magic phrase 'Why don't you talk to May Miller?'

May, producer in the Music and Arts Department of BBC TV Scotland, was not only accessible, she was interested in the project. Another wave of adrenalin hit me, and I spent one more night at the fax machine, sending her every possible, tantalizing detail about the eclipse I could find. I waited impatiently in London as May's team worked on a bearable production budget. Now I was talking daily by phone to Archie Lauchlan, the director assigned to the project. He told me later that he had also been gripped by eclipse fever whcn he'd seen the information come pouring out of the BBC fax machine in Scotland, and was as determined as I was to make the programme happen. The biggest concern in the minds of the team in Scotland was the thought of sending a crew halfway across the world to photograph a solar eclipse only

for it to come back with nothing, owing to some thought-
less wisp of cloud drifting across the sun during the three
crucial minutes of totality. Would it be possible to find a
location that was guaranteed cloud-free? A small area high
in the Andes, where Peru, Chile and Bolivia bordered each
other, seemed favourite. But then again these were countries with histories of political 'instability', where problems
might include the Shining Path terrorists (still active in the
mountains of Peru), entering Bolivia with valuable camera
equipment, and the ever-present potential nightmare of
dealing with *puna*, or altitude sickness. I just tried to put
these worries to the back of my mind.

Finally it all came together. On the morning of Sunday
30 October, having just finished my Halloween Special
Chill-out show at 5 a.m., I met up with the crew at
Heathrow at 7.30 a.m., minus a night's sleep, and with no
possibility of getting to bed until we reached Santiago some
two days later. Thirty-one flight cases of camera and sound
equipment had to be checked through to Chile, so there
was no time for pleasantries with the six-person crew,
none of whom I'd ever met before. They included Phil
Kay, an up-and-coming Scottish comedian, who was to be
the co-presenter. My first impression of Phil was of a tall,
gangly, long-haired young man who looked like a fugitive
from a heavy-metal band from Hull.

'You a rock musician?' demanded the immigration
officer at Miami Airport of Phil, who was first in line, in
front of me. 'Please don't say you're a comedian,' I
thought, 'it will make the situation even worse.' I have
had an intense paranoia about going through US Customs
ever since I was pulled over by them in Boston on my way
to a Rolling Stones gig in the late seventies. Then they'd
asked me, 'What is the purpose of your visit?', and I'd

replied innocently, 'I've come to interview Mick Jagger.' At which point I was hauled off for a strip search and interrogated as to whether I was bringing into the United States anything that was 'prohibited'. 'Like *what*?' I demanded in my best outraged BBC voice. 'Like *narcotics*?' replied the immigration officer. It was probably just as well that I had forgotten that I was carrying a bottle of 'slimming' pills, which were in fact prescribed speed.

The experience, which had caused much hilarity among the Stones at the time, had made me highly cautious about entering the United States during subsequent visits. On one occasion, when I had flown to San Francisco to interview the opera star Kiri Te Kanewa, I instructed the record-company publicist who came with me – it was her first visit to the USA – not to tell the immigration authorities what the purpose of our visit was. 'Just say we're on vacation,' I told her. Not a good plan. 'You've come from London to San Francisco just for *two days'* vacation?' asked the immigration officer suspiciously. And then he searched my bag. I remembered too late that I'd brought a home-made Christmas pudding wrapped in foil for friends in LA. I did not relish the prospect of trying to convince the US immigration officials that it was *not* a hash cake. But now, in Miami en route for Santiago, Phil Kay got through immigration with a classic 'Get your hair cut' admonition and nothing more.

Arica looked arid, barren and deserted. Not much sign of a rave. Not much sign of any kind of life. However, we didn't stop long – just long enough to meet up with our driver, Enriques, who was to drive our hired minibus to the next destination, Putre, some three thousand metres up in the Andes.

Chile has to have the weirdest geographical borders in

the world, apart from Israel. Pacific rollers crash on to its elongated stretch of western coastline, arcing way down to the Antarctic. But, when you turn to look inland from the sea, the Andes rear up like a pride of golden lions within a kilometre, or so it appears, of the blue-green ocean, dominating everything in sight.

With plastic canisters of diesel fuel loaded on to the roof rack of our minibus, we began our ascent of the lower slopes of the Andes. Within minutes of leaving Arica, the road began a series of hundreds of teeth-grindingly sharp hairpin bends. The weather was warm, the windows were open, and Enriques played an almost alarming variety of music from his cassette collection – from European classical to American garage punk. 'Drink much water,' he said, 'eat little. This helps with the *puna.*' So now, it seemed, we were to experience mountain sickness.

Lorena was our 'fixer'. We had met her in Santiago, and she was to accompany the crew throughout our trip. She was to 'fix' everything – hiring the minibus, booking hotels, interpreting, travel guiding, advising on diet; *and* she looked like she should be on the front cover of Italian *Vogue* – the sort of girl who could make a plain white T-shirt and a pair of jeans look like ultimate chic. It was Lorena who was to provide us with coca leaves to relieve the symptoms of *puna.*

The particular range of Andes peaks we were traversing seemed like an infinite number of pages in a pop-up book. No sooner was one array of peaks in our frame of vision than another, even higher, set leapt up from behind them, filling the golden horizon.

I'd had little opportunity to discover just why we were heading for Putre, a small mountain village, except that Lorena had managed to book us hotel rooms there. Bearing

in mind that the entire world of astronomy was probably
ascending to this part of the Andes to view the eclipse, and
had probably planned to do so for at least twelve months
beforehand, it seemed a miracle to me that we had anywhere to stay at all.

As Enriques grinded gears up through the mountain
road, Phil Kay nursed a hangover from a night on the town
in Santiago. 'I have four kinds of pain running around
my brain,' he said, but cheerfully. I noticed something
beginning to appear regularly on the Arica–Putre
'highway'. At first I thought they were Roman Catholic
shrines (after all, this *was* South America). Crucifixes were
staked out along the mountainside, many adorned with
fresh flowers. But these were not, as it transpired, shrines,
but graves. Whether people had died in the construction of
this fairly modern mountain highway or whether hapless
travellers had simply misjudged the bends and gone over
the side of the unbarriered, snaking, desert-dry road into
a ravine was unclear. 'I suppose you've done this trip many
times before?' I enquired chattily of Enriques. 'Oh no,' he
replied. 'First time. And,' he added, smiling, 'is worse
coming down.' '*Why*?' I asked quickly, panicking. 'Because
of brakes,' said Enriques. I presumed he meant 'lack of
brakes', or 'failure of brakes'. Which perhaps explained the
number of roadside graves. Or perhaps they were due to
the huge, killer-size, boulders poised threateningly on the
rocks above every bend in the road, ready and waiting to
topple, crash down and crush unsuspecting vehicles in
their path. So delicately did these boulders appear to be
balanced, it seemed as if the slightest engine vibration
could set off the equivalent of a desert avalanche.

We were travelling upwards towards the *altiplano*, a
huge stretch of high-altitude desert plateau, spanning the

borders of Chile, Peru and Bolivia. As the three-thousand-metre climb progressed, the colour of the giant slabs of Andes mountainside began to change. Pink rock appeared among the strata of golden ochre, and tinges of bright green, perhaps a hint of the copper-rich minerals beneath. The warm air began to freshen, and it was becoming thinner. Against Enriques's advice, I lit a cigarette. My lighter flared like a flame-thrower.

We reached the outskirts of Putre, stopped the bus, got out and admired the view. I felt heady, stoned – the awesome mountains had already wreaked some strange emotional effect on me. 'BIENVENIDOS PUTRE,' said large letters carved out of the mountainside above the town. Off-puttingly, atop the welcoming sign, was a huge metal-scrolled structure bearing the words 'Coca-Cola', which glinted rather obscenely in the late-afternoon sunlight. The European travellers and eclipse-watchers were to tear it down the next day, to great cheers from the camp-site ravers partying on Putre's hillside.

One day had been allowed for acclimatization before the final climb, another fifteen hundred kilometres further up into the Andes, to where we were to view the eclipse from the shores of Lake Chungaro.

The crew filmed the pre-eclipse sunset over the mountains of Putre. In the ten seconds it took for the sun to slip down behind the nearest peak, the temperature dropped as many degrees. I began to feel pins-and-needles sensations in my arms and legs, and even more light-headedness. Was this the *puna*? Lorena had told us during the drive up the mountain that *puna* was very much an attitude of mind. So I thought positively. I joined the crew for dinner in the hotel to find them all smiling rather beatifically. The coca leaves had arrived. 'Go on, then –

chop 'em out,' I said to Phil Kay, using the popular cocaine parlance.

The law appertaining to possession of coca leaves in Chile seems as woolly as the law concerning 'magic mushrooms' in the UK. As long as they're not 'processed' in any way, they're not illegal. Anyway, the whole point of taking coca leaves was medicinal, to counteract the *puna*. Officially. I was passed a handful of leaves under the table. 'It's like eating a mouthful of bay leaves,' Phil whispered to me. 'But don't swallow them.' I chomped away at what tasted like bitter dry twigs for a minute, and then attempted to spit them out. 'Naw,' said Phil earnestly, 'you've got to *keep* them in your mouth, *chew* on them for at least *ten minutes*.' I felt a bit like a koala bear getting to grips with eucalyptus for the first time. It was hard going getting any sort of high, but after a while I did feel a mild buzz, and the painful sensations in my arms and legs subsided. I wondered how many mounds of coca leaves it would take to refine into a gram of pure cocaine.

In the small town centre of Putre, the locals were getting geared up for their own eclipse celebrations, and they'd laid on as many 'attractions' as possible for the eleven thousand visitors who eventually wound their way up the mountain to this place no one had ever heard of before, but which was now designated as one of the best sites in South America from which to view the eclipse. A herd of llamas had been penned in the town square, presumably as a photo opportunity. With their arched, camel-like necks and protruding, petulant lower lips, the llamas looked bewildered and disgruntled – reluctant media stars.

Meanwhile, in 'downtown' Putre, a *gran fiesta* was getting under way. A makeshift outdoor nightclub had been put together, with an earth floor, a wall of bamboo on one side and corrugated iron on another. Around three sides of the square, three different bands played. On cue, as one finished, another started. Rather impressively, and efficiently. This was *altiplano* music, mountain music, played to be heard across vast areas of the high-altitude Andes. One musician had slung a bass drum over his shoulder, its circumference half the size of a house. Another played the *quena*, a square-shaped flute. Inexplicably, he wore a turquoise hooded sweatshirt with the words 'CALVIN KLEIN' in black letters on the front.

Their women danced in highly stylized fashion in thick woollen socks and flat soft-leather moccasins. Most of the men wore brown-and-white-striped vicuña ponchos and black Frank Sinatra-style fedoras. One of them, who looked like Oliver Reed, swirled me across the dusty dance floor. I didn't know if *altiplano* etiquette allowed me to return to my red plastic seat and bottle of Shopp, a litre's worth of local beer, without offending him.

It seemed that one sad aspect of the European dance club syndrome had found its way up the Andes: that of 'doormen', guest lists and ruthless dress policy. All sorts of semi-veiled faces stared wistfully in at the *gran fiesta* from the wrong side of the box office.

Meanwhile the young travellers had set up their camp on a steep hillside on the edge of the town. It seemed a miracle that so many should have travelled so far from all over the world to find this spot. But this was obviously going to be no ordinary camping party. An efficient-looking campfire had been set up, with a blackened saucepan hitched over it. What was boiling up in the saucepan looked like bright green melon balls in thick glue. 'San Pedro cactus,' one of the campers explained. 'Highly hallu-

212

cinogenic, and parts of the plants are laced with strychnine.'

Although the rave was now definitely going to happen, it was not to be until the next evening, after the eclipse. The travellers, however, wasted no time in getting into party mode. That first night in Putre, with the temperature now well below zero, five travellers were taken to hospital with altitude sickness, and one hapless girl was sent home with severe burns to her arms, having walked into the centre of the campfire believing she was besieged by devils. She was heard saying repeatedly: 'I'm so confused, I'm so confused.' One tall Englishman spent the night entirely naked, despite the temperature, rampaging up and down the hillside declaiming, 'I'm Vic Reeves.' Bad strong brown acid was officially blamed for this unexpected behaviour.

The film crew had more crucial matters on their hands – weather. A recce to Lake Chungaro early in the morning of the day before the eclipse had shown perfect conditions – clear skies, no hint of cloud cover. But now we were to travel back to the lake for the Real Thing. Our greatest fear was cloud, which could obliterate the eclipse completely and render the whole expedition a failure.

We left Putre in pitch darkness at 4.30 a.m. for the hour-long drive to the lakeside. The temperature dropped to teeth-chattering level, and even wearing three layers of leggings, four jumpers and two hats didn't in any way keep out the cold. Not that it mattered. Dawn broke to reveal a breathtaking scene, sub-zero temperatures or no. Lake Chungaro is ringed with snow-capped active volcanoes, the most visible, actually situated in Bolivia, conveniently smoking away like a chimney.

As the time for the eclipse drew closer, the cameraman,

Brian Jobson, set up his equipment on the mountainside above the lake and waited. And watched the skies. Extraordinarily for such a perfect vantage point, the crew was almost alone beside the lake. There were only two cars parked near our minibus, filled with Chilean families, wrapped in bright wool against the cold and, even two hours before the eclipse, singing and clapping and shouting in anticipation of the event. The lake itself was quiet, a few flamingos picking their way around its western edges, and large ducks making V-shaped ripples in their wake as they swam out from the shore. Lorena handed each of us a pair of protective glasses with pink cardboard frames and lenses of thick film to ensure that our eyes were not damaged by staring at the sun when it was eclipsed. As it came up over the lake, there was not the smallest hint of what was to follow.

The entire eclipse was to last an hour from when the moon first passed over the sun's surface. I realized that, for all my months of research and study, I hadn't really got a clue as to what it would be like. I had just imagined that full daylight would change to full darkness, planets such as Venus and Jupiter would be brightly visible for the three minutes of totality, and that would be the end of the experience.

It wasn't like that at all. To the naked eye, as the eclipse began, nothing in the sky looked at all different. There were a few clouds over the horizon, but they were too low to present a threat. A few more small white clouds hung around the necks of the volcanoes, like wispy white chiffon scarves. At the given word I put on the glasses and looked straight ahead at the lake. Nothing, but nothing, was visible, such was the strength of the protective film. Then I looked upward towards the sun. It appeared as a huge pure-white disc. Then a black disc appeared in its top left-hand corner, and began to bite into the white circle. It was strange to look at, and I began to think it was rather one-dimensional, and was perhaps going to be a disappointment. Without the glasses the lake looked much the same as it had at sunrise, except that now the beam of sunlight shining on its surface was becoming narrower and narrower. The sky was turning a deep shade of blue, and the wispy clouds around the volcanoes now threw dark shadows on to the snowy peaks.

I looked up again through the glasses. The flat black moon, or so it appeared, was blocking more and more of the sun's surface, until the sun itself looked like a crescent moon. Now that too was vanishing. I watched the sun becoming a smaller and smaller dot. There was a sense of climax approaching, an orgasmic sensation, a powerful sexual feeling which I found bewildering and unexpected. I also felt strangely embarrassed by it. Surely a solar eclipse wasn't supposed to be sexually arousing!

The moment of totality, with the moon exactly between the earth and the sun, had come. At a word from one of the crew, I took off the glasses, as it was now safe to do so, and looked up at the sky. At that moment I knew why I had travelled across the world, been magnetically pulled, dragged to this spot. Why I had persisted month after month in trying to see the eclipse, an unknown force drawing me to its path. What I now witnessed in the sky was undeniably the most beautiful spectacle nature has to offer. The moon was transformed into a shimmering black orb. Surrounding it was what is known in astronomical circles as the 'diamond-ring effect'. Which in no way describes the brilliance of the light now shooting out from behind the moon. It was a glimpse of the universe, of heaven perhaps, with unimagined colours flashing and tongues of fire flaring in a huge circle around the moon's surface.

It was like a ghostly lamp hanging from the sky, a spectacle granted only to the lucky few who had made the pilgrimage to see it. I promptly burst into a fit of uncontrollable sobbing, as sudden as it was unexpected. Brian, the cameraman, zoomed in on me, and I tried to hide my face in my two fake-fur hats. I looked up again at the sky, not wishing to miss a moment of the three-minute totality. I cried, I think, at the sheer beauty of the eclipse, but there were more emotions going through me as well. The sun and the moon were locked together, it seemed, held by some giant magnetic force, and I felt this overwhelming power holding me in its grip too. It explained the sexual sensation, the sun and the moon coming together as one and producing this violently beautiful image. The colours around the moon danced like fires, and they were colours I'd only ever experienced during the height of orgasm, and had never been able to explain or describe. I looked now at the lake and the mountains, which had changed colour to a deep blue, and oddly appeared to be in bas-relief, as though they were cut-out mountains, not real at all. The snow caps on the volcanoes had turned pink, and the chiffon clouds around them were black. Nothing could have prepared any of us for this.

I could understand now why the Incas worshipped the sun, why a Greek war had ended abruptly when the soldiers looked up and saw a solar eclipse. How easy it would be to start a religion based on what we were witnessing! The only image that for me even remotely compared with what we were now gazing at was a scene from *The Princess and the Goblin*, in which young Princess Irene, being pursued by goblins on a mountainside in the dead of night, only finds her way back home when her mysterious and beautiful grandmother shines a lamp from the top of their castle home, a light shining apparently in the sky, which only Irene can see.

As the totality ended, everyone who was assembled at Lake Chungaro hugged and kissed each other. We swigged a bottle of champagne and the local spirit, *pisco*, with the whooping, cheering Chileans. The emotional atmosphere of the eclipse had affected everyone. Looking back again through the pink cardboard glasses, I could now see the black disc of the moon slipping away from the surface of the sun. The morning sunlight over the lake returned, and the mountains looked real again. It was time to find the rave.

Ancient-looking buses began their laborious journey down from the *altiplano* to the coast, taking the travellers and ravers to Arica. The site for the post-eclipse party was perfect. It was to be held on a small islet, reached by a causeway, beneath a huge bluff called El Morro at the far end of this rather arid town and port on the edge of the Pacific. Night had fallen when we arrived, but the rave organizers had the perfect light show. The bright beam from a conveniently placed lighthouse on the island swung round and round to the German techno beat of the music, the sound being uniquely enhanced by the booming breakers crashing on the rocky shore.

Weary travellers from Putre arrived in small groups throughout the night. Every one of them could talk of nothing but the magic of the eclipse. They spoke of feeling a great energy during totality, and a sense of warmth and friendship towards each other afterwards which they felt

217

would become a permanent bond. Apparently I was not the only person to have sensed the sexual aspect of the eclipse.

During the journey down the mountain, back to the sea, Phil Kay was ruminating on the possibility of having sex during totality. 'Be a bit difficult for two people to have sex and watch the eclipse at the same time,' he decided. 'Your protective glasses would keep falling off!'

XVIII

I felt rather than saw Tony Byrne's presence, lying on a truckle bed parallel to mine in the hospital room in Havana. I sensed he wasn't asleep but worrying about what had happened, and what was *about* to happen. We had known each other for some years, but not well. A chance conversation at the wedding party of Eddy Temple Morris, a BBC colleague, at a club in the King's Road, Chelsea, just a few weeks before, had led to us coming to Cuba together. For Tony it had been initially a business trip and holiday combined, to check out the music scene. For me it had been an unexpected chance to visit a country that had always fascinated me, plus an opportunity to escape England at Christmas, the first since my father had died, and also to blot out my emotions regarding a finally and recently terminated five-year relationship. I was just running away.

After the assault, I'd tried to pick myself up off the ground on to my high-heeled pink suede shoes and realized that the crunching and searing pain in my right leg and my inability to put any weight on it gave unpleasant substance to notions of serious and/or permanent injury. Or, to put it plainly, I realized my leg was fucked. My cries of anguish and alarm had attracted not only the attention of Tony, who had been walking a few yards ahead of me with Angel's wife, Teresa, but most of the still-awake street population of Old Havana. Including curious children, off-duty policemen, lo-fi first-aiders, DIY paramedics, amateur ambulancemen, and wannabe junior doctors. A traffic jam after a freeway road wreck in Los Angeles is generally known as a 'spectator slowdown'. I had now become Havana's biggest free-admission after-midnight spectator-grind-to-a-complete-halt crowd-puller. Young and old, they argued and shouted, in to me totally incomprehensible Cuban Spanish dialect, tugged, pulled and pushed me, and loudly debated which was the best way to fold me into the back seat of a car. Without, I tried to insist, in any way touching or lifting any part of my right leg from hip to toe. I waved my arms about, glared ferociously, shook my head vehemently, screamed and swore. I had no idea where I was supposed to be going, or who was organizing the journey. The operation to slide me into the back seat of Angel's beaten-up Russian Lada took around two and a half hours, culminating, I believe, with me describing as cunts two Cuban cops who tried to slam the car's back door while my right foot was still protruding from it.

Tony told me afterwards that the first hospital I was taken to resembled an abattoir. As I was lying on my back surrounded by a sea of curious, strange faces looking down on me, I wasn't in much of a position to form an objective opinion on its facilities. Only on the pipework which adorned the ceiling. All that concerned me at the time was what is euphemistically known as 'pain management'. I knew that, each time I was lifted on to a stretcher, or raised on to an X-ray table, or rolled off a trolley or lowered into a wheelchair by a meddling if well-meaning but in any case totally unqualified and unprofessional wanderer-in-off-the-street, the chance of further damage and injury was becoming greater by the minute.

I had become public property now, being lugged here, dumped there, left lying on a hard metal stretcher elsewhere and, most alarmingly, being taken to another examination room by means of just a thin cotton sheet used as a body sling. It felt like being thrown out of the third floor of a burning building and agreeing to be caught at ground level by four blind men holding out a square of muslin the size of a postage stamp as a safety net. My black Joseph trousers had remained intact and in place throughout this involuntary tour of Havana's less palatable health care centres, but I was aware that the flower-pattern shirt I was wearing was gaping wide open at the front owing to a missing button, thus showing off a large area of bare torso and white Lejaby French bra. Not a particularly fetching display of decolletage.

This undignified scenario rather paled beside the ignominy of the next humiliation. When my bag had been snatched I'd been holding a half-full pack of Dunhill International cigarettes in my left hand. Nervously and quite unconsciously, I had clutched the red and gold packet so tightly, throughout the entire night's experience, that it was now almost completely crushed by the pressure of my metallic-blue varnished fingernails digging into it. But the cigarette packet as an object (any brand, full or empty) had always been something of a security symbol to me, and it was especially so on this particular night. So when, out of nowhere, a Cuban bloke with a miraculously perfect grasp of English approached me as I lay rolling and moaning and said, 'Could I have one of your cigarettes?', I was at least able to muster up both the strength and the fury to shout back at him, 'Why don't you just fuck right off!'

I lost count of the number of times I was shifted from table to trolley, and I had no comprehension of the discussions going on around me. Finally I was manoeuvred on to what felt like a more solid kind of stretcher, which had wheels under it, and I felt myself undergoing a gliding movement like the drawer of a filing cabinet being slid closed as I was shifted into an ambulance. More X-rays followed, more strange Cuban eyes looked down into mine. Then I was lying in a bed in a small, brightly lit room – a room where I was to spend the next nine, and as it turned out the most crucial, days of my life. I still had all my clothes on. Under my shirt my bra was unhooked at the back, half on and half off, but I couldn't pull myself up on to one elbow to free the straps. The pain in my leg was relentless, and I continued to clutch my thigh in the hope that I could knit the smashed bone back together just by positive thinking. I still didn't know what the diagnosis was.

The room in which I now found myself was decorated in a cool pale blue with a white ceiling. But I had no idea where it was, or what building or organization it belonged to. I was dimly aware that I'd been given a couple of painkillers when I had arrived, but ludicrously and inexplicably I had decided to hide them, to hoard them under a pillow in case the pain got worse. Pure animal behaviour – the reason a dog buries a bone, or scoffs food in case there is no more forthcoming! Then a man in a suit, wearing a bright red tie and spectacles that served to emphasize dark junkie-type rings round his eyes, appeared at the end of my bed. He spoke English, said he was a doctor, and announced rather sonorously that I needed an operation.

'*Operation?... I'm not having an operation!*' I screamed with all the indignation I had left in my energy cabinet. And not without good reason. Cuba, along with its sea, sun, sand, sex, drugs and salsa, is a Third World country with limited medical supplies. As well as having read warnings in every guidebook about the danger of having surgery in Cuba, I had seen enough at first hand in Romania not to risk the effects of used syringes or Aids-infected blood if a transfusion became necessary. Just as much to the point was that I was scared witless at the prospect of an anaesthetic. I hadn't fancied it during either of my experiences of childbirth – the first time probably because I was totally high and out of my tree on pethidine, and the second because the birth was quick and there just wasn't time. And, probably because of my interminable years of smoking, I had always been convinced that one whiff of whatever they make you inhale through that sinister black mask they stick over your mouth when you're anaesthetized would be an instant killer for me.

The doctor – the house surgeon as it turned out – shrugged at my outpourings. 'It is your decision,' he said. 'But I'm telling you that if you do not have an operation you will develop thrombosis. You have a very bad fracture of the femur.' He smiled curtly and added, 'It makes no difference to me whether you have this operation or not. I shall be working here at the hospital anyway. But you must make up your mind very quickly, or your condition will deteriorate fast.'

He told me that the clinic where I had been brought had a very high standard of medical care and that I would be in safe hands. And I thought, 'Well, he would say that, wouldn't he?' Exhausted though I was by the pain and shock of what had happened the previous sleepless night,

I forced myself to try to think my way calmly out of this dilemma, which was the worst I'd ever knowingly faced.

'Right,' I announced to Tony, 'I've got to get out of here. Let's get hold of the British embassy. The consul.' It was now around 7.30 a.m. on Monday, 23 December. I knew that in Britain almost every office and official establishment would have closed for Christmas. Fortunately there was a telephone beside my bed. Unfortunately all calls had to be routed through the different shifts of hospital switchboard operators, none of whom spoke English, or any language other than Spanish. Tony decided to check on Angel, and also engage Teresa's help to try to contact the British embassy. It transpired that I was now in a room at the Clínica Central Cira García, in an area of Havana called Miramar. This was an entirely private hospital catering only for tourists and diplomats. Angel, who had presumably brought me here, was not, as a Cuban, eligible for treatment. Hardly very egalitarian in its interpretation of the Communist creed, I thought. But the Cira García was just a medical equivalent of a dollar-only shop, the sort I'd seen in the Soviet Union. My room was well appointed by any standard, like a small hotel room, and manned by an extraordinarily large number of staff. Whether they were orderlies, physiotherapists, doctors, nurses, caterers or cleaners I had no idea, but they all streamed in and out, unannounced, eyeing me curiously and proclaiming '*Buenos días*', denying me any privacy. Not that I was too concerned on that score. All I wanted was to plan my getaway, and as soon as possible.

My only complaint about Cubana, the airline with which I'd flown to Havana, was that it did not provide any passenger maps, and I did not have much idea of the proximity of Cuba to anywhere else. Florida was obviously

224

closest, but the thirty-year US blockade meant that it was not possible to fly from Cuba to the United States . . . except on board those illegal 'ghost' flights I'd heard about which left every night from somewhere on the Cuban coast to Miami. Maybe I could get on one of those. Alex, my son, was at that moment en route from London to Rio de Janeiro, which was sort of in the same direction. Throb, the guitarist from Primal Scream, was on holiday with his wife, Anita, in Barbados, also in the Caribbean, so that *must* be quite close. I could get them to help me.

All delirious fanciful thinking on my part, I suppose. It hadn't really sunk in that not only had I had my bag with all my money, my passport and my exit visa stolen, but I couldn't even move. Don't anyone tell me there's no substance to astrology: I had never felt more like the fighting, determined Arian, fired up by the challenge of getting out of Cuba by whatever ingenious means it would take. But the plan was not exactly kicking off to a great start. All the phone lines to the British embassy were out of order, I was told. Finally Tony raised a second secretary to the British consulate. This rather harassed-looking grey-haired man didn't initially seem too impressed to be summoned to my bedside the day before the Christmas holiday. 'You may have got a broken leg, but people have *died* here,' he said. Whether he meant that British expats he'd dealt with had died in Havana or in this particular hospital he didn't specify.

Then, rather lugubriously, he told me of the unfortunate fate of another tourist wearing a rucksack like mine. Desperate bag-snatchers had come up behind him and attempted to cut off the straps with a machete. Unfortunately the tourist's ears got lopped off instead. I'd thought about nothing else for hours, but when it came to outlining my escape plans to this world-weary diplomat I felt a little foolish. But I launched into him, anyway. 'You know the British Forces Broadcasting Service, right? Well, I work for them, as well as for the BBC, right? And they've got a radio station at the British military base in Belize, right? Which is in the Caribbean, or Central or Latin America or somewhere really near Cuba, right? Well, you just call them up now, they'll know who I am, and they'll airlift me out of here and fly me back to London. You know what these pilots are like – they love a challenge, a mission of mercy, saving a damsel in distress. They'll be up for it . . . Double up for it.'

The diplomat didn't seem impressed by my outlandish plan. In fact he didn't even seem to regard it as outlandish. He pointed out that the British presence in Belize was shrinking, and he doubted that there would be a spare plane available for me.

'Look,' I said, breezily, 'I know all about "draw down" [gradual troop pull-out],' trying to impress the diplomat with my knowledge of British military jargon, 'but there's got to be enough of our guys there to cope with getting me out.' Our man in Havana shook his head solemnly.

Right, I would have to play my ace, then. With all the solemnity and dignity I could muster, and not knowing the state of my appearance – my make-up and hand mirror had been in the stolen rucksack – I announced the following to him. 'You may not know this – indeed I don't expect you to know this, and under normal circumstances there is no way that I would mention this to you – but I happen to be one of Prince Charles's, the Prince of Wales's, twelve ambassadors to the Prince's Trust. So will you *please* get on the case and inform HRH of my situation and I am sure he will organize a plane from the Queen's Flight to take me back to London immediately.' Ha, ha, that would do it. That would get the so-called out-of-order phones and faxes humming. *Now* there would be some action.

I was sure Prince Charles wouldn't mind me calling in a favour now after all the time I had – quite happily and willingly – put in for the Robin Hood outfit that is the Prince's Trust. But yet again the second secretary to Her Majesty's consulate looked strangely unmoved. 'He thinks I'm making it all up! He thinks I'm mad, delirious,' I thought.

The Grim Reaper of a surgeon reappeared at the end of my bed. 'Have you made up your mind yet?' he asked solemnly. 'Are you going to have this operation? You really don't have much more time to decide.'

Although I had absolutely no intention of letting him within a football field's length of me with a scalpel, I realized that if the worst came to the worst . . . Well, there was no point in rubbing him up the wrong way.

'Yeah, yeah, I'll let you know soon. Very soon.'

Gradually the whole wretchedness of the situation began to enwrap me like a dark, dense blanket. Although I still had no idea how serious my condition was, it was dawning on me that I just might not get out of Cuba for Christmas.

At Angel's, Tony was taking a really close look at the insurance policies that we had taken out to cover the Cuban trip. Meanwhile I began to dwell on the consequences of what had happened to me. What if I refused to have an operation? How serious was thrombosis? Was it life-threatening? I had no one but the surgeon's word for it that the break could be mended. What if he botched it up and I ended up crippled for life, unable to walk, unable to work, unable to support myself, an amputee perhaps? What if I got back to England to find that I'd made the worst decision of my life, a totally irreversible one?

The insurance company would not repatriate me at this time. It was decided that an operation to put a piece of metal ('Probably a bit of an old Russian Ilyushin,' some bright spark observed) and some screws into the bone would go ahead. I was not given any option, I made a private deal with myself not to smoke any more tobacco for the foreseeable future, the Grim Reaper suddenly became positively the Grin Reaper, smiling and shaking my hand. I looked forward now to what I'd heard was the good hit to be expected with the pre-med. Sadly, it was no big deal narcotically speaking, I have to report.

'Hi, Annie. How are you feeling?' It was now Boxing Day, and the phone beside my bed had rung at around 7 a.m.

'Who is this?' I felt surprisingly alert; and suspicious.

'My name is Pilar. I'm calling from London.'

I didn't know anyone called Pilar. 'So which paper is it, then?' I asked resignedly. There was a silence. 'The *Daily Star*,' came the reluctant reply.

'And how did you know about me being here?' I purred into the phone.

'I'm afraid I can't tell you that,' said Pilar pertly. She was, of course, observing the first rule of journalism: never reveal your sources. Still, I reckoned that as she'd got through to me in Havana first and had got the beat on the story, she might do me a few favours. I asked her to call various people at Radio 1. Throughout this whole escapade I was concerned that I was supposed to have been flying back to London on Christmas Night to do a live Radio 1 Show on 27 December, and that those in charge of the network very possibly didn't know what had happened to me. Well, Pilar certainly got that sorted. Just hours later Claire Sturgess from a late-night on-air studio at Radio 1 had got through to me, having read the first edition of the next day's *Daily Star*. 'What's all this about "may never walk again"?' she asked, sounding alarmed, and she read me a front-page quote from 'a hospital spokesman'. It was scenarios like this that had made me quit tabloid or, as it was once known, 'popular' journalism.

I was totally unprepared for the volume of response to Pilar's 'exclusive'. Early the following morning calls came through thick and fast from the *Daily Express*, Radio 4, the *Daily Telegraph*, Radio 1's news programme *Newsbeat*, and numerous agency reporters. I had no option but to pick up the phone in case it was family or close friends; it was impossible to screen calls via the switchboard.

Outside my room the sky shone a hot blue, and a palm tree neatly framed by my window waved its green and yellow leaves tantalizingly to remind me I was still in the Caribbean. I lay prostrate on my bed, my wrist wired up to a drip, with plastic tubes miraculously having grown out of my right thigh for 'drainage', as had been not very clearly explained to me. These tubes seemed to have an alarming amount of bright-red fluid running though them, but I assumed this was all part of the post-op parapher-nalia. I actually wasn't wearing any clothes, I think – just a sheet covering me from my tits down to the tops of my legs. There was no plaster or other evidence of the surgery apart from a wodge of cotton wool over the stitches. Although the entire female staff of the hospital had favour-ably exclaimed '*Bonita! Bonita!*' after studying my blue-varnished fingernails with obvious curiosity, I was missing my make-up bag and mirror rather badly. Fortunately my blue Italian mirror shades were still in my possession.

Pilar called again, now claiming to be my new 'bezzie' friend, and vowed that she would call every other day to see how I was. For which you can read 'follow-up'. What did she think I was – daft? When she then asked if it would be OK if someone came and took a picture of me recovering in my hospital bed, I told her that I thought this request was in extremely bad taste, especially after her report that I might 'never walk again' had frightened me, my family and my friends. I told her where to get off, and slammed the phone down.

I was now beginning to understand the hospital 'routine' at the Cira García. There wasn't one. Anyone could wander into my room at any time, unannounced. Most of the time the door was left wide open anyway. There was no such thing as respect for one's 'modesty' – not that I had much of that left by now anyway. I'd get a full body bath, including soaping all the intimate nooks and crannies, from either a male or a female nurse, depending on who was on duty. The main worry was who might come waltzing though the door while one was having warm water poured between one's outstretched bare thighs. I was becoming edgy. Understandably, I think, given that on one occasion a gang of journalists came streaming in through the door and announced, 'We are from Reuters and we have brought you some vegetables.'

My only means of gaining attention was to press a bedside buzzer. It played *'Für Elise'* – probably the first piece of music I could have identified as a child, as it was a piano piece practised endlessly by my next-door neighbour, Jennifer Baguley. *'Für Elise'* could be heard day and night echoing through the corridors of the hospital. I knew this because I was woken every hour on the hour throughout the night to have the drip altered and my blood pressure checked. It occurred to me how ironic it would be if *'Für Elise'* turned out to be the first and last piece of music I should ever hear.

Suddenly a young blond bloke appeared in my room. He was English and said he was from the *Guardian*. He didn't draw too much attention to the quiet burly chap who sidled into the room behind him. I spotted his cameras straight off, and slapped the shades on immediately. But I knew that, having got this far, there was no way this photographer would leave without snatching a picture. Inwardly I gave the pair of them points for ingenuity, for being in the right place at the right time, but I also knew I was trapped, caught in the cat-and-mouse chase of an ongoing international story on a slack news day over Christmas. At least, that is how I saw it at the time. I have no idea to this day what medication was being effortlessly fed into my body via the drip – an excellent idea for partying, I thought, an intravenous drip, endlessly balancing your metabolism with stimulants, uppers or downers – but I was mentally together enough to realize that, without the benefit of a stylist, make-up artist, wardrobe mistress or even a hand mirror, I was totally vulnerable in terms of what these shots were going to look like. I didn't want to come across as some pathetic mugger's victim. Even so, I was quite shocked when I eventually saw the pictures that were splashed in colour across the front page of the *Daily Express* and several other British national papers. Blue shades, blue nails, a skimpy bit of sheet, and precious little else. It all but made a lie of John Cooper Clarke's famous line 'You'll never see a nipple in the *Daily Express.'*

The *Guardian* bloke, however, once I'd forgiven him for smuggling in the photographer, became my personal guardian, warding off TV news crews and other media hacks who were apparently doorstepping the hospital. I was also picking up the cultural vibe that in Cuba people would come to visit you after an operation as though it were something to be congratulated on, like a christening or a bar mitzvah. Maybe they wanted to celebrate the fact that I'd survived. And so, when the hapless Angel trooped in, with him came all his relatives. I knew he felt guilty about what had happened to me, but not as guilty as I felt, seeing the poor man's weighted and plastered arm. It seemed a very primitive form of treatment for his broken collarbone. I thought back to the conversation we'd had before the attack, in which he had invited me to visit Chile, where he was going to be setting up a multi-purpose arts centre, and where both his sons were practising doctors. I was so tearfully touched by his visit that I could not properly respond. Even so, this social ritual, the mass visiting of the sick, which has largely disappeared in England, did amuse me.

I didn't know how to entertain these Spanish-speaking visitors as they lined up round the walls of my small hospital room, nor could I think what to say to them after we had all admired the bouquets of flowers which the media had thoughtfully sent me. My small Spanish vocabulary could have been greatly enhanced by the phrase book I had in my possession, but I couldn't read as my spectacles had been in the stolen bag. With the constant traffic of hospital staff, the room was fast becoming crammed with people. Then the police arrived.

The first wave was a team of regular cops, who wanted details of the attack, descriptions of my assailants and of the items that had been stolen. Routine stuff, though fairly pointless, I thought. I would not be able to positively identify my attacker. The police followed a particular line of questioning. Was the man or men who attacked me black? I replied that the guys I'd seen on the street corners immediately before I was robbed were dark – they certainly weren't blond, blue-eyed Aryans – but I wasn't buying into this potential racism shit.

The next day more police arrived, looking a touch more senior – larger badges, bigger handguns, but basically asking the same questions. Not that it mattered much now, given my situation, but my bag had contained some US $500 in cash when it was stolen, which I had changed from traveller's cheques when Tony and I had left our other London travelling mates, Mick P. and Johnny O., after visiting them in the resort of Varadero. The cash had been in denominations of $100, $50 and $20 notes.

What I had failed to realize was that the attention given to my misadventure by the international media was spelling disaster for the Cuban tourist industry. Even in the short time I'd spent in the country it had become apparent to me that tourism was Cuba's only real asset. Since the collapse of the Soviet Union, which had backed Cuba with one US $ a day per capita, the country was becoming more and more financially isolated, more and more dependent on incoming tourists' hard currency. It was being financially squeezed further each day by the recent US Helms-Burton legislation. Yet there was much evidence of inspirational defiance. 'SOCIALISMO O MUERTE' screamed the two-foot-high graffitti on the modern tower-blocked streets of Nuevo Habana.

Unbeknown to me, the British press had dragged El Presidente into the scenario. Fidel was reported to be sending me flowers. He was to visit me in hospital. He didn't, but his chief of police did. The substantial coverage of what had happened to me – not just in Britain, had reached friends as far afield as South Africa, Indonesia, the USA and via the Internet – had clearly worried the Cuban authorities. So the chief of police, who wore a bigger badge, toted a heavier handgun and smoked a fatter cigar than any of his lesser colleagues, now told me gravely how he and his fellow police officers had worked tirelessly day and night to catch my attackers and bring them to justice. To prove it – whaddya know? – they had got a result!

The police chief held out two passport-size, black-and-white, head-and-shoulders 'mug-shot' photographs of two young men, one of whom looked truly terrifying. He didn't have 'mad, staring eyes', as so many descriptions of violent criminals seem to feature; it was his mouth, twisted and contorted like that of a snarling, cornered animal, that was so disturbing to behold. He could well have been my attacker; on the other hand, he may well not have been. The same could be said of the less terrifying figure. It would have been easier to identify the muggers by handprints. My right arm above the elbow still bore the deep imprint of the hand that had grabbed me from behind in a painful outline of bruises.

But the police were not asking me to identify or verify the photographs. Identification was a fait accompli. The two blokes were under arrest and awaiting trial. The over-riding evidence that they were guilty of robbing me, stated the chief of police, was that my stolen money had been found in their possession. Or rather most of the money. They had come to return this to me. My curiosity took over. I began grilling the police chief. 'How and where did you catch these men? Where did you find the money?

Was there any trace of the rest of my belongings? When would the trial take place? If the two young men were to be found guilty, how long were their sentences likely to be?'

I was told that I would not be called as a witness; the two young men would be represented by defence lawyers, and if found guilty they faced between eight and fifteen years' imprisonment, depending on whether or not they had any 'previous'. In answer to my first question, the police chief intimated that a girl had grassed up the two young men and led the police to where they had stashed my stolen cash. And so now, if I would please sign a form to accept receipt of it, the police would hand me back my money.

Except that it wasn't my money. What the Havana police chief was counting out on to my hospital bed was the grubbiest collection of old greenbacks I'd ever seen. He dealt out the first hundred dollars or so in single-denomination notes. I was speechless. The implications were horrific. If two Cubans had been arrested purely on the basis of possessing an unreasonably large amount of US dollars, and these dollars were not mine, then there didn't seem much of a case to answer. Maybe these dollars came from a slush fund, for the purpose of face-saving and damage management on behalf of the Cuban tourist business. Well, you could understand that, couldn't you?

I had thought, and still do, about the culprit – not angrily or in terms of wanting vengeance, but wondering if he had any idea of the long-term effects on the person he had attacked. If he and his friend had not also assaulted and injured Angel, I might have thought that the attack on me had been perpetrated by someone who did not know his own strength, who had never intended to bring me down in such a vicious and brutal manner. I have no idea if the person who broke my leg was imprisoned, or if innocent men – since the general consensus seemed to be that the attack and robbery involved two people – have served a sentence so that law and order will have been seen to have been enforced in Cuba, demonstrating that the streets of Havana are safe for foreign tourists. I doubt if I will ever know.

Leaving Cuba to return, stretchered, to the UK on New Year's Eve was a nerve-racking as well as a painful affair. It was more like planning an escape from a prisoner-of-war camp than a return trip from a holiday. The embassy was edgy, worried that I didn't have all the correct documents to get through Emigration at the airport in Havana. A British nurse had been flown out to acccompany me back, and with her she had brought our flight tickets to London – Tony having stayed on in Cuba with me – but the Cuban officials were suspicious, questioning who had paid for these tickets. Again I was shifted from stretcher to stretcher, trolley to trolley, on to the flight at Havana, off in the next day's early-morning rain in Madrid by baggage handlers who blew their garlic-fumed breath in my face as they lugged me down the steps of one aircraft and up on to the next.

By now I had experienced my first 'Does he take sugar?' episode. The Iberia flight had finally left Cuba with me rather precariously balanced on top of and across six seats. When the stewardess pushed her drinks trolley past me, I leaned down and said, *'Dos Cuba libres, por favor, y dos botellas de vino rojo.'* I had not had a cigarette since arriving in the hospital in Miramar, but I was damned if I was going to give up other pleasures. The nurse leapt out of her seat in alarm. 'If you drink too much I won't give you your sleeping pills,' she threatened. This was too much.

'Listen,' I thundered at her, 'I normally live on a diet of painkillers, sleeping pills and alcohol, so please respect my wishes.' Rock 'n' roll she certainly wasn't, and nor did she understand what a taxing prospect it was to be going to run the phalanx of waiting reporters, photographers and cameramen at Heathrow which I had been tipped off to expect. But when I got there the strangest thing happened. I was lifted from the aircraft into an ambulance, and for the first time since I'd been attacked I broke down and cried. What prompted this was not some misty-eyed knee-jerk reaction to returning to 'Blighty'; it was purely and simply the sound of the ambulanceman's reassuring London accent saying, 'You all right, love?' I realized that now I would no longer have to gesticulate and worry about being manhandled, damaged, dropped or hurt by people with whom I could not communicate and whose language I could not speak. Well, not until I got caught up in the finer tangled bureaucratic skeins of the NHS, anyway!

I wrote this four months less a day since the attack. For the first time I had managed to get to my feet and hobble without crutches. On that night I met up again, for the first time since our carefree clubbing nights in Varadero, with Mick P. and Johnny O. Mick took me to a new venue in Notting Hill which was playing old-skool acid house and seemed to be mainly frequented by thirtysomething coke dealers wallowing in nostalgia for the good old days of 1988. For the first time since the attack I had been to a club, and enjoyed the experience, without the fear of being knocked off my crutches by a nudge or a brush with a stranger. And without the gnawing worry that I would have to negotiate a frightening staircase to reach the ladies' room or the exit. I couldn't have been more pleased, as though I had picked up where I had left off, clubbing and enjoying life, without that split-second incident which all but wrecked my life and caused untold anxiety and worry to my family and friends. I felt as if a circle had closed, Though I didn't know then that further complications were to set in, and my problems were far from over.

A tall, auburn-haired girl called Sarah introduced herself to me in the ladies' room and said, 'Thank you for all the many, many hours of pleasure you've given me.' Yeeessss! Back to form, I thought.

Lying in the hospital bed in Cuba, I had said to myself, 'If I get out of here and cured, then no one ain't gonna fuck with me no more.' I do feel different now – stronger, less intimidated by situations that previously would have frightened me. Like operating a studio desk and running the entire Radio 1 network in the middle of the night, completely alone and without any technical back-up. Now I realize that it might be scary, but it isn't life-threatening.

AFTERWORD

Sunday, 8.34 a.m. I've just returned home from the most unexpected night I could ever have imagined. At 1.50 a.m. this morning I discovered via the newsroom of the BBC that Princess Diana had been injured in a car crash in a tunnel in Paris. She had a broken arm and cuts. Dodi Fayed was dead, but Diana had *walked* away from the crashed car, and was *receiving guests*. This is what was said. At the BBC. By the newsroom, two hours before I was due on air at 4 a.m. Under normal circumstances I would never ever call the newsroom, situated in a different building from where Radio 1 broadcasts, more than five minutes before a bulletin. The only reason I found out about the Diana crash so early on this morning was through the conscientiousness of a dark, crop-haired young music enthusiast called Susan Masters. She had never worked with me before and was acting as producer on my first show for six weeks. I had been recuperating from a second operation after the attack in Cuba, this time to remove the metal pin that had been inserted in Havana, which had come dangerously adrift. Susan checked with the newsroom early only to ascertain where its studio position would be at 4.30 a.m., the time of the next scheduled newscast. Now she told me what had happened.

239

I had total responsibility for the musical content of my show, and I started pulling the running order around, taking out anything that might have been deemed 'insensitive'. Perhaps the BBC would regard as 'insensitive' a track I'd planned to play from David Holmes's new album *Let's Get Killed*, a track called 'Don't Die Just Yet' – great album, unluckiest possible release date in recording history: 1 September 1997.

Two o'clock came. Princess Diana was still just injured. There was no indication that her condition might be worsening or heading towards terminal. Now it was 3 a.m. The management called in by phone. Kate Marsh, Radio 1's editor, said to me, 'Darling, just be cool.' I said I would be, but it was still just Susan and me manning Radio 1. By mischance, all the senior management were out of London that weekend. I felt a not-unfamiliar icy calm take over. I was still juggling with the running order. Susan and I carried the box of tunes from the production office into the basement studio at twenty minutes to four. I felt the familiar womb-like sensation once I was in the studio, happy after all those weeks away to be going back on air live. On the computer screen that showed the running order for Radio 1 that day someone had posted a note: 'Annie is back, a nation rejoices.'

From the reports coming in it seemed that Diana's injuries were not serious. It crossed my mind to make some sort of joke about her breaking her arm and sharing my jinx – two Radio 1 producers, Chris Lycett and Chris Whatmaugh, had each broken a leg since my incident in Cuba. Tony Byrne had phoned earlier to say he'd broken his ankle the previous night. Join the club, Diana, join the club.

It was decided that we would go ahead with the plan

for a competition to give away tickets for the upcoming Primal Scream and Roni Size London concerts. Adam Orton, long-term Head of Shouts, the man who made witty sense for me out of the garbled, smashed, stoned listeners' phone messages on the show, had driven nine hours from Cornwall to come to the broadcast; he deserved to have some phone calls to answer. Then there was another call, from a different, unfamiliar, klaxon-shrieking in-studio phone. I didn't answer it; Susan did. As soon as the microphone was off and a record on, I was buzzing at her, 'Who was that? What is happening?' Unconfirmed rumours that Diana was dead, she said. What? *Dead?* From a broken arm? No, no, no way . . . This was from *whom*, I wanted to know? *What* source? The French government, apparently. Maybe this was a hoax, I thought.

Part of the BBC royal death procedure is to check. Always check with the BDM – broadcast duty manager – before making any on-air announcement, in case of a hoax. But now I was instructed by phone that the news bulletins would be stepped up. We had been taking bulletins on the half-hour; now they were to be every fifteen minutes. I was still hacking away at the running order, thinking, 'Not from just a broken arm and some cuts . . . But what if . . .' And here was the BBC's dilemma, as I saw it. Now that Diana had divorced Charles and been stripped of her Royal Highness title, did she really belong to the Royal Family, in respect of whom we had strict guidelines to adhere to, and instructions on how to proceed, in the event of a death? Which was to play specially selected sombre tunes back to back from two obit CDs kept in a special cupboard in the studio. For use, we thought, in the eventuality of the death of the Queen Mother. I had never paid too much mind to it, figuring that the palace was unlikely to issue a statement on the death of a member of the Royal Family at four o'clock in the morning. This situation, of course, was rather different.

I broadcast through 4 a.m., 4.15, 4.30. The klaxon studio phone had shrieked out again. Andy Parfitt, then assistant controller, now controller of Radio 1, had called. Susan wouldn't tell me till after 4.40 what he had said. '*Why* not?' I kept asking her. '*Why* won't you tell me what he said?' 'Do the next link, get to the next news junction, then I'll tell you,' she said. I thought maybe Andy had called because he'd felt that giving away Primal Scream tickets was inappropriate. But in fact he had rung in to say that Diana was dead. Confirmed but not yet announced. I played 'Take California' by Propeller Heads, a bit up-tempo perhaps, but I was running out of instrumentals, and Susan had no time to leave the studio to get more music.

I was making judgements about the music and the changing situation minute by minute, trying to work out what to do next. Thinking ahead. The official announcement still hadn't been made. Then Adrian Pearce, the newsreader, said it: 'Diana, Princess of Wales, is dead.' Now out came the obit CD, and I was told to play the same six tunes back to back, by Dreadzone, and Soul II Soul, and Massive Attack. The CD had not been used before, and the player skipped judderingly across the tracks. The newsroom fax machine had broken down, and now I was told to read out a handwritten Adrian Pearce-dictated quote from Mohammed Al Fayed saying that the Princess was 'irreplaceable'. Nothing about his son. Odd, that.

This was what was going though my head: just get to the next link, don't make any mistakes, play the right tune at the right speed, keep it simple. This is what you're paid for, to keep calm and keep broadcasting. Keep giving out the frequency, ninety-seven to ninety-nine FM, BBC Radio 1. People might have just tuned in, just woken up, heard this news, will be bewildered. Or just come in smashed, from a club, as a lot of them told me later they had. 'Ninety-seven to ninety-nine FM, BBC Radio 1, a news update coming up after this . . .'

I'd been at Diana's first-ever gig, her first solo public engagement, when she switched on the Christmas lights in Regent Street. At the men's shop Austin Reed. I was there because I had some tie-in with their groovy young men's boutique. I was the voice on their commercials. I'd come out of curiosity. It was pouring with rain, and I struggled to get through the crowd outside the store and the barriers and the police with my white invitation card clutched in my hand – no umbrella, drenched, hair plastered to my head. Inside Austin Reed there was a sort of wavy, higgledy-piggledy receiving line for Lady Di, not very well organized. Clement Freud was in the line next to me, and on the other side of me was Cilla Black. I remember deliberately not curtseying to Diana, and asking her if she listened to Radio 1. 'No, Capital,' she blurted straight out. Oh well, a bit of disingenuous honesty there, then. The press rushed in afterwards, demanding, 'What did she say . . . what did she say?' and I had thought then, 'How ridiculous, a nineteen-year-old with, by her own admission, one O-level, and they're hanging on her every word.'

The next time I saw Diana was at some charity lunch, in London, all women guests – and famous ones, like Shirley Conran, who swooped in wearing a fearsome big hat and in a far grander way than Diana. Diana just looked like she wanted to have a laugh. She'd catch your eye across the table and grin. 'Duran Duran still your favourite pop group?' I teased her on this occasion. 'Ooh, I tell all the bands they're my favourites now,' she said. Then it was Birmingham at the NEC. I'd got roped in to do the after-show TV interviews at a Prince's Trust concert. There was a late after-after-show party. Charles and Diana were still a couple then, but mingling separately in the crowd. I asked Diana if there had been one act she had especially enjoyed, and she said, 'Yes. Nigel Kennedy.' 'Like to meet him?' I asked. 'Don't move, I'll go and find him.' The world's most famous violinist and Aston Villa supporter was piling into the canapés at the far end of the royal reception area. ''Ere, Nige,' I said, 'Di wants to meet you.' I weaved him through the crowd to the middle, where Diana was still standing rooted to the crowded spot. She had done her homework and knew that Nigel had studied at the Juilliard School in New York, and commented on how she'd hated being at boarding school herself. Then a minion whispered in her ear. 'We've got to go now,' she said, 'to catch the train.' Nigel and I looked surprised. 'You'll never get a train out of Birmingham at this time of night,' we said. Diana looked acutely embarrassed. 'Um, well, we've got our own.'

Only two weeks before Princess Diana's death there had been an Elvis tribute night on TV. I'd been in Brighton, visiting friends. The flickering TV picture in the corner of Maria's sitting room had given rise to one of those 'Where were you when . . .' conversations, which then led someone in the room to pose the question: Who nowadays would attract international Elvis-level mourning? We all replied unhesitatingly: 'Princess Diana.'

My radio show was nearly finished. It was 6 a.m. I realized that the feeling of quiet grinding stress, the envelopment of icy calm, had happened to me before. Presenting the live TV tribute to John Lennon the day he was shot.

A week after Diana's death a caller phoned in to my show and said, 'Very sorry and all that, about Princess Diana, but have you still got any of those tickets for Primal Scream?'

EPILOGUE

The Mayans didn't believe that the sighting of a solar eclipse was a good excuse for a party. Quite the reverse. To them the 'black sun' effect meant that there were bad times just around the corner. I had cheerfully brushed this superstition aside, but in retrospect I was to be in for some far from happy days. Maybe it was coincidence, but . . . I was injured in a car accident on the M25 and got a crushed sternum through the pressure of the seatbelt.

Professionally I had survived another Night of the Long Knives at Radio 1, where Matthew Bannister had come in as controller to bring about some swingeing Birtian changes. The air of paranoia and mistrust had reached new intensity. I was instructed to go alone, telling no one, to a specially appointed secret room in the depths of Broadcasting House. There Matthew solemnly asked me if I would like to take over another slot on Radio 1. But he said that I must swear secrecy even from my then current producer, Pete Ritzema. I couldn't believe how grave the scenario had become with Matthew, a bloke I'd been used to having a lunchtime pint or two with in the Rising Sun pub across the street from GLR in Marylebone High Street.

The BBC's Stalinesque techniques were devised to prevent press leaks. Following my new secret appointment

I was phoned by the *Sunday Times* and asked if I knew whether I was to stay or to go. 'I'm so sorry,' I said slowly and sadly, 'I'm afraid I can't tell you.' The paper, along with many other publications, concluded that I was expected to be given the push. The next day a friend of mine said, 'I've seen a picture of you flashed up on breakfast TV with a great red cross all over your face. Have you been fired?'

I hadn't, but I'd almost had to bluff the press that I had. These were not easy times. Most of my colleagues were being sacked, or taking voluntary redundancy or early retirement. There was a plethora of unhappy leaving parties.

I was becoming increasingly concerned about the health of my father. He was in constant pain due to a botched prostate operation some years beforehand, but, ever cheerful, he never complained. My mother had died some twenty-five years earlier, and he had now only his younger brother, Bill, left from his own family. And me. Several times he was committed to hospital after a heart attack or pneumonia, and I tried to prepare myself for the worst. Over the years my love and utter respect for him had grown and grown.

I'd known when I was a child that my parents hadn't been very happy together, but my father alluded to this only once afterwards. 'We weren't really suited,' was all he would say. How chivalrous is that? I've tried to take many leaves from his book, and not putting people down or slagging them off – unless they really deserve it, of course – is a trait I hope I've inherited from him.

My father was attractive to women, and I often wondered whether he had contemplated a second marriage. It took years before I could bring myself to ask him about this. He replied, 'I didn't want to upset you!' I tore my hair out thinking of the possible happiness he had denied himself for my sake. And I certainly would have had no objections. But . . .

My father died two months short of his ninetieth birthday, in the early summer of 1996, in his sleep and peacefully I hope in his own house with his cherished garden of birds in full feather, and flowers and fruit trees in bloom. There's always a song, isn't there? That summer there were two that were never off the radio that will always remind me of his dying: quite inappropriately the 'Lager Lager Lager' song 'Born Slippy' by Underworld, and the Fugees' cover version of 'Killing Me Softly'. I found quite extraordinary escape and solace in Euro '96, on TV, and even found myself at Old Trafford with a couple of members of Primal Scream experiencing the thrill of my first international football match Germany *v.* Italy. Incidentally, other don't-play-this-to-me-or-I'll-burst-into-tears tunes are the following:

1. Judy Garland, 'Somewhere over the Rainbow' (my mother)
2. Bing Crosby, 'Where the Blue of the Night Meets the Gold of the Day' (early days – my father)
3. Frank Sinatra, 'Three Coins in the Fountain' (my mother)
4. Aretha Franklin, 'I Say a Little Prayer' (break-up of first marriage)
5. The Beatles, 'Hey Jude' (ditto)
6. Dion, 'The Wanderer' (birth of Alex)
7. Percy Sledge, 'When a Man Loves a Woman' (birth of Lucy)
8. The Who, 'You Better You Bet' (break-up of second marriage)

In the days between his death and his funeral, and for weeks after in the hot dry London days in June, the uncircling air refusing to move the hot curtains at Westbourne Park, my usual desire to get out of town and go back to the sea left me completely. I wanted to stay near my dad. Keep a sort of vigil. He'd chosen to be buried. I could not stop thinking about him being alone in the ground. At his funeral Lucy looked more upset than I'd ever seen her. Alex had stood over the family dugout space at Richmond Cemetery as the gravemen pulled a moss-green sheet over my father's life; his achievements, aspirations, bravery, dignity, loneliness, optimism. The days of drought continued. Good. As the months went on I found I could not bear the thought of rain soaking him, down in the ground.

One incident though gave me some comfort. As his only child, it fell to me to clear out his house. 'Try to find the silver flute,' my uncle Bill had told me. 'Your father wanted you to have it.' I looked everywhere in his three-bedroom semi in Twickenham for the flute, which had apparently bailed my grandparents out of trouble many times as they had repeatedly pawned it to pay off debts. I didn't want to turn the property over to house clearers without this one item my father had felt it so important to pass on to me, though he'd never mentioned it to me while he was alive. I searched the house from top to bottom in frustration, and in the very downstairs makeshift bedroom where he had died I said out loud, 'Oh, Dad, where *is* this thing?'

As soon as I had spoken, I was immediately drawn to one corner of the room, under a pile of old pillows. There in a dull-brown presentation box with worn green-velvet lining was the flute. On the top of the box is the inscription 'With the affectionate regards of the President, Vice Presidents, Committee and members of the Bleak House Club 1906'. And underneath, in ink on a paper label, is written, 'John J. Nightingale, 60 Friars Stile Road, Richmond, Surrey'. I've no idea what it's worth now – probably not much – but the fact that I felt my father's presence guiding me to it has helped a lot. And now I have learned what the Bleak House Club was, and this has helped solve a mystery for me. Apparently my grandfather organized a social club for Sanderson's employees and was also a Dickens-lover – hence 'Bleak House'. He often had musicians rehearsing in his house, and there is some evidence that his own grandfather was an organist and composer. Dudes groovin', blowin': good background to have, innit?

This information has come to light only recently. It goes some way to solving the mystery of why the middle-class, suburban, average, normal, run-of-the-mill, ordinary undistinguished young girl had her life taken over by music and is still in its passionate grip. It's genetic!

Tours with state-of-the-art DJs are being planned, compilations are being compiled for Creation despite my nowhere-near-total physical recovery from the Cuban episode. I have a scar as long as a scabbard down my right leg. I still have a pronounced limp. (That's pronounced 'limp' – sorry: irresistible, Spike Milligan joke. Another Aries, God bless him.) But, despite all that and my dubious abilities as a mixer, they still want me DJing in the clubs. Now I've been asked to open a night club called Nightingale in Palermo with some, um, well-connected Sicilians. I'm amazed. Ciao bella! Why not? See you there.